On Substantive Decriminalization

Based on both judicial practice and legal theory, this book examines the phenomenon of low acquittal rates in China from the perspective of substantive law and formulates the theory of substantive decriminalization.

In response to this pressing phenomenon, the author critically examines the prevailing tendency in the circle of criminal theory in China, which emphasizes criminalization over decriminalization and harm outcomes over behavioral process. The book attempts to think outside the box of procedural law, an approach that has yielded fruitful results but is limited in understanding decriminalization. Instead, it emphasizes the principle of substantive law, grounded in the modesty and restraint of criminal law and the protection of human rights. From the perspective of criminal class theory and criminal policy, the book proposes the theoretical framework of substantive decriminalization, which provides insight into the whole picture of the decriminalization mechanism of China's civil law and also has great practical relevance to China's criminal justice.

The title will be an important reference for scholars, students and legal professionals interested in the issue of decriminalization, legal theory and Chinese criminal law.

Liu Yanhong is Professor at the School of Criminal Justice, China University of Political Science and Law. Her research focuses on criminal law, the integration of civil, administrative and criminal laws, supervision law, and big data and Internet law.

On Substantive Decriminalization

Liu Yanhong

Routledge
Taylor & Francis Group
LONDON AND NEW YORK

First published in English 2024
by Routledge
4 Park Square, Milton Park, Abingdon, Oxon OX14 4RN

and by Routledge
605 Third Avenue, New York, NY 10158

Routledge is an imprint of the Taylor & Francis Group, an informa business

English Version by permission of China Renmin University Press.

British Library Cataloguing-in-Publication Data
A catalogue record for this book is available from the British Library

Library of Congress Cataloging-in-Publication Data
Names: Liu, Yanhong, 1970- author.
Title: On substantive decriminalization / Liu Yanhong.
Description: Abingdon, Oxon [UK] ; New York, NY : Routledge, 2023. |
Includes bibliographical references and index.
Identifiers: LCCN 2023024419 (print) | LCCN 2023024420 (ebook) |
ISBN 9781032598307 (hardback) | ISBN 9781032599052 (paperback) |
ISBN 9781003456773 (ebook)
Subjects: LCSH: Decriminalization--China. | Criminal liability--China. |
Guilt (Law)--China. | Criminal justice, Administration of--China. |
Crimina law--China. | Criminal act--China. | Criminal law--China.
Classification: LCC KNQ3878 .L585 2023 (print) | LCC KNQ3878 (ebook) |
DDC 345.51/04--dc23/eng/20230609
LC record available at https://lccn.loc.gov/2023024419
LC ebook record available at https://lccn.loc.gov/2023024420

ISBN: 978-1-032-59830-7 (hbk)
ISBN: 978-1-032-59905-2 (pbk)
ISBN: 978-1-003-45677-3 (ebk)

DOI: 10.4324/9781003456773

Typeset in Times New Roman
by KnowledgeWorks Global Ltd.

Contents

Tables

Introduction

How to achieve legitimate criminalization and reasonable decriminalization are the two core issues in the construction of criminal theory. In the course of China's development of the rule of law in criminal justice, numerous legislative, judicial and theoretical resources have been devoted to the issue of criminalization, depriving consistently the latter of due attention. Despite an exception in criminal law, decriminalization is a major content of the system of criminal theory in terms of constructing a comprehensive criminal law system. It is a natural embodiment of the substantive rule of law that acts with inadequate constituent elements or that are not illegal or culpable should not be treated as crimes.

The low acquittal rate is a salient feature of the criminal judicial practice in China. It on the one hand manifests the basic feature of refinement of Chinese judicial practices and on the other reflects the possible inculpation mindset. From 2012 to 2016, China's acquittal rate has been lower than 0.1% and such an extremely low rate demonstrates the discretion of the judicial practice department toward acquittals. In contrast, the acquittal rate is generally around 5% in civil law countries and about 20% in common law countries. The extremely low rate of acquittal casts light upon the status quo of China's judicial practice that emphasizes criminalization over decriminalization and is related to the fact that the judicial authorities at all levels in China take the "acquittal rate" as an assessment indicator. It is not only regarded as a proud achievement by local people's procuratorates and people's courts at all levels but is even cited as a major performance by the Supreme People's Court in its annual work reports. In recent years, the Committee of Political and Legal Affairs of the CPC Central Committee has required all units and local political and legal authorities to conduct a comprehensive review of various law enforcement and judicial assessment indicators, including the removal of the acquittal rate as an unreasonable assessment indicator. At present, the extremely low rate of acquittal has started to arouse vigilance among the theoretical and judicial practice circles of criminal law, where the majority believes that the sentence of not guilty is mainly dissolved by criminal procedures. The spirit of human rights protection, the principle of presumption of innocence and the concept of innocence until proven guilty are not given due respect in the judicial system; the rule of evidence adjudication in criminal proceedings is not strictly abode by, resulting in the failed exclusion of illegal evidence from the proceedings. The "withdrawal of prosecution" by the

DOI: 10.4324/9781003456773-1

procuratorate prevails in recent years and gradually replaces the court's "acquittal". The procuratorate often "does not prosecute due to doubts" after withdrawing the prosecution, which enables many cases that should be acquitted by the court to be dissolved in advance during the review and prosecution stage.

Nevertheless, the current understanding of the extremely low rate of acquittal in legal practice and theoretical circles is still limited to explicit phenomena. Through studying multitudinous criminal judgments in China, it is found that this issue entails further in-depth observations to unveil the deeply implicit information. As such hidden cases do not draw public attention like wrongful cases resulting from extortion of confession by torture or illegal evidence, they are covert "wrongful convictions" covered up by explicit ones. The name of covert wrongful convictions is attributed to the following two reasons: first, such cases are not publicly known; second, such cases should have been acquitted by the criminal substantive law but were finally convicted. Abolishing the evaluation indicator of acquittal rate not only requires the judicial authorities at all levels to foster an awareness of human rights protection in the criminal proceedings and strictly comply with the principles and rules of presumption of innocence, innocence until proven guilty, elimination of illegal evidences, etc., but also needs the judiciary to correctly interpret and apply the decriminalization mechanism expressly stipulated by the criminal law. To achieve the latter, a systematic study should be conducted on how the judicature in China interprets laws in pursuit of the ultra-low acquittal rate and dissection and analysis should be made on cases that are convicted but should have been exculpated to identify the realistic problems of legal interpretation and put forward corresponding countermeasures. On the basis of the empirical data of the criminal judgments, an analysis of the decriminalization mechanism of criminal law could provide a glimpse into the actual operation of China's criminal justice and reveal every problem that exists in the active criminalization and propose a feasible plan of reasonable conviction for the criminal justice in China.

Studies by domestic scholars about the decriminalization mechanism and relevant topics are mainly concentrated on procedural law and run through the entire judicial process to cover the public security organs, procuratorial organs and judicial organs, which have yielded relatively abundant and systematic theoretical outcomes. In contrast, the research on substantive law is relatively scattered and fails to tune into the data about the low acquittal rate in China's judicial practices. Besides, the criminal law of China is not compactly structured during its development and studies on the systematic construction of the decriminalization mechanism are also insufficient, suggesting that the decriminalization mechanism of civil law of China needs to be further investigated.

The substantive decriminalization theory based on the modest-and-restraint principle is a dogmatic path forged based on the current direction of the rule of law in China and the long-term studies on substantive rule of law. Against the theoretical backdrop that the construction of the system of criminal theory emphasizes criminalization over decriminalization and harm results over the behavioral process, efforts are made to sort out systematically the decriminalization-related issues from the perspective of the modesty-and-restraint principle and human rights protection, which is in combination with the criminal class theory and criminal policy, shape a relatively systematic theory of decriminalization that has been tested in practice. Decriminalization and criminalization are a set of adjudication activities that are mutually opposite and highly unified, which are contradictory in adjudication results but come under the umbrella of the same judicial adjudication procedures. The judicial authority is supposed to remain neutral in the process. An act that has the elements of a crime should be criminalized, while an act that satisfies the exculpation provisions of the criminal law should be decriminalized. Criminalization in form and decriminalization in substance is the core standpoint of the substantive decriminalization theory. Failure to exonerate the acts consistent with the decriminalization provisions obviously violates the decriminalization elements of the criminal law and is substantively unfair, which distorts the criminal law and contravenes the neutrality of the judiciary. Moreover, studies about decriminalization are limited to the field of criminal procedure law which could only take a peep into a single aspect of decriminalization in criminal justice practice and is unable to get the whole picture. Currently, the theoretical realm and practice circle ascribe the low acquittal rate completely to dissimilation of the decriminalization system in the criminal procedure law, which seems rather hasty in generalization. The crime circle of the criminal law must be confined within a certain range and its definitive property is the justification of punishment. The expanded crime circle is in essence the broadening of the punishment right and would inevitably encroach upon the realm of other laws and regulations as well as the private rights of citizens. In accordance with the basic concept of the rule of law and human rights protection, the crime circle shall be shrunk to maintain the character of modesty and restraint. The modern principle of *nulla poena sine lege* prescribes institutionally the demarcation of the crime circle. Under the guidance of this principle and upholding the value appeal of human rights protection, decriminalization excludes from the crime circle those acts that are not substantively illegal, not culpable, or with obvious minor circumstances and little harm, so as to narrow the crime circle. To break away from the field of procedural law and construct a theoretical system of decriminalization from the perspective of substantive law as well as deeply integrate the basic issues of decriminalization theory into the criminal class theory is undoubted of great significance for advancing the decriminalization theory and tackling the current imperative issues in practice.

Proceeding from a systematic reflection on the low acquittal rate in China, this research attempts to respond to practical concerns by virtue of the research results of theoretical issues, redefine the relationship between the theoretical study and practical operation of decriminalization and explore a systematic decriminalization mechanism of criminal law.

1 Legal Basis of Substantive Decriminalization Theory

Modest-and-Restraint Principle of Criminal Law

1.1 Risk criminal law cannot undermine the modest-and-restrained principle

The world has now entered into an era of "risk society". As a response, from economic criminal law to environmental criminal law and medical criminal law, criminal law demonstrates a growing tendency to afford protection to abstract and general legal interests at an early stage. All these "present challenges to the modest-and-restrained principle and are deemed as new major themes in the field of criminal jurisprudence". "As a result, the question of whether modesty and restraint can be maintained has been raised". Nevertheless, as greater efforts are being made to advance rule of law, it is impossible that the spreading of "risk society" concept and intrusion of risk criminal law into the traditional criminal law theory would undermine the modest-and-restrained principle.

The risk criminal law emerges in response to the raging of the concept of risk society. The risk criminal law is born to ward off social risks in pursuit of human security. It advocates the exertion of criminal punishment against acts that endanger social security, even if there is no result of infringement of legal interests. As its mission is to realize security instead of freedom, the risk criminal law is only expected to "meet behavioral needs of security policies", which therefore is also called "security criminal law". Under the risk criminal law, a crime "is expressed by failure to promote the formation of a secure state or the pace thereof rather than by imposition of sanctions under the precondition of the specific damage incurred. Crime is not a kind of specific damage but restlessness". However, the risk criminal law runs against rule of law. What the risk criminal law challenges is not the modest-and-restrained principle but the entire concept of rule of law in criminal justice and the principle of *nulla poena sine lege*.

The Nazi criminal law has long been acknowledged as defying rule of law and is therefore widely denounced. According to the analysis of the influences of Nazism on criminal law by German scholar Joachim Vogel, the criminal law tinged with Nazism manifests roughly the following features[1]: first, as the scope of punishment by criminal law continuously expands, the constitutive elements of crimes are also swelling, which take in an increasing number of behaviors as punishable acts; second, the criminal law is straying away from responsibilities. "In terms of legal

DOI: 10.4324/9781003456773-2

consequences, criminal consequences are constantly being created and divorced from responsibilities"; third, criminal law is becoming more and more subjective. As Nazism holds that unethical behaviors are illegal, the judgment of illegality grows increasingly subjective and personalized, while legal interests are tilting toward abstraction and spiritualization. Acts without value play an increasingly important role; "the actor himself, namely his personality, danger, and belief, is stressed, and the criminal law is developing toward the criminal law of the actor or even the criminal law of the concept". Fourth, there are legal concepts and general terms of increasing uncertainty in legislation.

The risk criminal law not only bears the mark of the aforementioned Nazism criminal law but also goes even further in many respects. First, the penalty scope of criminal law is continuously enlarged. The introduction of the risk concept has rendered legal interests under protection increasingly abstract and enabled criminal law to intervene at an early stage. However, what is more dangerous is that the risk criminal law also results in the broadening of punishment against traditional crimes, i.e., there is a tendency of applying the theory of risk across the board of the punishment of specific crimes. The risk criminal law requires not only to penalize extensively potential damage offenses that stand at its core but also to carry out "risk interpretations" about actual damage offenses in traditional criminal law. It promotes early punishment of nearly all crimes from the perspective of risk prevention and implements its important proposition of punishing people only with risks of endangering security of all crimes in the criminal law. As scholars have clearly pointed out, "A rapist would cause enormous anxiety, not just for himself but for others and society as a whole. If a response was not made until his act was completed to give rise to pernicious outcomes, it would be arguably too late. At this time, what is the benefit of imposing a severe punishment on him?" Therefore, in accordance with the theory of risk criminal law, "practical precautions and guarantee taken prior to the act could forestall the occurrence of harmful results". Such a view extends the tentacles of risk criminal law into all crimes of criminal law and fully exposes its nature of anti-rule of law. Second, the risk criminal law claims itself to have transformed the traditional culpability criminal law. In contrast to the traditional criminal law that takes "actual damage offense" as its core, the risk criminal law states unequivocally "potential damage offense is what the criminal law should focus on", thus transforming the traditional "culpability criminal law" into the "security criminal law". It is also pointed out that "criminal law must break through the traditional standard of an offense, and apply to certain circumstances some responses that are not based on culpability. Such responses emphasize more on the danger of doer than his liability". Obviously, like Nazism criminal law, the risk criminal law distances itself from responsibilities and totally deviates from the principle of criminal liability. Third, risk criminal law aims to prevent risks and regards all acts that hinder human security as illegal. As a result, risk criminal law determines whether a person is detrimental to social security by means of subjective understanding, and considers penalization objects at the level of "human as unsafe factors", thus fully exposing its subjectivity and the property of criminal law of the actor. Besides, risk criminal law deems that infringement upon legal interests is no longer a necessary constituent element but that "occurrence of a dangerous state is a necessary constituent element for punishing this behavior"; "it is the behavior itself that seems to be punishable rather than the result incurred by the behavior". This fully reveals the natural affinity existing between risk criminal law and discretionary principle. Disregarding the consequence of infringement of legal interests means that the act itself, once made, would be penalized, regardless of the result; placing emphasis on the act and the doer suggests that the inner motive, idea, concept and other subjective factors at the time of doing would become standards of penalty. Ultimately, this deviation from culpability would lead to extreme futility of act and moralism of criminal law. Fourth, risk criminal law attempts to address the security issue of the risk society by penalizing acts that cause risks to society. "An act must be safe to be allowed; if an act is proved possible to incur damage, the factual act shall be forbidden right away". Therefore, "risk" and "security" are key words in the risk criminal law. Nevertheless, it is these two words of the definitions remain extremely uncertain in the risk criminal law. Although the theory of risk holds that "risk and security are normative concepts", in fact, its founder Ulrich Beck also thinks that these concepts are unclear and indefinite. Beck points out that risk refers to a "peculiar real state featuring 'no longer-but-not yet' – no longer trustful/secure but not yet destroyed/devastated". "This modern concept of risk entails various decision-makings and attempts so that the unpredictable outcomes of decision-makings by citizens can be foretold and controlled". Clearly, Beck's concept of risk is not a description of reality but a prediction of the future; it seems not to indicate a specific catastrophe but to highlight the ability to control such catastrophe. This is different from the diverse so-called risk concepts that are used chaotically in today's academia. However, it is undeniable that Beck's concept of risk remains ambiguous. Perhaps the risk itself is destined to be defined in such a way that is difficult to capture its substantive content, which also compels Beck to definite this term repeatedly in a negative or oblique method. As later noted by Beck, "risk, after all, is not a specific object. It is invisible and imperceptible by human senses. It is the social construct and established mainly through knowledge, the public, participation of affirmative and negative experts, surmise of causality, sharing of costs, and system of accountability. It is an epistemic construct and therefore always carries an uncertainty". Beck's vagueness about the concept of risk buries the weakness in his theory of risk. "The concept of risk society has many loopholes of ambiguity. Due to this, many European scholars see Ulrich Beck as an advertiser who is more interested in building a sensational concept rather than as a rigorous sociologist that captures evidence from environmental tests". If the probability and contingency of the occurrence of risks are factored in, people would be more at lost about what "risk" and "security" are; when such dubious concepts are employed to judge whether an act is safe or might cause risks to society and on this basis determines whether a person should be punished, the uncertainty would be evidently further heightened.

Recently, some German scholars on risk criminal law have even argued that in response to "new challenges of the 'world risk society'", "the extension and DE-bordering (Entgrenzung) of criminal law" may be considered, namely making "criminal law is weighted towards solving issues related to prevention and security, and the resulting intervention in the acts prior to perpetrated crimes and suspected crimes", such as "pre-positioning of punishability in substantive criminal law", and "extension of preventive monitoring and removal of the guarantee of the right to freedom".[2] Such extreme concepts of risk criminal law intend to take criminal law as an instrument to control the society instead of merely as means of protecting human rights and fighting crimes. The essence thereof is the ubiquitous application of criminal law, but such criminal law without boundaries also constitutes the abuse of criminal law. The consequences would turn out, as Adam Smith had marked, "improper punishments, that is, punishments that should not be given or punishments that exceed the criminal negligence, are a kind of damage to the criminal law". This is equivalent to "damaging the law itself in the form of law", read by a Roman proverb. Ultimately, the criminal law would be dissolved and become the security law in the real sense, which is not a charter for good people nor for criminals. Therefore, what risk criminal law challenges is not only the modesty and restraint, the basic concept of criminal law, but also the maxim of *nulla poena sine lege*, the supreme principle of contemporary criminal law; or what it challenges is not the principle of *nulla poena sine lege* but the rule of law in criminal justice as a whole; or not just the rule of law in criminal justice but also the cause of rule of law in human society. Just imagine, how can rule of law and human rights exist in a country that tries to eradicate criminal law?

Evidently, the concept and practice of risk criminal law would prompt the mutation of laws and sabotage on rule of law. "The principle of *nulla poena sine lege*" is "the most important institutional component of the formal rule of law". Nowadays, all civilizations in the world set human rights and rule of law as national goals and take the principle of *nulla poena sine lege* that embodies the spirit of human rights protection and rule of law as the premier principle. The theory of human rights states "human rights exercise restraints on state power and confront state power". If the scope of punishment of criminal law is expanded blindly, the state's power of punishment would increase while the individual's rights to freedom decrease. In the face of a powerful state apparatus, individuals in weak positions should have the full right to contend with state power, namely the right to freedom that should not be infringed upon. Risk criminal law tries to achieve social security exactly by exceedingly confining civil liberties; under the banner of social security held high by risk criminal law, human rights are shelved. If the universal value maintains that society today is subject to rule of law, there is every reason to believe that the modest-and-restraint principle would not be challenged by the theory of risk society and risk criminal law. If "rule of law is most special and remarkable in its distribution of power but restraint of power exertion", what really makes rule of law in criminal justice unique is that it not only grants the state the power to punish but also restricts the arbitrary use of such power. A state is entitled to exercise the power of punishment to protect the legal interests of society, but the exercise hereof must be subject to certain restrictions. In detail, the criminal law shall not regard the so-called dangerous acts that would jeopardize social security as penalty objects but should confine the scope of punishments to the extent of absolute necessity. In other words, criminal law is a necessary means that have to be taken to maintain social order. This is the tenor of the modest-and-restraint thought of criminal law, which runs through the field of modern criminal law. Proceeding from the modest-and-restraint concept, the theory of modern criminal law has developed three specific principles: the principle of *nulla poena sine lege*, the principle of protection of legal interests and the principle of criminal liability. Three basic functions of criminal law are corresponding to these three principles, namely guarantee, protection and regulation. Therefore, the concept of modesty and restraint is not dissociated from the principle of *nulla poena sine lege* but exists as the conceptual basis of the latter, which explicitly reveals its role in commanding the overall criminal law.

In the view of Japanese scholars, the constant expansion of the scope of punishment by risk criminal law is "ironic" since such a practice equals to that "members of society exchange part of their rights and freedom for a safe social life" and signifies that "the risk of making and expanding the principle that 'if there is danger, there will be punishment' is acknowledged in the ultimate criminal legislation". If the criminal law allows security to take precedence over freedom, human right and rule of law to become its main concept, permits the general public to swap his freedom for the security of others (possibly including himself) and allows individual citizens to be punished for their already-determined rights and behaviors in exchange for uncertain social security, which means that human beings not only conduct self-injury with developing science and technology but also wrongly infringe upon themselves in the name of law. "Since all the changes happening in the world tend to add to the power of society and weaken the right of individuals, such erosion is not the kind of disaster that would disappear on its own but that will drag the society into an increasingly horrible vortex". Therefore, the concept and practice of criminal law that features "omnipresent risks" and "omnipresent criminal law" prove to be the greatest "risk" in the current "risk society". If we do not maintain ample prudence and vigilance in this regard, human beings may suffer a second trauma in addition to "social risks" brought about by the industrial society, namely the "risk of rule of law", which is undoubtedly more devastating than the former! How human beings think and make choices between rational development of science and technology and respect for nature and make more adjustments in comprehensive governance of the society and economic measures is a more effective means to deal with the risk society than criminal law – if we acknowledge Beck's theory of risk society as well. Consider, for typical risks that Beck and other risk scholars often mentioned, such as Chernobyl nuclear accident, environmental disasters, debate on human genetics, Asian economic crisis and current terrorist attacks, may not be prevented with the efforts of one single country's government or even the efforts pooled together by all countries around the world, how can the criminal law be expected to shoulder the responsibility of guarding against such political risks or major natural disasters caused by the development of science and technology? Humans cannot willfully wield the power of the criminal law simply because "we may solve conundrums in policy and law before the highly controversial issues can be settled such as justice, democracy or proper goals of the state", otherwise it would "end up in an extremely absurd situation that raises concerns in criminal policies, where crime control through the criminal law and police law is accepted as a mere placebo rather than its effectiveness". This approach would render the entire society "disruptively disorienting", and this should be given sufficient vigilance. In a word, even if we give certain credit to the formulation of risk society and risk criminal law, for example, to better remind us of coordinating the contradiction between social development and industrialization, the general value goal pursued by various civilizations and the modest-and-restraint principle are obviously impossible to shake. Interestingly, scholars in favor of risk criminal law are also aware that the blind expansion of the crime circle to prevent risks is not appropriate and suggest that we "are far from drawing such a conclusion that the prudent and inflexible criminal law with free rule of law, along with its evidence rules, the principle of culpability, legal and noble appeals as well as legal needs that are difficult to fulfill, is the most proper way to solve all risk issues that are lurking and on the rise in all areas of the risk society". In this case, it is in nature a pseudo-problem that the so-called risk society concept would challenge the modest-and-restraint principle. Moreover, "in the theory of modern criminal law in Japan, there is a tendency to expand the scope of application of the modest-and-restraint principle, and advocate applying this principle to the whole process "from legislation to rehabilitation". These indicate that against the backdrop of risk criminal law, the modest-and-restraint principle would not be challenged in theory or practice. On the contrary, in countries that advocate objective criminal law, like Japan, more attention has been paid to promoting and implementing it.

It should be noted that the author does not intend to totally repudiate the relevant theories and prepositions of the risk society doctrine but is prudent and skeptical toward the risk criminal law coming into being as the risk society theory penetrates into the criminal law field. What the author opposes is that the risk criminal law disregards civil rights like human rights and freedom in the mere pursuit of security and hereby hopes to sound an alarm to the possible consequential damage to the rule of law. Revealing the various problems of the risk criminal law may prompt us to reflect on how to strike a balance between social security and the proper application of criminal law to protect civil freedom. In the face of the criminal law of the enemy, risk criminal law and other criminal law theories from German shrouded in state authority, every scholar of criminal law should ponder over: Where would we ultimately lead the criminal law to? In fact, even in Germany, myriad scholars like Professor Schünemann also have become aware of the growing tendency of German criminal law to protect "world legal interests" and the resulting "crisis triggered by abuse and harsh demands on the criminal law" under the clamoring of such theories like risk society and criminal law of the enemy; "let the German criminal jurisprudence meet justice", they "argued paying attention to the plight confronted by the German criminal jurisprudence, including heading to dead ends and erroneous development". Facing the Western trend of thought in criminal law, we should not swallow it whole without discrimination under the so-called globalization context. Actually, the rule of law should and could only be a domestic culture and the globalized rule of law is questionable itself. Circumspect and skeptical analysis about whether "Western doctrines" should be introduced to China is obviously the rational attitude that Chinese scholars of criminal jurisprudence should have. Second, the above criticisms are not targeted at the opinions published by Chinese scholars under the heading of risk society, despite that the very minority about risk criminal law are correct and penetrating. Copinism is prevalent among Chinese scholars of criminal jurisprudence, who adopt the concept of risk society without discrimination or restriction. For example, many scholars would approach criminal law issues under the influence of such specious prepositions, which contains "against the background of risk society", although they may not have clarified the concept of risk society. Compounded by the polysemy of Chinese, numerous researchers interpret the risk in the risk society theory without real understanding as danger, threat, harm, distress and other similar words, and then by virtue of the social harmfulness theory, generalize the risk with specific meanings in the risk society as a ubiquitous concept of danger or harm; these have not only made it impossible for scholars against or in favor of the risk society in its true sense to start a dialogue with them but also given rise to the perilous variation of the risk concept in the risk society theory in China. In addition to misinterpreting the risk of the risk society as the risk allowed by the objective imputation theory, they also incorrectly regard the essence of the objective imputation theory as an embodiment of the value orientation of the risk society or believe that the objective imputation theory is built on the reality of the risk society and endorse the objective imputation theory on the ground of supporting the risk society theory, which is another "unconventional" misinterpretation of the risk society.

1.2 Violation of the modest-and-restrained principle leads to the generalization of the criminal law

Since the promulgation of the first criminal code in 1979 in China, the criminal legislation has been moving toward criminalization in the past 42 years. Whether the criminal legislation in China conforms to the modest-and-restraint principle and how this principle could be effectively implemented in future criminal legislation? These perhaps are the questions that criminal legislators as well as scholars and practitioners of criminal law need to consider. How the Chinese criminal legislation manifests modesty and restraint? This seemingly simple proposition implicates the following questions: What is the status quo of Chinese criminal legislation? Should the Chinese criminal legislation adhere to the modest-and-restraint principle? If so, how should Chinese criminal legislation reflect the modest-and-restraint? As the first two questions have been addressed in other articles,[3] the author will make a discussion here centering on the third question.

In light of the facilitation of punishment in the era of pan-risk and recent criminalization of Chinese criminal law, the philosophical questions on criminal justice by the English philosopher Hart in the middle of the 20th century appear particularly significant in the present age. Hart asked, "why is the punishment justified?" and "why should these doers be punished?" Apart from cut-and-dried answers in terms of retribution and deterrence, it is more urgent to look for an answer from the operable criminal legislation level in the domestic context. These two questions appear excruciating to scholars in favor of the modest-and-restrained principle, i.e., which behaviors should be stipulated as crimes if the modest-and-restrained principle is advocated? Throughout the European and American criminal law studies, this grand issue that bears on the justification of criminal legislation has been approached roughly by three theories: "harm principle" by English John Stuart Mill, the limits of the criminal sanction by the American Jurist Herbert L. Parker and the interest theory in the German and Japanese jurisprudence. Despite proceeding from different starting points, these three doctrines attempt to solve the same question, namely delimiting the reasonable reach of criminal legislation.

At the core of Mill's Harm principle, only when a man damages others' interests, would the society exercise jurisdiction over him and could such mandatory laws as criminal law govern; if a man's action does not affect the interests of anyone other than himself, or need not affect them unless they will, there is no room for any of the foregoing concerns. Parker pointed out based on his exploration about the "limits of the criminal sanction" that only actions that meet the following standards simultaneously can be defined as crimes by the criminal law: "(1) an action is significantly destructive to the society in the eyes of the majority of people and is not exclusive to a social class in any sense; (2) incorporating the action into criminal sanction does not go against the purpose of punishment; (3) restricting the action would not confine people's socially desirable behaviors; (4) it shall be addressed in a fair and nondiscriminatory way; (5) the action is controlled by criminal procedures which are not subjected to serious qualitative or quantitative burdens; (6) no alternatives to criminal sanctions are available to tackle the action". The interest theory holds that what laws protect are legal interests, and so is the criminal law, where only acts that infringe upon or threaten legal interests are crimes. The concept of legal interests is significant in determining the necessity of punishment and the rationality of punishment provisions. In criminal legislation, legal interests combined with the ultima ratio (last resort) feature of the criminal law play an important role in establishing the legal order of criminal law.

We may dig deeper into the above three doctrines. The harm principle requires that only actions that cause harm to other peoples' interests are defined as crimes and that power can be rightfully exercised to prevent the harm. The interests hereof actually refer to those protected by the law, i.e., legal interests; the harm to others evidently is an action that infringes upon or threatens others' interests. As a result, American scholars believe that, in accordance with Mill's harm principle, "the society would not struggle against the self-harm, thinking and any other behavior that cause no harm even if they should be condemned". Mill's *On Liberty* does not elaborate on the harm principle. His yardstick of crime merely proposed the harmfulness of crimes to other people at the level of value but failed to narrow down the expansive actions injurious to others that lacked objective standard as to what is harm. As Hershey noted, the core of the harm principle is "loss" but what is "loss" is indeterminate. The abstractness of the harm principle is exactly where its major defect lies, which makes the real connotation of a harmful act incomprehensible.

This is even more true of the interest theory. Early punishment in the risk criminal law causes the concept of legal interests increasingly abstract and ambiguous, which remains "the least accurately explained basic question in the criminal law". The absence of the substantive contents of legal interests incurs criticism and attack on legal interests from opponents and also makes it impossible to judge whether many acts infringe upon legal interests as well as answer what legal interests are jeopardized. Moreover, "discussions from legal interests are closely related to legislation but in the actual legislation process, which acts are serious enough to be criminalized is judged by the legislator", "when it is uncertain whether minor means (such as mere civil penalty) may adequately guarantee the results, the legislator also have the prerogative to exercise self-evaluation". Therefore, it is the legislator that determines the circumstances under which a violation of justice must be punished by criminal law, and so far legal interests merely play a symbolic guiding role for legislators and can hardly bring in practical effects. Based on above reasons, the legal interest is not ideally effective in demarcating borders of criminal law and is found not as able as hoped to answer questions what "has to" be punished by criminal law.

Compared with the harm principle and the interest theory, Packer's six principles are undoubtedly more concrete. However, these six principles are merely concrete in expressions rather than in substantive contents, let alone in their practicality. Some indicators such as items (5) and (6) are relatively specific and easy to operate; some indicators such as items (1), (2) and (3) are barely practical. For example, it is extremely controversial to select acts as significantly harmful to the society in the eyes of the majority. For items (2) and (3), these two indicators are equally debatable as the statement that an action is significantly harmful to the society, since they depend on the evaluation subject and standards. Besides, they touch upon the root of the game relationship between civil freedom and state power at the creation of criminal law and the fundamental issue of the legitimacy of criminal legislation, which are the goals that criminal legislation needs to strive to achieve instead of specific standards of criminalization. As for item (4), whether incorporating an act into the criminal sanction system is operable deserves obviously more attention, which determines the possible effect of criminalization. However, this question is distinctly not on the same level with "fair and non-discriminatory execution", as the latter seems more like an issue concerning criminal enforcement law and not a concern of the justification of criminal legislation.

At present, discussions of criminal legislation standards in Chinese criminal law theories are all based on the interest theory. Some scholars in China articulate that, the criteria of criminalization should be, "acts that directly harm legal interests and trigger other crimes and that are easily detected should be criminalized", and "crimes that seriously infringe upon or threaten major legal interests should be punished at an early stage". Some others hold that the criteria of decriminalization of Chinese criminal law should follow: crimes with "unclear legal interests" and "minor maliciousness" should be decriminalized; the former includes, for example, gathering to engage in licentious activities, stealing, insulting a corpse, gambling, and providing shelter for prostitution and the latter comprises partial offenders who prepare for a crime, partial offenders who attempt to commit a crime, partial offenders who discontinue a crime, euthanasia, concealing and harboring, bigamy, as well as other crimes. Obviously, the criminal legislation criteria proposed the Chinese academia, regardless of criminalization or decriminalization, all start from the interest theory of criminal law in German and Japanese; but the foregoing problems of the interest theory determine that such criteria of criminalization and decriminalization have internal deficiencies, such as what are serious infringements and threats of legal interests, what are unclear legal interests, what is minor maliciousness? All these questions have not been and are hard to be clarified.

The harm principle, Packer's six principles, and the interest theory all prove unable to effectively answer the questions: Which acts should be defined as crimes and which acts are to be defined as crimes in order to reflect the modest-and-restraint principle? Thus, the nature of the criminal act itself does come into play. Crime is an evaluation of evil acts, which not only entails value judgment – crime must be "malicious" – but also involves evaluation about the degree of "maliciousness". Besides, in response to the call for building a harmonious legal system, considerations should be given to the linkage between criminal law and other laws. The characteristics of law cannot innately satisfy the rigorous requirements imposed on science, and the selectivity of value, the study object of law, determines that law cannot be as precise and concrete as science.[4] In addition, as previously stated, what acts and doers should be punished matters not only at the technical level of legislation but is the philosophical inquiry into the punishment justification of criminal law. "The spirit of philosophy is persistently inquiry, doubt, questioning and meditation, rather than offering ready answers".[5] This also explains indirectly that it is rather unrealistic to propose head-on legislative principles which are more practicable than theories of Packer and other scholars.

That being the case, we might as well try another approach and address the modesty and restraint of criminal law from the negative side. As stated by Roxin, "although current researches on criminal jurisprudence cannot pinpoint the circumstances under which punishment intervention is necessary, we could delineate circumstances under which punishment is not justified by virtue of the auxiliary principle (namely modest-and-restraint principle of criminal law – author's note)".[6]

From the discussion of the above-mentioned scholars, we may readily find that they all agree that the criminal law should not be reduced to social administration law, harm prevention law, law of the legislator, priority guarantee law or law on paper. Additionally, the criminal legislation achieving the modesty and restraint is also subject to some common standards in the criminal law. For example, first, a victimless crime should not be punished. This is what Mill called self-harm acts, which may be harmful to the society but do not infringe upon the legal interests of any other people. If such acts are treated as crimes merely due to their social harmfulness, it would be in fact typical of taking criminal law as "harm prevention law". To this end, acts such as gathering to engage in licentious activities, taking drugs, whoring and prostitution should be excluded from the punishment of criminal law. By this standard, running a gambling house in the newly added Article 18 (2) of the Criminal Law Amendment (6) should be decriminalized. If the retention of the gambling crime in China is still a legacy of legislation or a tradition of criminal law or results from people's views on crimes, creation of the crime of running a gambling house is a far cry from the interest theory of criminal law, since such victimless crimes are at least unclear in terms of legal interests' infringement. The crime of gathering to engage in licentious activities in Article 301 of the criminal law should also be decriminalized. Second, acts to which other crimes are applicable should not be criminalized separately in criminal law, such as the newly created crime of offering bribes to a public official of a foreign country or official of public international organizations in Article 29 (2) of the Amendment (8). In the sense of applying China's domestic law, the foreign country public official and official of public international organizations do not belong to state functionaries of China, so Article 164 (1) of the Criminal Law pertaining to the crime of offering bribes to non-state functionary can be readily applied. Also, the newly created crime of dereliction of duty in food regulation in Article 49 of the Amendment (8) is also redundant and the act concerned could be exactly governed by Article 397 about the crime of power abuse or negligence of duty, which has been the case in judicial practice. There is no need to create the said crime of dereliction of duty against the surging food safety issues in China to showcase its importance. In fact, this is a legislative overlap and superfluity.

The modesty and restraint of criminal legislation is a serious problem that deserves deliberation; reflecting on all existing crimes in criminal law to ascertain what crimes should be retained or what crimes be removed rather than the creation of new crimes is probably an issue that criminal legislators and criminal theorists should inquire into continuously at present and in the future. If the consequential negative effects of criminal law expansion and willful criminalization are disregarded merely due to its convenience, the criminal law would ultimately "harm the law itself in the form of law", leading to abuse and the eventual dissolution of criminal law; if the criminalization of an act really solves major social problems such as wage arrears or forced eviction, it is also worthy of our reflection, "if a state can only make people do something with sticks and clubs, is there a vestige of honor to the state?" Relentless criminalization to regard the criminal law as a self-sufficient and powerful governance tool is an overestimation of the criminal law's capability in social governance; just as abuse of death penalty, the excessive use of criminal law will cause moral numbness, diminishing sense of guilty and weakening sensitivity to punishment, thus leading to nullity of the criminal law.

1.3 Conclusion

The modest-and-restraint principle of criminal law is the legal basis for constructing the decriminalization mechanism, which will not be shaken by the conceptual changes in the "risk society" or be silenced by the temporary inclination of legislative policies. Either the early legislation of environmental crimes or generalized criminalization of malicious wage arrears are grounded on the concept of active general prevention and deviate to some extent from the modest-and-restraint principle; in fact, even without these criminalization provisions, acts like environmental pollution and malicious wage arrears can be remedied or punished by civil or administrative measures and there are no institutional loopholes. Early and generalized criminal legislation may respond more to demands of social administration and make up for the shortage of civil and administrative relief; it exceeds the due positioning of criminal law and cannot effectively solve social problems, which is not quite necessary. Conversely, the more the legislation emphasizes active general prevention, the more necessary the modest-and-restraint principle is in guiding the restriction of criminalization or decriminalization in terms of criminal law interpretation and criminal judicial practice. Only in this way can the criminal law be prevented from overstepping its primary positioning as the "law of the last resort".

Notes

1 Vgl. Vogel: *Einflüsse des Nationalsozialismus auf das Strafrecht Von Professor*, ZStW 2003, S. 645ff.
2 Vgl. Sieber: *Grenzen des Strafrechts – Grundlagen und Herausforderungen des neuen strafrechtlichen Forschungsprogramms am Max-Planck-Institut für ausländisches und internationales Strafrecht*, ZStW 2007, S. 27.
3 See Liu Yanhong: *Risk Criminal Law Cannot Shake the Modest-and-Restrained Principle*, Studies in Law and Business, 2011(4); Liu Yanhong: *We Should Stop the Criminal Legislation of Criminalization*, Law Science, 2011(11).
4 [Germany] J. H. Von Kirchmann: *The Worthlessness of Jurisprudence as a Body of Knowledge*, translated by Zhao Yang, Journal of Comparative Law, 2014(1).
5 Song Mengxi: *Walking on the Path to Philosophy*, Dushu, 2001(6), SDX Joint Publishing Company, p. 103.
6 [Germany] Claus Roxin: *General Part of the German Criminal Law* (volume 1), p. 23.

2 Function of Substantive Decriminalization

Human Rights Protection

2.1 Mitigation of punishment: Embodiment of the human rights function of the decriminalization theory

Mitigation of punishment is a major embodiment of the human rights protection function of the decriminalization theory and dovetails with its fundamental concept through adjustment of the punishment degree. On February 25, 2011, China promulgated the Amendment (8) that highlights the mitigation of punishment by such contents as the abolition of the death penalty; this is also the first time that the criminal law reduces the number of capital offenses since its inception in 1997. The criminal law of China exhibits for a long time "a tendency toward severe punishments, with death penalty, life imprisonment and long-term imprisonment accounting for a considerable proportion, which runs counter to the trend of light punishment in the international community". Therefore, it is of undoubtedly great theoretical and practical significance to make an analysis on the human rights protection contents of the Amendment (8) and evaluate its advantages and disadvantages with reference to relevant international conventions.

2.1.1 Death penalty reform: Rule of law leap of the human rights cause

The current criminal law has too many capital offenses and unreasonable criminal charges, which has drawn criticism for a long time. Since the Chinese government signed the International Covenant on Civil and Political Rights (ICCPR) in October 1998, how to further improve the human rights situation in China has been a major concern of both the Chinese government and the society as a whole. Entering the 21st century, the academia has been calling on prohibiting the death penalty or even partially abolishing the death penalty, but no active response has been received in terms of judicial legislation. The new criminal law amendment addresses bluntly the death penalty, a sensitive and important issue in Chinese society; it repeals death penalty against 13 crimes for the first time and adds the prohibition on the use of capital punishment for the elderly at or above 75 years old, which makes a substantial progress in the death penalty reform and advances the human rights cause of China.

DOI: 10.4324/9781003456773-3

2.1.1.1 Gradual restriction of the death penalty

1 The Amendment (8) abolished the death penalty for 13 economic non-violent crimes.

The Amendment (8) abolished the death penalty for 13 economic non-violent crimes, accounting for 19.1% of all capital crimes. Before the promulgation of the Amendment (8), there were 68 capital offenses and the setting of the crimes was unreasonable in both the category of crimes and specific charges, where an excessive number of crime categories are punished with death penalty, particularly economic crimes (narrow sense) and property crimes, and capital punishment should not be imposed on such crimes as imparting criminal methods. Taking economic crimes as an example, the criminal law in 1979 included only one crime for which the death penalty is imposed on, namely the crime of embezzlement; later this number increased to 14 in the subsequent separate criminal law; instead of reducing the number of economic crimes punishable by death penalty, the current criminal law applied capital punishment to 19 crimes. The Amendment (8) confronted this major issue and dramatically cut down on the death penalty for economic and property crimes for the first time.

Specifically, the revisions in the Amendment (8) include five aspects: (1) in terms of smuggling crimes, the death penalty was canceled for crimes of smuggling cultural relics, precious metals, precious animals, precious animal products, ordinary goods and items. Meanwhile, to align the punishment with the crime, the original statutory punishment was increased appropriately so that the act with particularly serious circumstances is punished accordingly rather than indulging the criminals. (2) Regarding crimes of financial fraud, the death penalty was removed for the crime of bill fraud in Article 194 (1), the crime of financial certificate fraud in Article 194 (2) and the crime of letter of credit fraud in Article 195 and was reserved only for the crime of fraudulent fund-raising, maximally diminishing the use of capital punishment. (3) As for invoice crimes, the death penalty was abolished for the crime of falsely making out special invoices for value-added tax to defraud a tax refund for exports or to offset tax money and the crime of falsifying or selling falsified special invoices for value-added tax, achieving de-capitalization for tax administration in China. (4) The death penalty was repealed for the crime of theft. (5) The crime of imparting criminal methods, the crime of excavating and robbing a site of ancient culture or ancient tomb, the crime of excavating and robbing fossils of paleoanthropoids or paleovertebrates were removed. Besides, the application of capital punishment to the crime of teaching another person how to commit a crime is the most prominent manifestation of the unreasonable use of death sentences in the criminal law of China and there is actually no case of death penalty in judicial practice. The crime of excavating and robbing a site of ancient culture or ancient tomb, the crime of excavating and robbing fossils of paleo anthropoids or paleo vertebrates infringe upon the state's cultural relics management order and the state's property rights to cultural relics, so the violations in these two aspects shall not be deemed as "the most serious offenses" required in the ICCPR and the use of capital punishment does not conform to the spirit of human rights protection in the criminal law. The abolition of death penalty for the foregoing three non-violent offenses in the Amendment (8) should be regarded as positive.

2 The Amendment (8) adds the provision that the death penalty is not applicable to the elderly above 75 years old under certain conditions.

Article 3 of the Amendment (8) reads, "the death penalty shall not be applied to persons who have reached the age of 75 at the time of committing a crime, except for those that cause death by particularly cruel means". This suggests that the subjects against whom capital punishment is restricted are expanded from the previous people under 18 years old at the time of the crime and women that are pregnant at the time of the trial to cover those having reached the age of 75. By virtue of this provision, the criminal law may gradually approach the goal of restrictive application and ultimately complete abolition of capital punishment as stated in the ICCPR. For the elderly above 75 years old who have committed an extremely serious crime, the fixed-term imprisonment of a longer duration or life imprisonment could achieve the same deterrent effect as the death penalty and prevent crimes. Besides, the abolition of death sentences for the elderly above 75 years old echoes to the Chinese tradition of respecting and loving the elderly and the worldwide practice of caring for the elderly.

2.1.1.2 Reflecting on the reserved capital offenses

With the goal of gradual restriction till ultimate complete abolition of the death penalty set in the ICCPR as the standard, the crimes for which the death penalty is reserved in the Amendment (8) are analyzed. Further efforts may be made in terms of cancelation of crimes that warrant death penalty and the Amendment (8) still retains the application of the death penalty for some crimes that should have been exempted from death sentences, which should be deliberated on by the Amendment (8).

First, paragraph 1 of Article 6 of the ICCPR clearly stipulates "sentence of death may be imposed only for the most serious crimes". Although there are no further detailed explanations about the substantive condition of "the most serious crimes", it is pointed out in other relevant covenants that, the wording of "the most serious crimes" "should be understood that the scope of the death penalty should not go beyond intentional crimes with lethal or other extremely grave consequences". Therefore, it is reasonable that the criminal law of China retains capital punishment for crimes in serious violation of personal rights of citizens; in accordance with international practices, "crimes with other extremely serious consequences" generally refer to offenses that seriously endanger national security and public safety and some military offenses. Therefore, under the current situation, it is basically reasonable to retain the death penalty for crimes detrimental to national security and public safety and military crimes. However, for some economic crimes that are in essence only for profits, there seems no reason to retain the death penalty. What entails urgent reviews regarding the setting of capital punishment in China is the excessive charges of economic crimes punishable by the death penalty. For this end, the Amendment (8) abolished the death penalty for a dozen of economic and property non-violent crimes, which undoubtedly responds to the ICCPR and embodies the emphasis of the Chinese government on the citizens' basic human right: life right. These also fully prepare China for the scrutiny of the international community. However, if the provisions of the ICCPR were strictly taken as the yardstick, it could be found that the abolition of the death penalty for economic crimes in the Amendment (8) is far from enough.

Second, as the number of countries that keep and execute the death penalty is declining, China should make more endeavors to diminish the number of crimes that warrant capital punishment. The Amendment (8) abolished the death penalty for 13 crimes through criminal legislation for the first time since 1979, which seems to be a big step. Nevertheless, on the one hand, no or rare capital punishment has been imposed on some of the capital offenses abolished in the Amendment (8) in judicial practices, such as the crime of teaching another person how to commit a crime or the crime of financial certificate fraud. On the surface of it, the abolition of capital punishment for 13 crimes seems to signal a step closer by China toward controlling the death penalty, but "in terms of judicial application, these crimes are existent but seldom used or even never used". Therefore, "in fact, the abolition of these capital crimes would not result in fewer sentences of death in China". This indicates that how to actually restrict the application of capital punishment is the most important, which is precisely what the abolition of the 13 capital crimes is unable to achieve.

Last, since some progresses have been made for the abolition of the death penalty, sentences of death should also be repealed for crimes of the same nature and harmfulness in addition to the above 13 capital crimes. For example, the crime of smuggling the counterfeit currency and the crime of smuggling cultural relics all belong to smuggling contraband, but since cultural relics also carry the culture of a country apart from economic values and the latter only causes an intrusion into the national economy, smuggling cultural relics is to some extent more socially harmful than smuggling the counterfeit currency. However, the Amendment (8) abolished capital punishment for the crime of smuggling cultural relics but not for the smuggling of counterfeit currency, which makes us at a loss about the standard of abolishing or retaining the death penalty for some crimes. If the standard of the abolition of the 13 economic non-violent capital crimes is followed strictly, the death penalty should be repealed for more economic crimes.

To sum up, in accordance with the application conditions of the death penalty in the ICCPR and the spirit of restriction and gradual abolition of the death penalty, as well as in combination with the standards of abolishing capital crimes by the Amendment (8), the death penalty should also be repealed for many economic crimes for which the death penalty remains to be imposed, such as the crime of smuggling counterfeit currency, the crime of smuggling goods and items prohibited by the state from importing and exporting, the crime of counterfeiting currency and the crime of fundraising fraud. If the Amendment (8) could abolish the death penalty for a wider scope of economic crimes, better outcomes would be achieved for sure.

2.1.2 Sympathizing with the elderly and children: New direction of the cause of human rights under the rule of law

The Amendment (8) has added many provisions about lenient treatment regarding punishments for crimes committed by minors and the elderly, maximally realizing the human rights protection of minors and the elderly. This demonstrates that the criminal law of China has achieved the mitigation of punishments from multiple aspects to reflect the humanitarian spirit of the criminal law.

2.1.2.1 Revisions in the Amendment (8) about lenient treatment of minors and the elderly

1 A person under the age of 18 at the time of commission of the crime cannot be a recidivist. Article 6 of the Amendment (8) reads that Article 65 (1) of the criminal law is amended as, "n of minors vict sentenced to fixed-term imprisonment or a heavier penalty commits a crime for which a fixed-term imprisonment or a heavier penalty shall be given within five years after finishing serving his sentence or being pardoned, he shall be a recidivist and be given a heavier penalty, unless it is a negligent crime or he commits the crime under the age of 19". This article stipulates that a minor under the age of 18 cannot be ruled as a recidivist.
2 For a convict under the age of 18 or above the age of 75, probation shall be announced if the probation conditions are satisfied. Article 11 of the Amendment (8) makes a modification and improvement to Article 72 (1) of the criminal law. Specifically, the following three aspects are modified. First, the conditions for the application of probation are revised. The probation conditions provided for in Article 72 of the criminal law state "if, according to the circumstances of the crime and demonstration of repentance of the convict, it is certain that probation will not result in further harm to society". It is amended in the Amendment (8) as more concrete conditions, including "(1) the circumstances of the crime are minor; (2) demonstration of repentance; (3) not likely to commit any offense again; (4) announcing the probation will have any major adverse impact on the community where the convict lives". Second, subjects to which the probation must apply are added. Article 11 specifies that where a convict sentenced to criminal detention or imprisonment of not more than three years meets the above four substantial conditions of probation, probation shall be announced if he is under the age

of 18 or attains the age of 75, which affords greater protection to the minors and the elderly. Third, provisions about the execution of probation are added. On the one hand, the decision to announce the probation for a convict shall take into consideration of the impact that his probation may have on the community he lives in and the availability of effective supervisory conditions; on the other hand, when the probation is announced, in light of the crime committed, the convict may be ordered at the same time not to engage in certain activities or enter certain areas or premises or get in touch with certain people within the probation period.

3 A person attaining the age of 75 may be given a lighter or mitigated penalty if he commits an intentional crime. This is also the provision of Article 1 of the Amendment (8) and equivalent to the abolition of capital punishment for people above the age of 75, which are both aimed at better protecting the elderly. Besides, the provision that a lighter or mitigated penalty "may" be given indicates that if an elderly person commits an extremely serious crime and shall not be given a lighter or mitigated penalty, no lighter or mitigated penalty may be carried out; meanwhile, as a negligent crime is less condemnable itself, it is obviously proper to prescribe a lighter or mitigated punishment.

4 A person under the age of 18 that has been sentenced to fixed-term imprisonment of not more than five years or a lighter penalty may be exempted from reporting such an offense. Article 100 of the criminal law stipulates that "Anyone who has been subjected to criminal punishment shall, before being recruited in the army or employed, report to the unit concerned about the fact; he may not conceal it". Nevertheless, Article 57 (3) of the Law on Protection of Minors sets forth that "a minor that has been subjected to detention or imprisonment shall not be discriminated against in returning to school, further education or employment". Therefore, Article 19 of the Amendment (8) stipulates that one paragraph is added to Article 100 as paragraph 2, "whoever is given a penalty lighter than imprisonment of five years for a crime committed under the age of 18 shall be exempted from the reporting obligation as mentioned in the preceding paragraph". It is stipulated explicitly that a person under the age of 18 is not required to report his prior convictions, which establishes a system to eliminate the criminal record of minors. This could protect the minors' rights of employment and education from being restricted due to previous delinquency and may help them return to the society to start a new life, which embodies the human rights protection spirit of the criminal law and protection of minors.

2.1.2.2 Comments based on the Beijing Rules and the Inter-American Convention on Human Rights

1 The revisions about the lenient treatment of minors in the Amendment (8) profoundly reflect the harmonious unity of the humanitarian spirit in the juvenile justice and the crime prevention purpose of the criminal law.

Paragraph 4 of Article 1 of the United Nations Standard Minimum Rules for the Administration of Juvenile Justice ("the Beijing Rules") promulgated on November 29, 1985, reads that "juvenile justice ... shall be conceived as contributing to the protection of the young and the maintenance of a peaceful order in society", which has laid down the most important principle for the juvenile justice so far: the principle of two-way protection, namely protecting the interests of the minor delinquent and the interests of the society. China has always upheld the criminal policy of "dominance by education and supplement by punishment" for minor delinquents. Article 44 of the Law on Prevention of Juvenile Delinquency prescribes that "The principle of education, probation, and salvation shall be implemented for minor delinquents when investigating their criminal responsibilities, and the principle of dominance by education and supplement by punishment shall be insisted on". After its creation, this criminal policy has become a guiding policy for tackling minor delinquency cases in judicial practices and complied with the judicial and reform systems for the minor delinquency. It can also be credited as a compass for applying laws to minor delinquencies; how to reflect and implement it when interpreting and applying relevant provisions of the criminal law for juvenile crimes is an unavoidable question when interpreting relevant provisions. Therefore, the principle of two-way protection in the international convention is essentially consistent with China's criminal policy regarding juvenile delinquency, and the latter is considered by Chinese scholars to be an extension and expansion of the former. In view of this, the criminal principle of "dominance by education and supplement by punishment" should be thoroughly implemented in the formulation and improvement of criminal legislation.

The Amendment (8) modified for the first time comprehensively the content of criminal treatments on juvenile delinquents. First, in addition to the prior condition, a person "under the age of 18 at the time of committing a crime" is not a general recidivist, which truly carries out the policy of "dominance by education and supplement by punishment". Second, no leniency was ever granted to the application of probation to minors in the past so that some juvenile offenders with misdemeanors were unable to enjoy special criminal policies that belonged to their age but were put into jail and contaminated by other criminals which generally led to more serious criminal personality or graver crimes after being released from prison. Drawing on previous experiences, the Amendment (8) adds a provision that probation shall be given if the convict under the age of 18 meets the probation conditions, which has greatly mitigated the punishment for juvenile crimes. Third, juvenile offenders were required previously to perform the obligation of reporting prior convictions just like adult criminals, which is not only too cruel but also strongly retributive for juveniles who have not started their life and have a long way to go. The Amendment (8) incorporated the suggestions from the theoretical and practical departments and added a paragraph that a convict given a penalty lighter than imprisonment of 5 years for a crime committed under the age of 18 shall be exempted from the obligation of reporting prior convictions, which realized humanitarian justice toward juvenile offenders and general prevention of crimes to the greatest extent.

Nevertheless, the provision about exempting juveniles from reporting prior convictions in the Amendment (8) also has certain flaws and shortcomings. Since it is stipulated that a convict given a penalty lighter than imprisonment of 5 years for a crime committed under the age of 18 shall be exempted from the obligation of reporting prior convictions, those sentenced to an imprisonment of 5 years or a heavier penalty for a crime committed under the age of 18 are also obligated to fulfill the reporting obligation, which is still somewhat stringent. A more appropriate approach is to set an upper limit, such as more than five years but less than ten years, and no commission of a new crime within a certain time after serving the sentence (such as five to ten years). In this way, the system to eliminate the criminal record of juveniles would appear more effective and humane, circumventing the problems caused by the one-size-for-all standard of five-year fixed-term imprisonment. Considering the status quo that "the judicial practice in China is on the whole relatively conservative regarding the application scope of the juvenile criminal record elimination system", the judicial practice shall handle liberally the provision of Article 19 of the Amendment (8) instead of imposing some additional so-called repentance and other substantive restrictions. Besides, although the provision in the Amendment (8) allows conditionally juveniles not to fulfill the obligation of reporting the criminal record, under no circumstances are adults exempted, so there is still a long way to go to improve the criminal record reporting system in the criminal law of China.

2 The provision about lenient treatment toward the elderly in the Amendment (8) signals the human care in the justice for the elderly and the civilization and progress of China's criminal law.

On the one hand, there was no provision in the criminal law on the lenient treatment of crimes by the elderly prior to the promulgation of the Amendment (8) and relevant judicial interpretations are also quite rare, where individual clauses in judicial interpretations might touch upon it. In terms of physiological conditions, the elderly are similar to juveniles, with the latter still immature and the former already on the decline; the same effect is that their capacities of recognition and control are relatively on the weak side. However, these two types of people with similar conditions face entirely different criminal treatments, which clearly contravenes the equity principle in the application of criminal law. The provisions about lenient treatments toward the elderly represented by the abolition of the death penalty for crimes committed by the elderly make sure that both the elderly and juveniles are equally given lenient punishments, which in essence fulfills the equity principle in the application of the criminal law and maximally protects the legal rights and interests of the elderly.

On the other hand, the provision about the abolition of capital punishment for the elderly. Among the provisions about lenient treatments toward the elderly in the Amendment (8), the most striking is no imposition of the death penalty on the elderly attaining the age of 75. Nevertheless, this provision is also the most controversial treatment for the elderly.

First of all, against the backdrop that the abolition of the death penalty has become an irreversible global trend, and that most countries in the world have abolished it through legislation or introduced a moratorium on the death penalty despite retaining it, there are people in China worried that abolishing the death penalty for the elderly attaining the age of 75 would indulge the elderly to commit crimes and hinder the crackdown on crimes. Such concerns are completely redundant. If an elderly attaining the age of 75 commits an extremely serious crime, the life sentence instead of the death penalty is imposed, which would certainly last a long time; for the elderly already deprived of freedom and whose physiological and psychological conditions are on a downward trend along with the age, his criminal capacity has actually been deprived. Under such a circumstance, the use of punishment against freedom over the death penalty also achieves the purpose of special prevention of the crime; moreover, since the death row is under consideration, the crime committed must be extremely grave and the punishment against freedom would be unlikely to be short, so the long sentence would turn out the harshest punishment against the elderly afraid of loneliness and solitude. Therefore, even if from the perspective of retributive criminal law, the abolition of the death penalty for the elderly attaining the age of 75 does not indulge crimes. An analysis of the purpose of the general prevention of crimes suggests that the Amendment (8) aggravates the life sentence while relaxing the death penalty, so as the elderly above the age of 75 do not have many days left, the long sentence against freedom poses a deterrence no less than the death penalty and is equally effective; furthermore, Article 3 of the Amendment (8) attaches a condition to the provision about the elderly attaining the age of 75 exempted from death, namely "unless he has caused the death of another person by especially cruel means". This suggests that the death penalty may be carried out for the elderly who cause the death of another person by particularly cruel means even if he is over the age of 75 at the time of committing the crime.

Second, our provisions about the commutation of the criminal liability of elderly offenders could go back to ancient times. "The relevant legal provision originated at least from the Western Zhou period and underwent the development of the Spring and Autumn period, Warring States, Han Dynasty, Wei, Jin and the Northern and Southern Dynasties as well as Sui Dynasty to form a relatively complete system in the Tang Dynasty. In accordance with the relevant regulations of the Tang Dynasty, an offender reaching the age of 70 could be given lenient treatments; an offender that should be sentenced to death for the crime of treason, insubordination or homicide committed at or above the age of 80 should be reported to the emperor for ruling, and those convicted of theft and intentional injury could atone for their crimes with money while those convicted of other crimes would not be investigated for criminal responsibility; the offender attaining the age of 90 would not be investigated for criminal responsibility even if he committed a capital offense. The lenient treatment system toward the elderly offender has been carried forward by later generations, especially in the Song, Ming and Qing dynasties. The criminal law of the Republic of China still retained lenient treatments toward elderly offenders. For example, the Criminal Law of the Republic of China promulgated in 1928 and amended in 1935 recorded: a convict attaining the age of 80 should be given a mitigated punishment and not sentenced to death or life imprisonment".[1] Under the Chinese cultural tradition of respecting the old and cherishing the young and against the legislative history that lenient treatment toward the elderly has been a common practice in the criminal law of China, the provision of the Amendment (8) about restriction of the death penalty for the elderly attaining the age of 75 would easily win recognition of the public and find implementation; this is also an eloquent embodiment of the criminal legislation that Chinese legislators have factored into the traditional culture of sympathizing with the elderly and the young as well as the international trend of prohibition of capital punishment.

Last, concerning the age of the elderly for whom the death penalty shall not be inflicted, which is widely debated by all walks of life, the author holds that this is not the crux of the problem. Should the elderly attaining the age of 60, 65, 70, 80 or 90 be exempted from capital punishment? Different parties put their own spin on this issue. The debate is naturally grounded. Article 2 of the Law on Protection of the Rights and Interests of the Elderly ("Law on Protection of the Elderly") coming into effect from October 1, 1996, stipulates that "the elderly referred to in this law are citizens at or above the age of 60". Article 21 of the Law of the People's Republic of China on Public Security Administration Punishments prescribes that "those over 70 years old" are the elderly. The Amendment (8) sets the age of the elderly exempted from capital punishment at 75 years old rather than 60 years old or 70 years old, respectively, set forth in the Law on Protection of the Elderly and the Law on Public Security Administration Punishments. This shows that the Chinese criminal legislators disapprove exclusion of all elderly offenders satisfying the age requirement of the Law on Protection of the Elderly from the death penalty but in consideration of the combination of special prevention and general prevention of crimes and coordination of human rights safeguards and social protection, reckon into both the basic human rights of the elderly and accommodate the actual need of combating crimes before designating the age of the elderly at 75 years old instead of 60, so as to strike a balance between protecting the rights and interests of the elderly and fighting crimes. Of course, lowering the age to 70 years old perhaps would appear more practically significant than the currently prescribed 75 years old. In accordance with the World Health Report in 2008 released by the World Health Organization, the average life expectancy of Chinese people is 72 years old, with that of men only at 70 years old and that of women at 74 years. Considering the foregoing average life expectancy, the stipulated 75 years old is obviously divorced from reality. Moreover, empirical studies have revealed that from 2006 to 2008, only two people were aged from 70 to 74 years old according to the statistics on criminal cases of the elderly (over 60 years old) handled by the investigation and prosecution departments. This suggests that there are few criminal cases of the elderly at or above 75 years old in judicial practices, which further validates that the abolition of capital punishment for people attaining the age of 75 at the time of trial is insignificant in practice.

2.1.3 Improvement of non-custodial sentences: The future blueprint of the cause of human rights under the rule of law

2.1.3.1 The Amendment (8) adds community corrections for the improvement of non-custodial sentences

The Amendment (8) has made numerous revisions and supplements in standardizing the non-custodial sentence and perfecting its execution measures. Article 2 of the Amendment (8) stipulates that one paragraph is added to Article 38 of the Criminal Law as paragraph 2, "in light of the crime committed, a convict sentenced to control may also be prohibited from engaging in certain activities, entering certain areas or places or contacting certain person during the term of execution" and meanwhile "one paragraph is added as paragraph 4: whoever violates a restraining order as provided in paragraph 2 shall be punished by the public security authority in accordance with the Law of the People's Republic of China on Public Security Administration Punishments". Article 11 amends the previous condition for probation that "a probation may be granted if it is certain that probation will not result in further harm to society" to four concrete conditions; paragraph 2 is added: "when probation is announced, in light of the crime committed, the convict may also be prohibited from engaging in certain activities, entering certain areas or places or contacting certain persons during probation". Articles 15, 16 and 17 also refine, respectively, the execution conditions, probation period and execution method regarding commutation and parole. However, among all the revisions and supplements of non-custodial sentences, the biggest highlight is the punishment of community corrections.

First, Article 2 of the Amendment (8) stipulates that paragraph 2 of Article 38 of the Criminal Law is amended as paragraph 3 and the previous provision that "where a criminal is sentenced to control, the sentence shall be executed by a public security organ" is amended as "criminals sentenced to control shall be subject to community correction". Second, Article 13 of the Amendment (8) prescribes that Article 76 of the Criminal Law that "any criminal whose sentence is suspended shall, during the probation period for suspension of sentence, be subjected to observation by a public security organ with the cooperation of the work unit to which he belongs to or of a grass-roots organization" is amended as "a criminal whose sentence is suspended shall be subject to community correction during the probation period for suspension of sentence, and if none of the circumstances as set out in Article 77 of the Criminal Law occurs, the original sentence shall no longer be executed upon expiration of probation, which shall be announced to the public". Third, in Article 17 of the Amendment (8), the previous Article 85 of the Criminal Law that "subject to supervision by a public security organ during the probation period for parole" is amended as "a convict released on parole shall be subject to community correction during the probation period for parole according to law, and if none of the circumstances as set out in Article 86 of the Criminal Law occurs, the original sentence shall be deemed to have been fully served upon expiration of the probation period for parole, which shall be announced to the public". The above provisions about the three articles in the Amendment (8) have codified the community correction into the Criminal Law, which is stipulated applicable to criminals sentenced to control, criminals whose sentence is suspended, and criminals released on parole.

2.1.3.2 Comments on the punishment of community corrections based on international conventions

How to effectively achieve mitigated and humane punishments while ensuring social security? In the game between human rights safeguard and social protection, relevant international conventions of the United Nations not only require its member states to maximally prohibit and gradually abolish capital punishment but also devote itself to advancing the movement of replacing custodial sentences with non-custodial sentences for criminals subjected to a life sentence. This is a far cry from the provisions about non-custodial sentences in the Criminal Law of China. The primary non-custodial sentences set forth in the Criminal Law and the Criminal Procedure Law of China comprise control, suspension of sentence, parole and execution of the sentence outside prison, which are to be executed (control) or supervised (parole) by a public security organ or observed by a public security organ with the cooperation of the work unit to which the criminal belongs to or of a grass-roots organization (suspension of sentence). However, such provisions are too general and abstract and are often poorly implemented regarding how the observation and supervision should be carried out to practically regulate the non-custodial offenders. Therefore, since the promulgation of the current criminal law in 1997, despite the lack of provisions about community corrections in Chinese laws, the community correction pilot programs have been rolled out step by step in practices under the guidance of relevant normative documents. The Notice about Launching Experimental Work on Community Corrections issued by the Supreme People's Court and the Supreme People's Procuratorate, the Ministry of Public Security and the Ministry of Justice on July 10, 2003, stipulate that "the judicial and administrative organs should take the lead in organizing relevant units and community grassroots organizations to carry out experimental work on community corrections and better supervise and observe offenders serving their sentences in the community along with the public security organs". The provinces and municipalities also enacted some local documents to direct the experimental work on community corrections at various places. However, two points are evident. First, the community correction, as an execution method of non-custodial sentences, implicates the restriction of citizens' personal freedom. Although community corrections have distinct social work elements, the overarching feature still lies in penal sanction. The penal sanction measures related to the restriction of personal freedom should be prescribed by "the legal institutions of the country" rather than administrative rules, otherwise, their legitimacy can hardly hold ground. Second, although the provisions about probation for parole and suspension of sentence in the Criminal Law include relevant content about community corrections, key issues such as their legal status, execution method, applicable objects and application subjects are not elucidated, which is detrimental to the promotion and implementation of community corrections and contrary to the requirement in the international convention that "the use of non-custodial measures should be part of efforts towards depenalization and decriminalization" "instead of interfering with or delaying efforts in that direction". Penalization of the community correction in the Amendment (8) not only establishes its legal status to provide the sufficient legal basis for the future community correction work in China but also showcases China's emphasis on depenalization and endeavors to reduce offenders in prison, which is conducive to actively promoting depenalization in judicial practice.

It should be noted that community correction is a complex system and entails numerous and complicated issues. Limited by its topic and length, this article only makes a rough evaluation on the penalization of community correction and does not touch upon other issues that are to be explored separately. Some scholars believe that the community correction "does not relate to the substance of conviction and sentencing" so its legislation should "be led by the amendment of the criminal procedure law, with the local legislation then catching up". This view essentially deems community correction merely as an execution method of punishment and impertinent to the substance of conviction and sentencing, and as a result, the community correction should be stipulated by the criminal procedure law, which is debatable. First, as an execution method of punishment, whether the community correction should be prescribed by the criminal law or the criminal procedure law has no differences in principle. The criminal procedure law may lay down the execution method of punishment, such as executing the death penalty by shot or injection, but the criminal law could also provide for the execution of punishment, such as passing the probation in Article 76, commutation procedure in Article 79 and parole procedure in Article 82, which are all related to the execution of punishments. If the foregoing view was applied, wouldn't all these provisions be set forth in the criminal procedure law? However, the facts are just the opposite. This demonstrates that the criminal law could work to specify relevant issues about the execution of punishments, which is also a consistent practice in the criminal law of China. Therefore, it is entirely justifiable to incorporate the community correction into the criminal law. Second, if a discussion was made on which penalty execution content should be written into the criminal procedure law and which into the criminal law, it could be concluded that the community correction should be regulated by the criminal law. Contents related to the substance should fall under the criminal law, while questions about procedures should be clarified by the criminal procedure law. As an execution method of punishment, community correction is on the one hand indeed a procedural issue but, on the other hand, encompasses many contents of the substantive law, such as legal provisions that the convict should comply with during the period of community correction, probation period and treatment of failed assessment, the procedure of community condition and conditions for carrying out the community correction. All these are substantive contents closely related to the criminal law. Besides, the substantive contents about suspension of sentence and parole, including legal obligations of the criminal on suspension of sentence or parole, probation period and treatment after probation, are all stipulated by the criminal law. Therefore, some scholars point out, "compared with the Criminal

Procedural Law, the work of community correction has closer ties to the Criminal Law, and issues confronted during the experimental work on community correction all pertain to the criminal substantive law and could be roughly addressed by amendment of the Criminal Law, including issues of 'applicable objects and application subjects', adjustment and improvement of punishment contents, expanded application of community correction and demarcation of legal obligations of offenders serving their sentences in the community".[2] As the community correction involves similarly numerous substantive contents, it is natural that it should be set forth by the criminal law. Of course, from the completeness of legislation, it would undoubtedly be more proper that the community correction is prescribed briefly as an execution method in the criminal procedural law and elucidated for its legal obligations, observation and other substantive contents in the criminal law.

Certainly, it is also unrealistic to expect the penalization of community correction to greatly reduce the number of inmates. If excessive expectations are placed on the legislation of community correction in the Amendment (8) to elevate the human rights protection level for criminals in China instead of actually implementing various measures to reform the criminals through labor and creating job opportunities for them to return to society, the realization of human rights protection goal in the criminal law of China remains a distant prospect.

2.1.3.3 Legalization of "leniency for confession to crime" as a lenient sentencing circumstance and comments

In practice, the criminal justice system of China has always advocated "leniency for confession and strictness for resistance". The so-called confession is undoubtedly in a broad sense, including voluntary surrender and confession in a narrow sense (the confession mentioned in this article refers to the meaning in a narrow sense). At the level of the criminal law, the criminal legislation in China has always only stipulated voluntary surrender but not confession as a statutory lenient circumstance for sentencing; confession is only a discretionary circumstance for lenient sentencing, which merely exists at the level of criminal policies and could barely have compulsory legal effects in judicial practices. This leads to some judicial organs in judicial practices to consider and grant lenient treatment after the criminal truthfully admits his crime while some judicial organs fail to handle the case leniently and the criminal "is sentenced to life imprisonment" even after confessing all crimes that have not been grasped by the judicial organ. The various conundrums ranging from difficulties in solving cases, interrogation and collecting evidence in judicial practices are inextricably linked to a certain extent with the difficulty of implementing the policy of leniency for confession.

For this end, Article 8 of the Amendment (8) stipulates that "adding one paragraph in Article 67 of the Criminal Law as paragraph 3: a criminal suspect who truthfully confesses to his crime may be given a lighter penalty although there is no voluntary surrender as mentioned in the preceding two paragraphs; and may be given a mitigated penalty if any especially serious consequence is avoided for his truthful confession". This provision symbolizes that the criminal law of China for the first time legalizes confession as a lenient sentencing circumstance like voluntary surrender, truly materializing the criminal policy of "leniency for confession and strictness for resistance". This will greatly inspire the offender and positively impel them to actively cooperate with the detection activities of the judicial organ and encourage them to voluntarily confess their crimes. From the perspective of criminal litigation, legalization of leniency for confession as a lenient sentencing circumstance will contribute to reducing and eradicating the negative impacts of the right to silence. Therefore, this provision in the Amendment (8) can help encourage and guide the criminal to truthfully confess his crimes and continue the spirit of the voluntary surrender system of the criminal law.

2.1.4 Summary

Although the abolition of the death penalty in China has greater symbolic significance than actual effects at the current stage, it signals that we are making progress and full of hope on the long road to the complete annulment of the death penalty. Instead of entirely decriminalization and mitigation of punishment, the Amendment (8) also aggravates the life sentence, tightens commutation conditions, highlights protection of people's livelihood and strengthens crackdown on underworld crimes as well as criminalizes such behaviors as dangerous driving and malicious wage arrears since the criminal legislation at the current stage develops in the direction of criminalization rather than decriminalization; despite that relevant provisions in the Amendment (8) about the light penalty or lenient sentencing circumstance have various flaws, such as "overcautious" provisions about human rights protection toward juveniles and the elderly and legalization of "leniency for confession" attracting criticism due to violation of the basic concept of modern criminal justice, such shortcomings are unable to disrupt the main theme of human rights protection embodied in the Amendment (8) nor undermine its extraordinary achievements in pressing ahead the human rights cause in China. As a fruit borne by the cause of human rights, the Amendment (8) will endure for its significance and compared with all prior amendments is the best and most influential.

2.2 Social security and personal freedom: A dilemma of the decriminalization theory

Peace is surely beautiful but is the hardest to achieve for human beings. The current world is plagued by the spread of terrorism and grim situation of counter-terrorism. Against this background, the Chinese government has also reinforced the crackdown on and governance of terrorist crimes. From 1997 to the present, several amendments of the criminal law have enacted provisions about terrorist crimes; the Amendment (9) has further added a number of new crimes related to terrorist crimes and revised the scope or gravity of punishment of original terrorist crimes to weave a closely knit criminal net over criminal laws. The Counter-terrorism Law of the People's Republic of China on December 21, 2015 ("Counter-terrorism Law"), presents comprehensively and systematically stipulates the system, mechanism, means and measures of China's counter-terrorism work, which provides solid legal guarantees for China to legally fight against terrorism. The past 20 years following the enactment of the current criminal law saw the evolution of legislation about terrorist crimes in a trend from single to multiple charges, from punishment of substantive to preparatory acts and from light to severe penalties. However, the changing world patterns may dash people's habitual expectations on the rule of law and may also abort their familiar crime governance model. The frequent terrorist crimes worldwide are more competitions and conflicts among world civilizations due to cultural and religious differences as said by Huntington than criminal laws. Leaving aside whether it is feasible to resolve the conflict of civilizations in human society with the rule of law, merely in view of the counter-terrorism means of the rule of law in criminal justice, "when the security of a country is threatened, is its citizens' freedom at great perils" has become an extremely realistic question. Against this backdrop, a major question facing the law-based governance of terrorist crimes is to analyze the value position and pros and cons of China's criminal legislation about terrorist crimes between security and freedom and discuss how the governance of terrorist crimes strikes a balance between safeguarding social security and protecting civil liberties.

2.2.1 Criminal sanction system for terrorist crimes: A study of criminal legislation over 20 years

Terrorist crimes are divided into exclusive charges and related charges. The former refers to those that are only or mainly constituted by terrorist crime activities, whose names often contain the word "terrorist", so its denotation is clear and would not prompt a dispute about "whether a charge belongs to the terrorist crime". Naturally, there are also a few crimes that are publicly recognized as terrorist crimes based on the background of counter-terrorism, such as hijacking aircraft and releasing dangerous substances, although their names do not have the word "terrorist". Some other crimes involve the criminal means often used by terrorist criminals, such as intentional homicide and explosion, which are terrorist crimes but at the same time more ordinary criminal offenses, so they belong to related charges of terrorist crimes. This article mainly focuses on exclusive charges and may also involve related charges in a few places.

From the first terrorist crime of forming, leading and participating in terrorist organizations stipulated in 1997, the Amendments (3), (8) and (9) to the criminal law in the past 20 years have increased the number of exclusive terrorist crimes from 1 to 9, with the range of related charges broadening as the overall number of criminal offenses increases. The criminal law has been continuously expanding the punishment scope of terrorist crimes and toughening punishment (lowering the requirement for constituting a recidivist and gradually increasing the statutory penalty). For a political country built on the foundation of constitution, the state of emergency is a touchstone to verify and measure the development of its rule of law; as for its criminal law that punishes criminal offenses, terrorist crimes are a litmus test for the progress of rule of law in criminal justice. How to evaluate

China's criminal legislation, particularly the system of terrorist crimes established by the Amendment (9), matters the deep-seated issues of law-based governance of terrorist crimes in China.

2.2.2 Value orientation of China's legislation about terrorist crimes: Security or freedom

"Value implication represents the active pursuit of the certain social public. Legislation cannot circumvent value issues and value is the ultimate reason why legislation is meaningful".[3] The legislative values of the criminal law in modern society comprise security and freedom. The security criminal law touts "the value of security, for which the traditional criminal law is transformed to broaden the crime circle and set abstract potential damage offenses"; "The liberal criminal law still adheres to the concept of rule of law, gives priority to human rights protection and sticks to the restrictive function of criminal law". The risk criminal law theory originating from the risk society advocates the security as the leading value that the criminal law of the modern society should champion and the criminal law system constructed on the basis of this concept is called security criminal law; the human rights protection theory that abides by the free rule of law concept of the classical legal school and the principle of *nulla poena sine lege* claims that freedom is the dominant value that the past and modern society should continue to pursue and the resulting criminal law system is called the liberal criminal law. In light of the high incidence of risks in modern society, the risk criminal law coming into being under the influence of the risk society theory possesses a huge market; while the liberal criminal law advocated by the traditional criminal law theory more closely reflects the characteristics and needs of criminal law, so there is a trade-off between them. The "9.11" attacks dealt an immediate impact on the security and liberal order of all countries around the world. "On the one hand, the harm to innocent people, destruction of the social order of various countries and impact on the international security situation caused by the terrorist crimes themselves; on the other hand, responses taken by various countries to terrorist attacks, particularly the 'counter-terrorism wars' led by America that have seriously affected the human rights safeguard and protection worldwide".[4] In contrast, the setting of crimes and provisions about sentencing in China's criminal legislation about terrorist crimes effectively protect citizens from attacks of terrorist crimes and bring the governance of terrorist crimes onto a more reasonable track of rule of law in criminal justice. Nevertheless, this by no means suggests that our legislation about terrorist crimes should blindly cater to the general trend of "expanding the application scope of the criminal law" and "reducing traditional due process and protection means" that countries around the world are taking against terrorist crimes, nor indicate that the laws about terrorist crimes oriented toward security are not worthy of reflection. Therefore, an examination about the choice of security and liberal values in our legislation about terrorist crimes may facilitate achieving a balance between the protection of national and social security and the assurance of citizen personal freedom in the course of terrorist crime governance. By an analysis of the criminal legislation about terrorist crimes in China, it is fair to say that the value orientation of giving priority to security has always been upheld.

2.2.2.1 Relevant legal documents explicitly stipulate that the legislative value of terrorist crimes is "security"

The Counter-Terrorism Law of China embodies the value concept of giving priority to security. First, the legislative purpose is security value. Article 1 of this law states, "for purposes of preventing and punishing terrorist activities, improving counter-terrorism work and safeguarding national security, public security and the security of people's lives and property, this law is developed in accordance with the Constitution". Article 6 prescribes, "counter-terrorism work shall be conducted in accordance with the law by respecting and safeguarding human rights and protecting the lawful rights and interests of citizens and organizations. In counter-terrorism work, citizens' freedom in religious belief and ethnic customs shall be respected and any discriminatory deeds based on regions, ethnic groups, religions and other causes shall be prohibited". Although this law clearly requires that the counter-terrorism efforts shall not neglect citizens' freedom to protect the lawful rights and interests of citizens from being infringed upon, the legislative purpose of safeguarding national security and social security established in Article 1 has laid down the value concept that security is paramount; what Article 6 intends to highlight may exactly make up the shortcoming of Article 1 in over-emphasis on security value and alert the bottom line of the rule of law that should be observed in the counter-terrorism work. In a nutshell, despite that the Counter-Terrorism Law of China also stresses respecting and safeguarding citizens' human rights, it is the national and social security that serves as the primary and ultimate value pursued by this law. Second, the concrete counter-terrorism measures set forth in the Counter-terrorism Law also embody the concept that security value comes first. Article 30 is created for terrorist convicts released after serving their sentences and stipulates that the prison or jail shall conduct a "social danger assessment" of the terrorist convict; if the convict has social danger upon assessment, the prison or jail shall offer a "settlement and education" proposal to the court, where the settlement and education are organized by the provincial people's court and assessed each year; if the convict still has danger upon assessment, he or she shall continue to receive settlement and education, which may be removed when the convict does have repentance and no longer endangers the society. The provisions on "social danger assessment" and "settlement and education" actually authorize the court, procuratorate and government to carry out compulsory measures, that is, imprisonment, on citizens, which seems contrary to the relevant contents of the Constitution. Article 37 of the Constitution of China articulates, "the personal freedom of citizens of the People's Republic of China is inviolable. No citizen may be arrested except with the approval or by decision of a people's procuratorate or by decision of a people's court, and arrests must be made by a public security organ. Unlawful detention or deprivation or restriction of citizens' personal freedom by other means is prohibited, and unlawful search of the body of citizens is prohibited". Despite in the name of education, settlement and education in fact deprive detainees of their personal freedom, which are equivalent to compulsory measures in nature. Besides, there is no time limit on the settlement and education. Compulsory measures that deprive citizens of personal freedom should only be implemented following a judgment of the people's court in accordance with the criminal procedure law and should be subject to a definite time limit instead of being determined based on the "social danger" of the settled convict. Therefore, the nature of settlement and education is questionable, which may be illegal in procedure and unconstitutional in content and is somewhat similar to indeterminate sentence or security sentence under the theory of social defense. This provision belongs to typical counter-terrorism legislation with security as the absolute value orientation. However, no matter what means is taken to combat terrorist crimes, the government must ensure that the counter-terrorism measures respect citizens' freedom and do not encroach upon the legal bottom line of human rights and, on this basis, shoulder other responsibilities to citizens.

The criminal legislation in China regarding terrorist crimes also manifest the value of giving priority to security. First, the Amendment (3) was formulated in response to the actual need of crackdown on terrorist crimes by the international community after "9.11". The Amendment (3) draft pointed out that the draft was prepared "for the purposes of cracking down on terrorist activities, better safeguarding national security and social order and protecting people's lives and property security"; meanwhile, "in view of the regulations of the UN Security Council, countries should criminalize the act of providing or raising funds for terrorist activities", so the draft criminalized the act of providing money, property or other financial supports to terrorist organizations. In short, the purpose of the Amendment (3) is to meet the call of the counter-terrorism committee established by the United Nations after "9.11" to various countries to intensify prevention of terrorist acts at home and abroad and in various regions, effectively combat international and domestic terrorism crimes and ensure national and social security. Second, the Amendment (8) has revised the punishment scope of special recidivists in Article 66 of the criminal law and adds convicts of terrorism crimes and crimes of a gangland nature as special recidivists. Since the enactment of the Amendment (3), the number of terrorist crime cases has risen and some terrorist convicts released after serving their sentences committed terrorist crimes again who seriously jeopardized the national and social security. However, in accordance with the prior provisions of the criminal law, only a convict that committed crimes of endangering national security twice would be punished as a special recidivist, which is not conducive to crackdown on terrorist crimes. In order to "broaden the scope of special recidivists, and toughen punishments for terrorist activities and crimes of a gangland nature", Article 66 of the criminal law has been amended. Third, the legislative concept of the Amendment (9) about terrorist crimes is also security. Legislators pointed out: as "multiple severe violent terrorist cases have occurred in some places in recent years and cybercrimes also exhibit new characteristics, it is necessary to proceed from the overall national security perspective and take into account of the linkage and coordination between the criminal law and the counter-terrorism law, the counter-espionage law and other draft regulations on national security to amend and supplement relevant provisions of the criminal law". Obviously, the three amendments are all aimed at punishing crimes and protecting the people and tasked with safeguarding the national and social security, which ensures their consistency with the purpose and mission of the criminal law in Articles 1 and 2 and also testifies to the resolve to fight against terrorist crimes and protect the national and social security and interests.

All in all, either the Counter-terrorism Law, the basic law of China against terrorism, or the several amendments of the criminal law that make special legislation on terrorist crimes demonstrate that the public security is the primary value upheld by the counter-terrorism legislation in China.

2.2.2.2 The concrete charges of terrorist crimes reflect the absolute security value

The exclusive charges of terrorist crimes in the current criminal legislation in China all serve to implement the criminal policy of cracking down on terrorist crimes at an early time. This means that the charges of terrorist crimes are applied not to overt terrorist criminals in many cases but to merely potential "terrorist criminals", while the so-called potential terrorist criminals might be real or just might be ordinary citizens that have not been identified as terrorist criminals. "The penalty distribution has been created to pose effective deterrence to future crimes". Deterrence aimed at other potential criminals refers to "general deterrence", while deterrence targeted at arrested offenders denotes "special deterrence"; "in extreme cases, general deterrence would justify the punishment for innocent people", so general deterrence mainly reflects the security value of the criminal law. The terrorist offenses prescribed by the criminal law of China, particularly the Amendment (9), embody exactly the security value of the criminal law.

First, the criminal law touting the security value is prone to use uncertain legal concepts, while the criminal law pursuing the value of freedom places special emphasis on the clarity of *nulla poena sine lege*. In the case of terrorist crimes, the most uncertain legal concept is "terrorism". According to incomplete statistics, several hundreds of definitions about terrorism are in use in the international academia. However, the peculiarity of terrorist crimes renders it impossible to nail down a universally accepted definition of terrorism or precise definitions of terrorist crimes, terrorist activities or terrorists, which has greatly compromised the affirmation and combat of terrorist crimes. The same question has also been haunting the legislation of terrorist crimes in China. The current Decisions on Relevant Issues Concerning Strengthening Counter-terrorism Work and the Counter-terrorism Law all take the word "terrorism" as the core basic concept of terrorist crimes but fail to ascertain what "terrorism" is. The ambiguity of the basic definition of terrorism-related crimes would directly affect the accurate application of relevant terrorist offenses, but this is exactly the characteristic of security criminal law since vague provisions are easier to interpret and apply and conducive to fighting terrorist crimes and protecting national and social security. One derivative of the *nulla poena sine lege* principle is the principle of clarity. Equivocal laws would cause citizens unable to predict their own behaviors and inevitably lead to misjudgments due to numerous ambiguous concepts, which is a violation of the *nulla poena sine lege* principle. Meanwhile, such ambiguous legal concepts would pose challenges to the practice of terrorist crime governance.

Second, the criminal law in pursuit of security value is inclined toward criminalization, expansion and prepositioning of crimes. Taking the Amendment (9) as an example, its legislation about terrorist crimes concerns about the criminalization of new terrorist activities and broader punishment scope and higher punishment degree for existing terrorist crimes. Since the crackdown in the aftermath of terrorist crimes can hardly remedy the huge losses incurred, it is generally believed by the international community that the fight against terrorist crimes should center on "how to effectively prevent them in advance", which is also an important consideration in China's legislation about terrorist crimes. (1) In response to such legislative requirements, five exclusive charges of terrorist crimes have been added in the Amendment (9). Preparatory acts of terrorist crimes are prescribed as crimes, thus adding the crime of making preparations for terrorist activities; whoever advocates terrorism or extremism or instigates terrorist activities by way of preparing or distributing any book, audio or video materials or any other article advocating terrorism or extremism or by instructing or issuing information is convicted of the crime of advocating terrorism and extremism or instigating terrorist activities; whoever, by using extremism, instigates or coerces the public to sabotage the implementation of the marriage, judicial, education, social management or any other system determined in national laws is convicted of the crime of using extremism to sabotage the implementation of laws; whoever forces anyone else to wear the costume or symbol that advocates terrorism or extremism in a public place by means of violence or coercion is convicted of the crime of forcing others to wear the costume or symbol advocating terrorism or extremism; whoever illegally holds any book, audio or video materials or any other article while obviously aware that it advocates terrorism or extremism, if the circumstances are serious, is convicted of the crime of illegal holding items advocating terrorism or extremism. The core behavior of terrorist crimes is violent attacks, such as terrorist assassination and terrorist bombing attacks. The criminalization of preparatory terrorist acts fulfills the legislative requirement of the international community for advance prevention of terrorist crimes. (2) The Amendment (9) adds the crime of failing to perform the information network security management obligation, the crime of illegal use of the information network, the crime of providing assistance to information network criminal activities and the crime of organizing or providing financial support to illegal assembly. The first three belong to crimes of information network security but are also highly relevant to terrorist crimes. In terms of the governance of terrorist crimes, a very important link in advance prevention of terrorist crimes is how to take effective measures to collect information about terrorist activities, how to boost cooperation among intelligence departments worldwide to build an information security net against terrorism as well as increase the crackdown on cybercrimes to share information about counter-terrorism. Therefore, the first charges are created separately for accessories to cybercrimes by augmenting the obligations of the network service provider and network user for security administration or legal use of information network to foster a secure network environment and make it possible to combat cybercrimes and increase its odds. The crime of organizing or providing financial support to illegal assembly does not contain the word "terrorism" but could actually be subsumed under the exclusive charges of terrorist crimes. Although assembly is a neutral word and means a gathering or meeting, illegal assembly alters the nature of the assembly behavior. However, there is no applicable basis for what constitutes an illegal assembly in the Law of the People's Republic of China on Assembly, Procession and Demonstration, nor in the Amendment (9). From the analysis of the legal interests of this crime, an act that disrupts social order seems all able to be convicted. This charge also furnishes a convenient channel for criminalization and punishment for the governance of terrorist crimes, since once a suspicious gathering that may endanger the public order is detected, the person who organizes and provides financial supports for several times could be inculpated. It is quite obvious that legislators create this charge to achieve timely crackdown on such behaviors with the intention of nurturing an orderly social environment free from terrorism. Therefore, this charge is a newly created terrorist crime to effectively achieve advance prevention of terrorist crimes. (3) Although some crimes are not new, the Amendment (9) alters the contents of existing crimes to greatly expand the punishment scope of terrorist crimes, which also is a response to the legislative requirement on prevention of terrorist crimes. For example, the crime of illegally producing or selling special espionage devices or eavesdropping or secret photographing devices in Article 24 and the crime of refusing to provide relevant evidences about any other person's commission of a crime of espionage, terrorism or extremism in Article 38 of the Amendment (9) increase the objects of crimes and broaden the punishment scope. Despite without the word "terrorist", some charges are in fact created to fight against terrorist crimes from the perspective of legislative setup and applicable scope of the charges. The crime of failing to fulfill the obligation of information network security management, the crime of illegal use of the information network, the crime of providing assistance to information network criminal activities, the crime of organizing or providing financial support to illegal assembly and the crime of organizing or utilizing any superstitious sect, secret society or cult organization or using superstition to cause any other person's serious injury or death all give consideration to prevent the occurrence and spread of terrorist crimes. Among these crimes, the first four are newly created and the last one is a revision of the prior crime to expand its punishment scope. Besides, the first three cybercrimes are newly created to combat network terrorist crimes. In a word, to safeguard the public security and punish terrorist crimes, the Amendment (9) criminalizes some acts to broaden the punishment scope of the criminal law against terrorist crimes.

The legislation about terrorist crimes in the Amendment (9) realizes the foregoing criminalization and expansion of punishment scope by adding new provisions of the criminal law and also extends to the stage before actual sabotage of legal interests for advance intervention, namely prepositioning of crimes. The crime of making preparations for terrorist crimes is preparatory behaviors before the start of formal terrorist activities and is prescribed as a criminal activity. Since the act of making preparations for terrorist activities belongs to preparation for a crime and terrorist crimes are felonies, the preparation for a crime is punishable in criminal laws of many countries. Nevertheless, what kinds of acts should be affirmed as the "preparatory" behavior? "In the field of criminal substantive laws, criminal culpability could be traced to time points before the criminal act is carried out". Similarly, the prepositioning of punishment is also manifested in another four exclusive charges of terrorist crimes, which do not incur any actual harm but are merely prepositioned behaviors with the danger of terrorist crimes. Therefore, the affirmation of such behaviors might also be challenging. Could casual and occasional references to terrorism be confirmed as "advocacy"? Should boycotting intermarriage between different ethnic groups due to religious beliefs be deemed as "using" extremism to undermine law enforcement? Could leering at others to hint them to wear costume of terrorist be affirmed as "coercion"? Could solely holding a terrorist book without subjective cognition be identified as "illegal possession"? What is extremism, what costumes and signs can be determined as "terrorist or extremist costumes or signs", what items could be considered "terrorist or extremist items" and what behaviors could be affirmed as "advocating terrorism or extremism"? The legislation about the crime of organizing, leading or participating in terrorist organizations suggests, "the criminal sanction could be extended to so-called 'status offenses', in other words, the single status of 'organization member' constitutes a crime",[5] which is also a type of crime prepositioning.

In brief, the imputation of terrorist activities in the criminal law of China as well as amendment of existing terrorist crimes all aim to expand the punishment scope, and so does the prepositioning of punishments against terrorist crimes. By this, the security value of the criminal law has been amplified while its function of protecting citizens' freedom and human rights takes a backseat. To achieve the purpose of governance of terrorist crimes, traditional principles of rule of law, such as the principle of last resort, the principle of clarity as well as the principle of *nulla poena sine lege,* are weakened and often are sacrificed for irrational punishment needs. The criminal law that should have the stability quality of law becomes increasingly "flexible", which is exactly the characteristic of security criminal law. However, the excessive flexibility will "lead the law to a regrettable or even perilous direction" and directly result in "obliteration of the criminal law". The punishment scope of the criminal law has been further broadened, the security value been accentuated and its purpose "has distinctly shifted to prevention and security where the state starts to intervene before a crime occurs and the suspicion of the specific crime against a doer has been dispelled". All these may be effective for the governance of terrorist crimes but perhaps are signals that need to be tackled with caution in terms of human rights protection.

2.2.3 "Limited counter-terrorism": Rule of law objective of terrorist crime governance under the dilemma

In the course of terrorist crime governance, if countries around the world, including China, do not abstain from the goal of building a country under the rule of law, some questions need to be addressed circumspectly and pondered over from the jurisprudence, including how to ensure that terrorist offenders do not undermine the democracy and freedom of a state and how to minimize the risk of violating "core values of rule of law", namely "dignity and freedom of human beings" in the process. Terrorist crimes are horrible because of their violent means, destructive consequences and indeterminate targets. To protect the safety of civilians and peace of the society, it is imperative to deter and punish terrorist crimes with necessary legal means. However, could we safeguard the security of the majority at the cost of the innocent minority? Could the judiciaries be given unlimited authorities for secret arrest and assassination to thwart leakage of information about the counter-terrorism campaign? Such questions are essential because terrorist criminals are often hidden among ordinary civilians. "Those powerful measures, either overt or covert, employed to deal with terrorists and protect civilians are also often likely to harm the freedom and rights of the protected civilians, which just plays into the hands of terrorists. Therefore, counter-terrorism decisions are difficult to be made". Back to legislation of terrorist crimes, should the counter-terrorism legislation be security-oriented to crush terrorism at an early time or freedom-oriented to maximally ensure the citizens' freedom and human rights? This is also a dilemma.

However, a decision has to be made though difficult. Based on the limited state argument regarding post-World War II democracy reconstruction of German and in view of the characteristics of terrorist crimes and the property of the criminal law, it is appropriate to put forward the "limited counter-terrorism theory" as the governance model for terrorist crimes. To ensure the legitimacy of terrorist crime governance methods, it is necessary to establish the "limited counter-terrorism theory" based on the "limited state theory". Counter-terrorism governance means that the state apparatus must be granted certain powers to deter the terrorist crimes and punish terrorist offenders. However, the questions are how much powers should be given to contain terrorist crimes? Could the state apparatus be given indefinite powers for the purpose of fighting terrorist crimes? "Who gave permission for the state to exercise such powers?" "Could humans impose judgment on humans?" These questions should be considered upon the establishment of the governance model for counter-terrorism. At present, there are many violations of human rights in various countries in order to control terrorist crimes. For example, after "9.11", the legislation of some countries allowed the long-term detention of foreign citizens without basic guarantees; some new counter-terrorism provisions may not provide the legal protection recognized by international human rights law at the national level, while the purpose of these international human rights laws is to prevent human rights violations, in particular legal safeguards to prevent and prohibit torture and ill-treatment; the special rapporteur on freedom of expression highlights that the war on terror is being used by authorities in many countries as a means of imposing restrictions on the Internet and publications; on March 22, 2002, the national security department of Georgia arrested two Georgian Chechen activists working with refugees in the Pankis Canyon on suspicion of ties to Al Qaeda because they were the only Georgian citizens that went on a pilgrimage to Mecca in 2002.[6] Such examples defy enumeration.

In order to prevent the expansion of counter-terrorism powers and avoid undue violations of civil liberties and human rights by state power, the efforts to fight terrorism with law-based means must be grounded on the "limited state" theory for the reconstruction of democratic countries after World War II and restrict the expansion and misuse of state power in the counter-terrorism process. After World War II, elites in the European intellectual circles continued to reflect on why World War II broke out and moreover pondered over the urgent problems confronting the social democratic reconstruction in Europe after World War II. Europeans were keenly aware of the democratic responsibility of the society and the necessity of restating democracy in Europe. The priority in the agenda of rebuilding European democracy was to "stem the resurgence of totalitarianism" and "ensure that post-war democracies were limited states firmly built on individual rights"; while the security value advocated by the limited state theory took human rights as its moral basis. This indicates that all countries should establish the "limited counter-terrorism theory" and stress that the counter-terrorism power of a country must be subject to certain constraints and effectively exercised within the scope of democracy and freedom. For this reason, the "limited terrorism theory" is unfolded on the following three levels: recognize the limitations of "law-based counter-terrorism" model, where the "law-based counter-terrorism" should not be excessively advocated, at least not as the primary means against terrorism, regardless of the feasibility of "war against terrorism"; recognize the limitations of "criminal (law-based) counter-terrorism" and limitation of the rule of law in criminal justice since too many terrorist crimes and too harsh penalties against terrorism will only lead to the loss of national freedom and the security at the expense of freedom is meaningless in the rule of law; the legislation about terrorist crimes should follow "the concept of security value on the premise of freedom" and waives the legislative goal dominated by security.

2.2.3.1 "Limited counter-terrorism theory" level 1: Concept of limited law-based counter-terrorism

In the current international community, "law-based counter-terrorism" has become the primary principle and direction of terrorism governance. However, the counter-terrorism efforts under the rule of law should not kill the golden goose. A state that fights against terrorism with various means, particularly law-based ones, should not exhaust all tricks and must use with caution legal means adverse to human rights protection; those already in use should be practiced conscientiously and prevented from expansion. For this end, the "concept of limited law-based counter-terrorism" should be established; otherwise, the counter-terrorism under the rule of law will not only be doubted for its legitimacy but also produce unsatisfactory outcomes.

For a long time, "we have paid too much attention to the normal society and firmly believe in the power of human rationality and the orderly development of the society".[7] However, such a way of thinking has been shattered by the occurrence of terrorist crime. Terrorist crimes are not behaviors in a normal society but are considered to be between war and crime and belong to a kind of abnormal events. They are highly uncertain, unexpected, unconventional and global, which are typical risk features of the risk society. The rule of law can merely resolve the problem of order rather than the problem of risk; thus, terrorist crimes as the top risk of the human society could only be tackled by other means. One solution to the risk in the risk society is the distribution of responsibility instead of the simplified rule of law. Terrorist crimes, one of the most serious social risks spreading around the world, have many causes; correspondingly, the governance of terrorist crimes should follow the same solution to risks in the risk society. This means that in the face of terrorist crimes, the discussion should be based on the mentality of cause-countermeasure in the criminology, and in light of the cause, efforts should be made to assign responsibilities and mechanisms for solving the problem.

In the current era, the fundamental risk in the classic industrial society further escalates into "a conflict of responsibility distribution" in the risk society, and the outbreak of this conflict "entails how to allocate, prevent, control and recognize as well as deal with the accompanying risks in the production process", such as "nuclear technology, chemical technology, genetic research, threats to the environment, over-militarization and growing impoverishment outside western industrial societies". The global grim situation of terrorist crimes today is inseparable from a series of international political moves and conspiracies orchestrated by Western countries and also is an embodiment of human beings being mired in the Hobbesian war. Behind the terrorist crimes are the deepest-seated and toughest racial, cultural, political and economic problems. For example, the terrorist incidents in the Middle East are directly related to the Western forces' apathy to the Afghan issue and their support for the Soviet Union's invasion of Afghanistan that further exacerbated the situation there.

The international community has been making attempts to offer good recipes to sanction terrorist crimes through various international conventions, but facts have proved that the law-based counter-terrorism fails to obtain expected outcomes. To this end, the plan of responsibility distribution based on risk resolution must eliminate various causes that lead to terrorist crimes to effectively control terrorist crimes, rather than simply resorting to the rule of law. Terrorist crimes as a result of multiple causes must be resolved through joint efforts and all countries should foster the concept of mainly relying on joint efforts to combat terrorism while realizing the limits of counter-terrorism under the rule of law. Besides, Western powers that cause terrorist crimes must be endowed with more responsibilities instead of making excessive demands on other countries in the name of the United Nations to enact laws to sacrifice citizens' personal freedom in exchange for security. Regarding the counter-terrorism, "those politicians that intend to restrict civil liberties are obliged to elucidate whether the measures they propose could actually increase security"; if no, they should reach a consensus on the view of limited law-based counter-terrorism so as to push forward counter-terrorism through synergy. Naturally, the specific measures of synergistic counter-terrorism need to be determined by governments through negotiation with high political, legal and management intelligence. This ticklish problem cannot be addressed by one country nor by the rule of law; meanwhile, it may only be sorted out after resolving the underlying international political and economic conflicts.

2.2.3.2 "Limited counter-terrorism theory" level 2: Concept of limited criminal counter-terrorism

One traditional characteristic of Chinese laws is to equate the "law" with "punishment".[8] Therefore, under the precondition of advocating a limited use of law-based counter-terrorism, the law-based counter-terrorism is highly likely to be deemed as an equivalent of criminal counter-terrorism. The peculiarity of terrorist crimes and the criminal law as a double-edged sword require the criminal governance of terrorist crimes to uphold the principle of *nulla poena sine lege* and stress the limitation of power by rights, namely limiting the state's mobilization of punishment power by the protection of citizens' rights. Therefore, the "concept of limited criminal counter-terrorism" should be brought about, where the criminal legislation about terrorist crimes should incorporate the concept of prudence and modesty when the model of counter-terrorism under the rule of law is established and adopted; the governance of terrorist crimes should be "outsourced" to other legal fields so as to make sure that the last resort trait of the criminal law is not lost and its rule of law foundation not undermined.

Therefore, the special traits of terrorist crimes determine that controlling terrorist crimes by the criminal law is tantamount to milking the bull. Terrorist crimes are characterized by a well-knit organization system, well-equipped arms and well-trained personnel and are extremely cruel, violent and ferocious, whose harm and influence on the evolution of world civilization, political situation, economic development, ecological environment and human life and health are comparable to or even to some extend exceed wars; wars are generally targeted at the "hard" target of the hostile country, while terrorist crimes are aimed at "soft" targets such as innocent civilians and civil facilities; moreover, wars often cherish the lives of soldiers to ensure the continuity of combat effectiveness, while terrorist crimes always use human bombs regardless of common ruin. Therefore, terrorist crimes are by no means simple ordinary criminal offenses and are underestimated if with the intention to solve them by the criminal legislation, criminal litigation or criminal law enforcement. Terrorist crimes would not only lead to casualties and enormous economic losses in the victimized countries or regions but also achieve far greater psychological and political goals by "conveying information and images" themselves: the terrorist violence disseminates fear and horror and after the propaganda of media stings the sensitive economic and political system of modern society that is then subjugated to political blackmail", so terrorist crimes are a type of "asymmetrical and quasi-warlike" non-ordinary criminal offenses. Therefore, even if under the model of law-based counter-terrorism, it is noteworthy that the criminal law, a conventional tool for combating crimes, has limited effects against abnormal terrorist crimes.

That being the case, it is reasonable to abandon the view of omnipotence of criminal law upon terrorist crime governance with the criminal law and establish the "concept of limited criminal counter-terrorism", where the criminal law must be applied prudently and modestly to combat terrorist crimes.

First, terrorist crimes are a type of "crimes of belief as political offenses", to which the criminal law has limited effects so it must be used with caution. Leaving aside whether terrorist crimes are wars, they are by no means ordinary criminal offenses merely in terms of law-based governance. Terrorist crimes are typical "crimes of belief as political offenses", namely they are political offenses and also have strong religious complexion. Most scholars think that terrorism and terrorist crimes are political and those without political motives or intents are not terrorist crimes. Therefore, terrorist crimes are first of all political offenses that are carried out for the purpose of disrupting the basic order of the state but at the same time are not just ordinary crimes intended to overthrow the state or government and are conflicts triggered when "the pervasive ethical complex" is continuously "brought into another group of people"; meanwhile such ethical complex is bonded by "religion". Therefore, terrorist crimes are both political offenses and crimes of belief. The offenders of crimes of belief have the greatest esteem for the religion they believe in and are willing to give up everything for it, including their own lives. Terrorists attempt to convey their radical religious thoughts by the methods and means of terrorist crimes and then fight against the ideology, beliefs and values of the civilized world. "For most terrorist organizations, their primary goal is to build an 'authentic value and religious order' around the world". Afghanistan, the hub of the global terrorist network, has impressively revealed to mankind the inner spiritual drive of terrorists. Laws, including criminal law, as a governance tool in a civilized society, have a strong instrumental character, particularly the criminal law that has always been used as a means of combating crimes. However, the court may imprison a person with terrorist thoughts by declaring him guilty but cannot force the terrorist to drop his terrorist thoughts. Terrorist offenders have a firm self-identity and remain adamant to their religious sects and political beliefs, who are less likely to alter their spirit and personality even if getting physically eliminated; this is why human bombs are willing to come forward to sacrifice their lives. Against the ferocious and cruel acts perpetrated by such terrorist offenders, the criminal law has undoubted limited deterrence.

Second, the time lag in the emergence of terrorist crimes makes their reconnaissance and prevention extremely likely to infringe upon human rights, so the criminal law must be applied modestly. Terrorist crimes are well-organized, thoroughly planned and highly confidential; once occurring, they often lead to a large number of casualties and seriously affect national construction and social development. However, terrorist activities are subject to lengthy orchestration and difficult to detect in the early stage, whose high risk and destructiveness would usually show in a very short time before the activity is carried out; this is also an important reason why terrorist crimes are difficult to control. Take the 2014 terrorist incident in Kunming of Yunnan province in China as an example. Before its occurrence, the criminal investigation organs did not detect any signs. This also explains why the legislation about terrorist crimes in various countries, including China, is always formulated for abstract potential damage offenses. However, the problem is that the crackdown on terrorist crimes at an early stage by virtue of legislation can easily lead to unjust, false and wrongly convicted cases or cases of human rights infringements. (1) There are often no obvious evidences for such crimes, so it is difficult to determine whether the suspect is really a terrorist criminal when the activity has not been carried out. The Muslim boy pencil box case vividly illustrates the violation of citizens' human rights by counter-terrorism efforts. It can be seen that in the counter-terrorism practice, there exist human rights risks when the terrorist activity has not been conducted and the evidences available cannot affirm the terrorist crime and incriminate the suspect. (2) The criminal procedure law of China stipulates that interviews for cases of crimes endangering national security, terrorist crimes and particularly serious bribery crimes must be approved by the investigation organ, which are possible factors breeding unjust, false and wrongly convicted cases of terrorist crimes. This is not just a conjecture. For example, the research report reveals that the above "three types of cases" are at risk of arbitrary interpretation, which has become a shield for some case-handling organs. The foregoing provisions of the criminal law and arbitrary interpretation and intervention of relevant agencies in the handling of terrorist crimes undoubtedly make it difficult to protect the human rights of defendants in terrorist crime cases. (3) The conviction culture of the criminal law of China has been to eliminate all evil, and as the old saying goes, justice has long arms. "For a long time, the philosophy of criminal justice guiding civilians and judicial officers has been 'never let off a single bad one'. Based on the experience of western countries that have relatively complete judicial systems, Shen Deyong tried to persuade the public to accept the fact: to prevent unjust, false and wrongly convicted cases and never wrong a good person, there is a possibility to 'let off' some bad guys. This is the price that is bound to pay". Under such circumstances, once arrested, the suspects of terrorist crimes are extremely difficult to be exculpated. "Why is acquittal so difficult? The most fundamental reason rests on the thought of presumption of guilt. Why are illegal evidences difficult to be excluded? The crux of the problem is the production of evidence". "Without the presumption of innocence or the exclusion of illegal evidences, to protect the human rights of terrorist crime suspects would naturally become a problem". The case of Wang Bingzhang in China that has drawn limelight in the international community is an example, which was criticized by the United Nations Human Rights Committee due to evidence issues. This demonstrates that to ensure impeccable conviction and sentencing of terrorist crimes, the criminal justice in China must guarantee the availability of reliable and sufficient incriminating evidences; if without sufficient evidences, suspects of terrorist crimes can only be acquitted.

If the world pattern and unfair world political and economic order remain unchanged and people from different cultures do not show tolerance or understanding to each other, our understanding and governance of terrorist crimes can only stay at an irrational level. Using the criminal law prudently and modestly to combat terrorist crimes can help formulate more reasonable counter-terrorism strategies in a rational way. Criminal law is a heteronomous means of social control with material coercive power. Excessive reliance on the punishment to control terrorist crimes is like asking a tiger for its skin. "Replace violence with violence without knowing the error". Therefore, the criminal legislation about terrorist crimes in various countries should foster the concept of "limited criminal counter-terrorism" and abandon the practice of regarding the criminal law as the most powerful means against terrorist crimes.

2.2.3.3 "Limited counter-terrorism theory" level 3: Concept of limited security value

Regarding serious terrorist crimes, the criminal legislation of various countries seems inclined to stress more on ensuring social security than the freedom protection function of the principle of *nulla poena sine lege*. The criminal law "increasingly becomes a tool to rein in acts that seriously disrupt social and national order" and a tool "providing auxiliary supports to international and domestic policies" that "assist in" fighting terrorist crimes. The criminal legislation of various countries respond to the counter-terrorism needs of our era with least delay and most extensive coverage and fully reflect the value of the security criminal law in punishing crimes to protect the people. The problem is that seeking the security value at the expense of freedom is not justified; if the rule of law in criminal justice breaks away from civil liberty to achieve the protection of national and social security, the security earned in this way is also meaningless. The close-knit criminal legislation about terrorist crimes and improper security precautions would lead to a crisis in the human rights protection function of the criminal law. Therefore, after the law-based counter-terrorism means are retired to the backseat, the limits of the rule of law means in criminal justice should be further recognized and "the view on security value on the premise of freedom" should be established, which is also the core of the "limited security value concept".

In terms of worldwide counter-terrorism, after "9.11", the domestic legislation of various countries and regional counter-terrorism conventions of international organizations have all been continuously beefing up counter-terrorism endeavors, "even exceeding the need of security and freedom protection", thus causing "it impossible to truly respect and ensure basic human rights". Counter-terrorism would undoubtedly require paying the price of human rights to some extent and security interests must be conditioned on restricting or even sacrifice certain basic rights, but such sacrifices must have a limit, namely establishment of the "view on security value on the premise of freedom". The genuine security relies on the formation of an environment where human rights are fully realized, respected and protected. When fundamental freedoms are trampled on, no room of democracy, alienation and complaints would turn into politically motivated violence, there is no way to fulfill the goal of genuine security.

"The view on security value on the premise of freedom" entails preventing too many crimes in the criminal legislation of terrorist crimes and confining the legislation of terrorist crimes within a reasonable range to prohibit its excessive invasion into civil liberties. The legislation of terrorist crimes is a means of the criminal law that the state uses for the purpose of security, where the state sacrifices the personal rights and freedom of civilians to protect the society. If a country "emphasizes on the whole over the individual, this would inevitably give birth to authoritarian criminal law", which is also an "intolerant law". When the criminal law prescribes what clothes to wear, what books to read and what to say as crimes, the security value would then prevail everything and the personal freedom room of civilians would be greatly squeezed. "Sacrificing freedom for security" may eventually undermine the mass base which is not conducive to the isolation of terrorist crimes. Hence, the position of "expanding the circle of terrorist crimes" in the criminal legislation to "strengthen counter-terrorism operations" should be denounced.

On the one hand, the appropriateness of existing terrorist crimes should be reflected upon. The terrorist crimes prescribed in the criminal law of China should be analyzed one by one for their legitimacy. For example, whether the increasingly heavier punishments are appropriate for the crime of organizing, leading and participating in terrorist organizations; whether the addition of property punishment to peripheral or early terrorist crimes such as the crime of advocating terrorism go against the principle of balance between crime and punishment; whether it is advisable to stipulate the assistance to terrorist crimes as the crime of providing financial supports to terrorist crimes to make the accomplice a principal offender; whether the diction "illegal assembly" depicted in the crime of organizing and providing financial supports to illegal assembly is too vague and is "unclear and invalid" due to violation of the derivative principle of the *nulla poena sine lege*; after the crime of fabricating and intentionally spreading false information is added in the Amendment (9), whether the crime of fabricating and intentionally spreading false information about terrorist crimes in the Amendment (3) needs to be retained; whether the creation of terrorist crimes related to possession contravenes the traditional culpability principle of the criminal law; whether too many potential damage offenses of terrorist crimes have been criminalized. However, one concept that should be established is that "majority criminal law scholars have a skeptical and negative attitude about the expansion of the scope of criminal law and intensification of punishment that legislators are committed to", and that the criminal law is required to "protect civilians from arbitrary legislation" based on the principle of *nulla poena sine lege.* This shall act as the yardstick to reflect on the existing legislation about terrorist crimes.

On the other hand, whether new terrorist crimes should be added should be treated with caution. Our future legislation about terrorist crimes should take criminalization and penalization prudently; terrorist activities are at best be governed by existing crimes and there is no need to add new charges in the short term. Meanwhile, other suggestions about terrorist crime legislation that covertly expands the punishment scope of the criminal law should also be addressed prudently. For example, some scholars claim, "the Amendment (9) provides for a series of new crimes related to terrorism and extremism, which mainly concern about preparatory acts or instigating acts of violent and terrorist activities, and does not prescribe the implementation of violent and terrorist activities as separate crimes. Due to the lack of special counter-terrorism charges in the current criminal code of China, criminal activities with violent and terrorism colors can only be convicted and punished in accordance with ordinary crimes such as crime of intentional homicide, crime of intentional injury, crime of kidnapping, and crime of bombing, which can barely reflect the peculiarity of counter-terrorism work. Therefore, violent and destructive crimes should be separated from relevant chapters and sections of specific provisions of the criminal code and in combination of their particular purpose of crime commission, are subsumed under a special charge—crime of terrorist activities that is to be set forth in Chapter 2 Crimes of Endangering Public Security in specific provisions of the Criminal Code of China".[9] This is a statement of criminalization that continues to expand the circle of terrorist crimes. The core means of terrorist crimes are mainly violence such as killing and explosion, but this does not mean that the criminal law should add exclusive charges for terrorist crimes corresponding to these common core means of terrorist crimes. Crimes of homicide and explosion have already been existent in the criminal law. For example, violent crimes out of the motive and purpose of terrorism have no particularity when evaluated from the elements of criminal offenses, so there is no need to separately stipulate like "crime of terrorist homicide" or "crime of terrorist explosion"; they are different from ordinary homicide and explosion crimes in that the motives, purposes and means of terrorist crimes are far more cruel and dangerous than those of ordinary criminal offenses; besides, the latter makes good sense from the perspective of the science of crime countermeasures and synergistic governance of terrorist crimes and there is nothing special about the affirmation of crimes of homicide and bombing in the criminal law. In the early founding days of the People's Republic of China, there was no legal basis for conviction and sentencing in practice so they are highly arbitrary, and all crimes were modified by the word "counter-revolutionary", which has been derided in history. For terrorist crimes, it is also necessary to oppose adding the word "terrorist" to all crimes, which would lead to a generalization of terrorist crimes and has no practical benefits.

The principle of *nulla poena sine lege* and its concept of human rights protection are the essence of the rule of law. Only through delineating the reasonable range of terrorist crimes and formulating laws about terrorist crimes with dual functions of freedom and security can we guarantee the operation and development of the rule of law of a country. Blindly imposing harsh punishments and preventive criminal law is futile and will damage the personal freedom of ordinary citizens, while "the security without human rights and freedom will be meaningless". Therefore, the concept of "security value on the premise of freedom" should be implemented in the legislation about terrorist crimes; the criminalization and penalization of terrorist crimes as well as the mentality of early crackdown should be treated with caution to maximally ensure that citizens have more freedom, prevent the criminal law from converging to the law of war in the "battles" against terrorist crimes and rationally foster the concept that the security value must be based on the realization and protection of the personal freedom of citizens.

It should be noted that the above three layers of the "limited counter-terrorism theory" are of restrictive and progressive relationships. The sequence of above three layers suggests that the governance of terrorist crimes shall mainly depend on joint efforts supplemented by the rule law; then under the model of law-based counter-terrorism, the last resort nature of the criminal law shall be ensured without willful use of the criminal law to combat terrorism; last, if the criminal law has to be applied for counter-terrorism, it is necessary to establish the "view on security value on the premise of freedom" to make sure that criminal legislation reasonably confines the punishment scope for terrorist crimes, take behaviors and their outcomes as the imputation basis as required by the traditional culpability criminal law, remain vigilant about the thought about omnipotence of the criminal law and protect the freedom and human rights of terrorist crime suspects and ordinary citizens from legislation to judicial practice. Terrorist crimes could seriously impede the peace and development of mankind. China is now also plagued by frequent terrorist crimes and faces great challenges in the fight against terrorist crimes. No mercy shall be given to crackdown on terrorist crimes and counter-terrorism means in any form must be supported and recognized by the public. Advocating the limited counter-terrorism theory does not mean ignoring the harmfulness of terrorist crimes nor condoning them. However, in the face of terrorist crimes as "new types of wars" or "quasi-wars", the reasonable counter-terrorism governance model should be solving them with political wisdom by the international community and all sovereign countries, with the rule of law means only playing an auxiliary role. Meanwhile, all countries should make it clear that "there is no compromise between human rights and counter-terrorism" and "the threat of terrorism must be suppressed but the country should prevent counter-terrorism measures from violating human rights". Under the principle of the modern rule of law, the norm of the overall legal order is to protect the basic human rights of the public, so the criminal legislation should be used with caution to resist terrorist crimes. Even if the criminal law is mobilized, it should also be ensured that "the exercise of the ruling power of a country must be bound by the constitution and laws" and finally "converted to concrete protection of the people's basic human rights", so that the criminal legislation and application of the criminal law always uphold the freedom value of the criminal law of a law-based country and follow the concept of security criminal law on the premise of freedom. Only in this way would the rule of law progress of the human society not change its original track due to terrorist crimes. During the construction of the overall national security concept of China, the above goal of rule of law pursued by the terrorist crime governance may perhaps advance the overall governance of national security along the law-based governance track.

2.3 Conclusion

The development of the human rights protection function of the criminal law in China is going through a bottleneck period and confronted with the inherent disadvantage of infeasibility in practice despite with rich connotations. The decriminalization theory undoubtedly offers a critical opportunity to break the deadlock and invigorate the human rights protection function of the criminal law. Statute laws are the important crystallization of human wisdom but the topics of criminalization and decriminalization that are inextricably linked to personal interests can hardly be exhausted; although there are reasons to believe that legislators are in a mind of upholding justice and fairness, we have to admit that legislators have too many difficulties to cope with the complex social situation, or even make unreasonable judgments. The formation of criminalization mentality in judicial practice, of course, may be ascribed to the factors of the judiciary itself but in the final analysis has legislative reasons. The system construction of the decriminalization theory is of great significance for reflecting on the purpose of legislation and responding to judicial conundrums, and its expansion of the human rights protection function in the field of criminal law is worthy of expecting.

Notes

1 Zhao Bingzhi: Whether the Elderly Should Be Exempted from Death for Committing Crimes, *Legal Daily*, October 27, 2010, p. 12.
2 Wu Zongxian: *On Community Correction Legislation and Criminal Law Amendment*, Justice of China, 2009, No. 3.
3 He Yuejun: *Study on the Legislative Mechanism of Risk Society*, China Social Science Press, 2013, p. 125.
4 Ni Chunle: *Special Litigation Procedures for Terrorist Crimes*, Mass Publishing House, 2013, p. 8.
5 See Scales v. United States, 367 U.S. 203, 226-29 (1961), quoted from Liu Tao, see note [5], p. 125.
6 *Human Rights Watch* interviews with attorneys for both the defendants, Tbilisi, April 2002.
7 Lin Dan: *Ulrich Beck's Risk Society Theory and its Influence on China*, People's Publishing House, 2013, p. 169.
8 See Liang Zhiping: *Law' Defense*, Social Sciences in China, 1986, No. 4.
9 Zhao Bingzhi, Du Miao: Criminal Law Amendment (9): Prepositioning of Legal Interests Protection to Weave the Counter-terrorism Legal Net, *Procuratorial Daily*, September 28, 2015, p. 3.

3 Impacts of Criminal Legislation on Legal Dogmatics

Based on the Substantive Decriminalization Theory

3.1 Impact of criminal legislation on legal dogmatics

Legal dogmatics is a methodological paradigm presented by the self-conscious development of current legal researches in China and is an interpretation of the normative nature of law and its possibility from the philosophy of right. Legal dogmatics is not a "meditative" legal research paradigm and can interact with legislation and justice and has the functions of interpreting and guiding legislation, and self-reflection in the process.

Legal dogmatics is based on legal texts, and respecting legal texts or legislation is its basic characteristic. Formal rule of law and substantive rule of law are two propositions that often collide in legal dogmatics, but most of the final conclusions are that the formal rule of law is the basic pattern of the rule of law, and substantive rule of law is the supplement to formal rule of law. Only on the basis of formal rule of law can we pursue substantive rule of law.[1] Legal dogmatics cannot be divorced from legislative stipulations and can only be revitalized by respecting legislation. Despite relatively rich philosophical speculation, legal dogmatics carries out philosophical discussions with legislation as the starting point. At the same time, legal dogmatics also has an irreplaceable function in interpreting and reviewing legislation, which may reinforce theoretically matters that are expressly stipulated and deduce and justify matters that are not expressly stipulated in the law.

On the one hand, legal dogmatics may reinforce theoretically matters that are expressly stipulated in the law. The essence of law lies in reason, which determines what the legislation should include. Some clauses of the ever-changing criminal norms may remain unchanged after hundreds or thousands of years, while some other clauses need to be continuously adjusted with the elapse of time, which should all be explained by legal dogmatics. Of course, the interpretation of legislation by legal dogmatics is not static, and even the same provision may have different connotations under different backgrounds. But even so, the function of legal dogmatics in interpretation of legislation can still endure mainly because legal dogmatics pays attention to system and logic, where the purpose of system construction is to form a set of relatively stable standards and logic is to furnish eloquent methodological supports for reasoning.

DOI: 10.4324/9781003456773-4

On the other hand, legal dogmatics may deduce and justify matters that are not expressly stipulated in the law. In the absence of express provisions in the law, the legal dogmatics may independently promote further development of the law through the rigorous logical reasoning and theoretical justification rather than passively leaving it alone. The further development of the law by the legal dogmatics is an extreme exception, which would not destroy the stability of law; in contrast, successful continuation of law could make legislation quickly adapt to changes in social life if being transformed into legislative stipulations. Moreover, for unreasonable legislative stipulations, legal dogmatics also has the function of criticizing, guiding the legislation to abolish and revise unreasonable provisions.

3.2 Characteristics of China's criminal legislation in the past 40 years of reform and opening up

Over the past 40 years after the reform and opening up policy was introduced, as the national politics has become more powerful and the economy has become more prosperous, the criminal law of New China has sprung up from nothing and grown from rough to detailed, from imperfect to increasingly complete. During this process, the criminal legislation manifests two characteristics: extensive legislation and symbolic legislation.

From 1979 to 1997, the criminal legislation of China showed extensive features. Extensive criminal legislation mainly refers to the first criminal code of New China, the 1979 Criminal Code, which was formulated under the guidance of the rough and cursory legislation concept and manifested the lack of legislative techniques in the initial stage of criminal legislation in China. This legislation concept believes that the law should be formulated in a crude way to maintain its applicability to complex realities … the cursory legislation concept advocates that "justice has long arms" and that the "crude" legislation is a good formula to achieve "non-omission" of justice. The guiding legislative ideology of "rough over detailed" and "crude over meticulous" for the criminal law in 1979 is the product of specific historical background and conditions. Facing complicated political struggles at home and abroad in its early days, the inexperienced rules of new China had a greater need for the convenience of law than the clarity of law; the crude criminal code could be interpreted at the discretion of its users, which of course could help better combat crimes to protect the interests of the country and society. Therefore, "as the main body or main part of China's current criminal legislation, the criminal code features most distinctively in legislative technique flexibility, non-concreteness and poor operability. This has been the consensus of the Chinese criminal law academic circle". The crudeness of the 1979 Criminal Code is firstly manifested in the fact that it did not specify the types of crimes in an elaborate and precise manner but lumped crimes of different natures into one chapter and articles that should have been separated into one article: "The description of crimes was simple in many articles and most of the necessary descriptions of the elements of crime were lacking; the penalties prescribed were too heavy". Moreover, the 1979 Criminal Code only stipulated 130 crimes and set forth the analogy system in Article 79 of the general provisions that "crimes that are not expressly stipulated in the specific provisions of this law could be convicted and punished with reference to the most similar articles in the specific provisions", thus breaking through the barriers for the arbitrary determination of criminal acts.

In response to the above-mentioned shortcomings of the 1979 Criminal Code, the Standing Committee of the National People's Congress established three guiding ideologies for the revision of the 1997 Criminal Law, namely the current criminal law: to formulate a unified and relatively complete criminal code; to maintain legal continuity and Stability; for some originally relatively general and principled regulations, try to ascertain the criminal behavior and make specific stipulations. To this end, the 1997 Criminal Law abolished the analogy system, established the principle of *nulla poena sine lege* as the basic principle of the criminal law and made the provisions on crimes more rigorous and detailed. Narrative facts about a crime were used extensively to replace blank facts about a crime and obscure wording was reduced maximally and such words as serious circumstances, flagrant circumstances and others were clarified to the greatest extent. However, the 1997 Criminal Law did not fundamentally get rid of the rough and cursory features of the 1979 Criminal Code and still showed extensive features on the whole. This could be found in the following two aspects. First, there are still many pocket crimes, for example, the crime of picking quarrels and provoking trouble derived from the crime of hooliganism, the crime of illegal business operation derived from the crime of speculation, the crime of endangering public security by dangerous means and the crime of disrupting production and business operations. These crimes were vaguely worded in connotation and extension and became the vanguard in punishing illegal and criminal acts in practice, which have eventually developed into pocket crimes. Second, since the "1997 criminal legislation was relatively rough and abstract, the supreme judicial organ formulated numerous judicial interpretations that far outnumbered the articles of the criminal law. Without these judicial interpretations, the judiciary could hardly handle the case".

The period from 1997 to the present witnesses the symbolic criminal legislation in China. The symbolic criminal legislation suggests that the 11 amendments promulgated by the legislature following the 1997 Criminal Code were drafted under the guidance of the symbolic legislation concept, which reflects the arbitrariness and poor operability of legal norms in the fledgling stage of criminal legislation in China. Along with the reform and progress of society, many new crimes need to be addressed urgently by criminal legislation; to punish crimes of sabotaging the socialist economic order, terrorist crimes, crimes of corruption and dereliction of duty and ensure the smooth progress of socialist modernization as well as protect the security of lives and property of the state and civilians and maintain the public order, the legislature in China has enacted 11 amendments from 1997 to 2021, increasing the 413 crimes to the current 483 crimes. The creation of new crimes has greatly expanded the punishment scope of the criminal law and transformed the criminal legislation model from the traditional draconian but not rigorous model to rigorous but not draconian and even strict and draconian. However, under the influence of many international human rights conventions, and the reform trend of mitigated punishment in the world, the punishment of these new crimes is not heavy or even very light. For example, regarding the crime of dangerous driving in Article 133 of the criminal law that has been added by the Amendment (8) in 2011, the punishment prescribed is detention plus a fine. Consequentially, in the 20 years since the promulgation of the Criminal Law in 1997, the criminal legislation in China starts to display symbolic features. Symbolic legislation refers to the legislation that conveys the legislators' attitude, sentiment and stance of defeating crimes and threats but does not exert or can hardly exert substantive regulatory effects.[2] By this, legislators are simply aimed to meet the expectations of the society, and "gradually subsume publicly recognized risks into the legal norm system of symbolic legislation", but the actual punishments of crimes fail to have the effect of combating and preventing crimes.

In the past two decades, the symbolic feature of criminal legislation in China is primarily manifested in terrorist crimes, cybercrimes and environmental crimes. Take terrorist crimes for example. What opened the prelude to the symbolic criminal legislation are the three new terrorist crimes added in the "Amendment (3), including the crime of providing financial supports to terrorist activities, the crime of distributing false and hazardous substances and the crime of intentionally disseminating false terrorist information. Subsequently, the Amendment (8) in 2011 added the provision that a convict of terrorist activities could be punished as a recidivist; the Amendment (9) added five terrorist crimes, and revised factual descriptions of terrorist crimes in the paragraph 1 of Article 120, Article 283 and Article 311 of the criminal law and toughened the punishment prescribed. However, although the law has long arms, counter-terrorism efforts can hardly work. So many charges for terrorist crimes have not effectively curbed terrorist crimes and the high incidence around the world testifies the weakness of criminal governance. Terrorist crimes are not ordinary criminal offenses but are the result of political, economic and cultural conflicts among different countries, societies and races; they are not legal problems of a society under the rule of law but are risk problems of a risk society, or even quasi-wars in human society; the means of the rule of law can only solve the order-related problem, but cannot solve the problem of risk or even quasi-war.[3] However, in light of the requirements for crackdown on terrorist crimes in real life and in timely response to people's emotional desire for security, the amendments of criminal law in China still adopt various measures such as criminalization and expansion of punishment for legislation of terrorist crimes. Such legislation is more to address the declined 'perceived security' of civilians and attempt to protect their 'peace of mind' than to safeguard their specific interests, which is more reminiscent of symbolic legislation". In brief, the legislation on terrorist crimes fully reflects the counter-terrorism stance of the Chinese government, so it is symbolic rather than substantial legislation.

The reason why symbolic legislation has become the main feature of criminal legislation in the last two decades is closely related to the influence of the responsive legislative concept. Among the countries entering the modernization stage, countries such as the United Kingdom and the United States led the trend of the world's modernization process by adopting an "endogenous" modernization model and, thus, were the first to suffer severely a series of crimes represented by corruption crimes. Britain, the birthplace of world industrial revolution and even modernization, bore the brunt of the serious challenge of corruption. As a response, the United Kingdom and the United States changed their long-standing common law traditions and resolutely chose the statute law model, gradually forming a "preventive" legislative strategy.[4] Such legislation responding to the realistic needs of combating crimes and the urgent needs of crime prevention often pays too much attention to the comforting effect such as relieving people's anxiety and calming their mood, making criminal legislation focus on responding to social needs and become more open and elastic. It may seem like a legislative model but actually has actually evolved into a policy model of national governance, so symbolic provisions have gradually increased. Slavishly proactive and timely response to the demand for combating crimes has made it difficult for legislators to summarize the actual state of crimes and then rationally formulate legislation, so it's comforting effects are given more prominence than actual effects and expression of stance over legislative operation. Consequently, symbolic legislation has become a salient feature of criminal legislation.

The extensive criminal legislation in the early stage is not only pertinent to technical features but also concerned about substantive contents, while the symbolic criminal legislation in recent years implicates substantive features but also are closely related to the legislative technique. Either the technical form or actual effect, they are all intimately related to the quality of legislation and to some extern, signifies that the criminal legislation in China needs to be improved.

3.3 Reasonable demarcation of the crime circle based on good law and governance and enactment, revision, abolition and interpretation

3.3.1 Legislative path of the decriminalization theory: Good law and governance and enactment, revision, abolition and interpretation

There is a gap between the extensive and symbolic features of criminal legislation in the past 40 years of reform and opening up, and the requirements for scientific legislation in the new era. Although the criminal law is a routine law-making field, as the fundamental law of China, it strengthens that criminal legislation is a major event in promoting and developing the socialist rule of law and also an important task to improve the criminal law; the special status of criminal law determines that the scientific law-making work in the field of criminal law still needs to be intensified. In combination with the trait of the criminal law, the criterion for promoting high-quality criminal legislation by scientific law-making is whether good legislation and governance have been achieved; the specific path is the enactment, revision, abolition and interpretation.

First of all, the criterion for promoting high-quality criminal legislation by scientific law-making is whether good laws and governance have been achieved. General Secretary Xi Jinping emphasized, "the law is of great value in the governance of a country, and good laws are a prerequisite for good governance"[5]; efforts should be made to "advance the development and guarantee good governance through good laws, and integrate the core values of socialism into the various links of legislation, law enforcement, justice and law compliance to develop the socialist rule of law into good laws and governance".[6] To this end, the scientific approach to law-making must be upheld. Therefore, scientific law-making first requires that laws enacted are good so as to achieve good governance on this basis. Considering the trait of the criminal law, whether the criminal law formulated by legislators is a good law is subject to the following three basic criteria: (1) clearly prescribed law, (2) fair and just law, (3) effective law. The first two concepts need not be elaborated; the so-called effective law highlights the protection of legal interests and stresses the infringement and threat of behavior on the interests protected by criminal law and its consequences, but symbolic legislation is often divorced from the acknowledgment of legal interests and predisposed to recognition of behavior norms or ethical order. For example, concerning the crime of forcing others to wear costumes or sign advocating terrorism or extremism stipulated in the Amendment (9), the punishment is not based on infringement of legal interests or consequence without value, nor specific harmful consequences of terrorist crimes, but based on the illegal behavior of wearing clothes or signs related to terrorism, which belongs to normative violations and acts without value. But in fact, "the purpose of criminal law, at least its main purpose, is not to protect the state itself or to maintain ethical order, but to protect the life, body, freedom, and property of individuals", because only these legal interests fully reflect the "security needs of citizens" or the "protection needs of citizens". In other words, protecting specific legal interests is more in line with citizens' needs for security than protecting citizens' peace of mind, and sometimes "the symbolic legislation in response to the call of the people not only fails to relieve the anxiety of the citizens, but even exacerbates it in some cases". In order to make criminal norms more effective, the concept of legal interests should be strengthened to prevent the symbolic legislation from diluting the connotation of legal interests, particularly criminalization-oriented criminal legislation. The guiding function of legal interests must be brought into play, and illegal acts that do not cause actual harmful consequences should not be incorporated into the scope of the criminal normative system.

Secondly, the specific path to promote high-quality criminal legislation with scientific law-making is to simultaneously promote enactment, revision, abolition and interpretation. Good law and good governance are more about value appeals, whose implementation must rely on some specific paths. General Secretary Xi Jinping pointed out, "It is necessary to ensure and promote the sustainable and healthy development of the economy with high-quality legislation. We should cater to the needs of building a new system for an open economy and put in place unified fundamental laws on foreign investment. We should make early arrangements on law-making authorization for areas where the reform and opening up policy is piloted first. Legislative items on intellectual property protection, biological security, land system reform, and ecological civilization construction must be considered as a whole and the law enactment, revision, abolition and interpretation should be pressed ahead simultaneously".[7] As far as criminal legislation is concerned, it is also necessary to promote high-quality criminal legislation in an all-round way through concurrent enactment, revision, abolition and interpretation so as to realize criminal legislation in a scientific way.

"Enactment" refers to criminal law-making in China. The creation of new crimes and formulation of new stipulations should be conducted cautiously and modestly, without undue hastening or over-reaction; the criminal law should be used effectively to combat crimes under the compliance with the modest-and-restraint principle to prevent it from being reduced to a "social administration law" instead of the law of the last resort. Although the modest-and-restraint principle does not mean that the smaller the punishment scope, the better, it does not mean remaining indifferent to the punishment scope of the criminal law while raving about the modest-and-restraint principle or believing that the broader the punishment scope, the better in the context of the activation of legislation. In particular, an excessive number of *mala prohibita* crimes are made criminal in China's criminal legislation as 99% of the crimes in the 11 amendments are *mala prohibita*. Crimes such as dangerous driving, running casinos, organizing and leading pyramid schemes, sitting in an exam on behalf of others, are not necessarily wrong by their very nature but are wrong merely because there are laws prohibiting them. The proper criminalization of these acts helps to achieve the administrative purpose of the state but excessive criminalization makes people think deeply about "Is there any principle to determine what behaviors should be stipulated as crimes and what behaviors should not be stipulated as crimes?" This shows that how to reasonably set up new criminal norms is an important problem to be solved by scientific criminal law-making.

"Revision" refers to the timely rectification of unreasonable criminal norms. For example, whether the principle of *nulla poena sine lege* in Article 3 of the criminal law should be replaced with the classic expression "no crime or punishment without express stipulations by law"; whether clauses about joint crimes in Article 25 of the criminal law should add the provisions about joint crimes of negligence; whether the classification of joint offenders from Article 25 to 29 should be changed to be solely based on the division of labor or on the function so as to avoid various problems caused by the mixed use of these two classification standards in the current criminal law of our country. For some symbolic legislative crimes, the guiding role of criminal legislation and criminal norms in the science and theory of criminal law, criminal justice and criminal law practice should be strengthened to prevent legal provisions from existing only in names in the criminal judicial practice and make sure that the stipulations of criminal legislation are brought into effect.

"Abolition" indicates the timely elimination of criminal norms that are not in use. In the criminal field, the quality of legislation should be improved to ensure and facilitate that civilians could realize fairness and justice in every case. For this reason, it is necessary to carry out criminalization legislation to meet the legislative needs of the risk society for the prevention of crimes and not relinquish the fundamental legislative value of post-crime punishment with legal interests as the core concept. At present, the criminal legislation in our country is mainly prone to criminalization regarding terrorist crimes, computer crimes, information crimes and big data protection crimes; at the same time, some criminal norms that are no longer used, especially some individual crimes, should be abolished or namely decriminalized. Only when enactment and abolition are carried out simultaneously to maintain the fundamental balance between criminalization and decriminalization, can criminal legislation be scientific. "Abolition" includes the abolition of some provisions that are unreasonable and unused in the general provisions of the criminal law. For example, Article 95 of the criminal law has no practical effect in judicial practice, because the article uses miscellaneous provisions with obscure connotation and extension, namely "other injuries that cause grave harm to a person's physical health", after enumeration in the first two paragraphs; either disability, disfigurement or injury of organ functions are ultimately determined in accordance with the Human Body Severe Injury Identification Standards so the provisions in Article 95 are not operable and can be abrogated. Moreover, "abolition", more fundamentally, suggests the repealing of some crimes that have not been used for a long time in the specific provisions of the criminal law. In the Criminal Code of 1997, a considerable number of crimes have been outdated and are no longer applicable along with the development of national economic and criminal policies or criminal theories, which have even lost the meaning of expressing the legislators' sentiment or stance. For example, the crime of falsely declaring the capital to be registered in Article 158 and the crime of false capital contribution and surreptitiously withdrawing the contributed capital in Article 159 have actually expired due to the introduction of a series of economic policies encouraging innovation and entrepreneurship or cancellation of requirements on the company's registered capital. Also, along with the enactment of the policy allowing two children for all couples in the communiqué of the Plenary Session of the Central Committee of the Communist Party of China in 2015, the crime of illegally performing contraception operation in Paragraph 2 of Article 336 of the criminal law to combat behaviors that undermine family planning will undoubtedly be phased out because of changes in the national demographic policy and progress of the times, and this article and the crime concerned will become a new zombie clause and zombie offense in the near future.

Scientific criminal law-making could advance the law-based operation of the judiciary. If the "rule of law government construction" "sets an example for the construction of a rule of law country or rule of law society",[8] criminal legislation in a scientific way would play a central role in the judicial practice of a rule of law country. Efforts should be made to make the criminal legislation more scientific and boost the binding effect of legislation on judicial practice to put an end to zombie clauses like undue defense in Paragraph 3 of Article 20, scarecrow clauses like the crime of refusing to pay labor remuneration in one paragraph of Article 276 or empty clauses with only the numbers of clauses instead of any substantive content like Article 199 of the criminal law after the revision in the amendments. If such clauses or crimes cannot be abolished, revisions shall be made; if revisions are not possible, they should be applied in a timely manner, such as the self-defense clause. In brief, clauses that are left unused for a long time are a waste of legislative resources and a compromise of legal authority. If things go on like this, the cause of the rule of law in China will also be impeded.

"Interpretation" refers to the timely interpretation of unclear criminal norms. From the perspective of the needs of criminal legislation, the interpretation of China's criminal law has always emphasized authoritative interpretations over doctrinal interpretations. Legislative interpretations and judicial interpretations of criminal law are not only numerous and lengthy but also have given rise to the habit that "the criminal law does not apply without interpretation"; authoritative interpretations have formed a secondary law system outside the master law, while "the application of the criminal law, as the master law for conviction and punishment, depends on the secondary law system outside the criminal code, which is predominated by judicial interpretations".[9] Such interpretations ensure the correct implementation of the criminal law, effectively avoid differences and disputes about the provisions of the criminal law in judicial practice and maximally realize judicial fairness. However, the over-concentration of discourse power in legislative and judicial interpretations has stunted doctrinal interpretations and academic disputes, which damps down the enthusiasm of the academia to innovate socialist rule of law theory. In fact, the doctrinal interpretation of criminal law by scholars plays an important role in judicial decisions. For example, in a civil-criminal case, the judge boldly quoted scholars' opinions to substantiate how to coordinate the civil judgment with the effective criminal judgment.[10] Also, in the judgment of a death due to beauty treatment, the judge boldly adopted the objective imputation theory to analyze whether the speaker's acts had created risks not allowed by the law.[11] The practice of these judicial decisions has effectively promoted the guiding role of doctrinal theory to practice and effectively unleashed the positive effects of scholars' interpretations. However, this kind of practice is still very rare in China. The doctrinal interpretation is mostly underestimated, making it difficult to form a system of academic discourse; the academic confidence of Chinese rule of law theory is deeply affected, resulting in an estrangement between the academic discourse and political and legal discourse. In the future work of criminal legislation in our country, endeavors should be made to give full play to the enthusiasm of scholars and promote the application of doctrinal interpretation of law. Only in this way can we "in the process of constructing the theoretical system of the socialist rule of law with Chinese characteristics" "adapt the academic discourse system for the jurisprudence to China's conditions, keep abreast with the time, put it into practice and cater to the needs of the public to coordinate with the political and work discourse for the rule of law and create a rule of law discourse system and theoretical system with Chinese characteristics".[12] Without the doctrinal "interpretation" of law by scholars, criminal provisions, no matter how scientific, are unable to forge a criminal law discourse system with Chinese characteristics.

All in all, the enactment, revision, abolition and interpretation work entails the timely criminalization of new illegal acts, timely modification of unreasonable criminal norms, timely abrogation of criminal norms not in use and timely interpretation of unclear criminal norms. The criminal legislation should be adjusted dynamically to redress the various unreasonable phenomena facing the criminal legislation in China such as enactment without abolition, minor revisions and numerous enactments as well as the emphasis on authoritative interpretation over doctrinal interpretation so as to help shape the scientific criminal law-making system. Through the enactment, revision, abolition and interpretation, the criminal law will be developed gradually into a law with unequivocal provisions, effectiveness, fairness and justice and ultimately into a good law in the real sense so as to achieve good governance; the scientific law-making should be implemented to promote the high-quality criminal legislation and press ahead with the socialist rule of law system.

3.3.2 Three decriminalization concepts from China's criminal legislation

Over the past 40 years of reform and opening up, China's criminal legislation has changed from being extensive to symbolic, reflecting the characteristics of the era transitioning from the traditional planned economy to reform and opening up, which responds to the political and social situation of risk societies at home and abroad. General Secretary Xi Jinping pointed out in his speech at the Symposium on Philosophy and Social Sciences that "the development strategy of philosophy and social sciences is not yet very clear, the discipline system, academic system, and discourse system are poorly constructed, and academic originality is not strong"; at the same time, General Secretary Xi Jinping stated briefly, "those that fall behind get beaten up, those that are poor go hungry and those that have no right to say get scolded. Figuratively, for a long time, the communist party has led the people to solve the three major problems of 'being beaten', 'starving' and 'being scolded'. After several generations of unremitting struggle, the first two problems have basically been solved, but the problem of 'being scolded' has not been rooted out. Striving for the right to speak internationally is a major issue that we must resolve."[13] To this end, we should "adhere to the guidance of Xi Jinping's important exposition on the rule of law in the new era, and apply it throughout the entire field of legal research and discipline development, timely update legal research content, research methods and paradigms, to further accelerate the construction and improvement of the legal discourse system with Chinese characteristics in the new era".[14] Although the discourse system of criminal jurisprudence with Chinese characteristics is not as easy to spread and exert influence as international jurisprudence, criminal legislation and criminal governance are parts of the human rights situation that the international community is concerned about, so the construction of its discourse system has its own particularity and significance. The development of criminal legislation from extensive to symbolic then to scientific legislation emphasizes the realization of good laws and good governance through the enactment, revision, abolition and interpretation of the law, which is in line with the scientific standards and paths of criminal legislation, and will effectively promote the innovative development of the criminal law discourse system under high-quality criminal legislation.

The current research about criminal jurisprudence is in an unprecedented new era. "The new era is an era of inheriting the past and opening up the future, and continuing to secure the great victory of socialism with Chinese characteristics under new historical conditions".[15] How the Chinese criminal jurisprudence in the new era "inherits" the legacy of the former Soviet-Russian criminal jurisprudence, "carries on" the Chinese cultural traditions of the criminal law, "draws on" the experience of German and Japanese criminal jurisprudence to "build" a criminal law discourse system with Chinese characteristics and how China transforms from a country importing discourse concepts in the early stage to an exporter and promotes the amelioration of the criminal law discourse system via the scientific rule of in criminal justice are issues that the Chinese criminal law theorists should deliberate on.

Scientific criminal law-making can promote the formation and development of the criminal law discourse system with Chinese characteristics. The criminal law discourse system is the system of criminal law concepts that originate from the provisions of the criminal code; the concepts of theoretical researches on criminal law are an extension or expansion on the basis of the concepts in the provisions of the criminal code. The "concepts and axioms in the science" of criminal law studied by scholars "are by no means the product of arbitrary and rash conclusions, but are truly existent and finally formed after long-term and profound exploration". For example, although there is no concept of punishment in the chapter on property crimes in the specific provisions of our criminal law, combined with the analysis of crime facts in this chapter, the intention and acts of punishment are the core of property crimes, so the punishment concept for property crimes is precisely an extremely important concept of criminal law derived based on criminal legislation and judicial practice of property crimes.

Based on Chinese experience and Western examples of the law and the reality of Chinese issues and the independence of Chinese consciousness, some criminal law academic discourse systems with Chinese elements that can promote Chinese rule of law culture have been formed under the guidance of Chinese criminal legislation.

3.3.2.1 Leniency combined with strictness

The provisions about recidivism and self-surrender in Chapter 4 Sentencing of China's Criminal Code, especially commutation and parole, are a penalty system established according to the criminals' different situations about education through labor. In order to give full play to the positive functions of commutation, parole and other systems, China has put in place the criminal policy of combining leniency with strictness, emphasizing that "overall planning and all-round consideration should be made for coordinated use of leniency and strictness". The combination of leniency and strictness has a long history in Chinese legal culture. Historical documents such as *Shangshu·Lvxing* (Classics of History·Penal Law of Lv), *Zhouli·Qiuguan Sikou* (Rites of the Zhou·Autumn Offices Senior Overseer of Penal Affairs), *Zuo Zhuan* (The Commentary of Zuo), *Book of Jin·Criminal law* and *History of Ming Dynasty·Criminal Law* all have written expressions embodying the spirit of combining leniency with strictness. Although there is no wording of "combining leniency with strictness", the contents demonstrate such a spirit. Chinese traditional culture emphasizes harmony and moderation while the combination of leniency and strictness is neither too strict nor too lenient and is a concept of criminal law discourse with Chinese characteristics formed by "using local resources and cherishing our own traditions". To a certain extent, this concept is helpful to "restore China's legal tradition and establish a rule of law compatible with China's modernization" and also has guiding significance for the formation of China's criminal governance model and conceptual system. What needs to be explained is that the combination of leniency and strictness is a criminal policy of China, not criminal legislation. The best way to deal with the relationship between policies and laws is to incorporate policies into laws through the legislative process, so that the ruling party's governance philosophy and methods can be implemented in the whole country. Policies are often formulated within the ruling person and do not have the will of the country, while laws are universal and apply to all citizens; just as the new development vision of the Party that can directly lead the construction of rule of law in China if being written into laws.[16] Nevertheless, this criminal policy has obtained the authoritative confirmation by the supreme judicial organ in the form of judicial interpretation, so in light of the secondary law status and role of criminal judicial interpretations in China's criminal normative system, the criminal policy of combining leniency and strictness has been recognized as quasi-criminal legislation in China. The further expansion and research by the criminal law theorists have made the combination of leniency and strictness a basic concept throughout the criminal judicial practice in our country; meanwhile, the traditional Chinese cultural elements contained in this concept and the value connotation of the rule of law civilization in the human world make it both national and global, which has tremendous influences in shaping the image of China's rule of law in criminal justice and promoting China's rule of law culture going global.

3.3.2.2 Equality in the application of crime and penalty

This refers to the principle of equality in application of crime and penalty as stipulated in Article 4 of China's criminal law, which states that the law shall be equally applied to anyone who commits a crime, and that no one shall have the privilege of transcending the law. The principle that all people are equal before the law is one of the essential principles guiding China's socialist legal system, and its creation is closely related to the development of the socialist market economy in China since the subjects of market economy are equal civil subjects and identity and class pose a barrier to market economic activities. Therefore, "in 1978, the law circle initiated an extensive discussion on several major legal issues including equality before the law under the slogan of 'everyone is equal before the law'. Over the 40 years since reform and opening-up, relevant researches have shifted from ideological contention deeply influenced by class discourse to abstract theoretical research in which class discourse has been fading away, to technical and concrete practice". An important manifestation of this practical turn is that Article 4 of the 1997 Criminal Law regards it as one of the three basic principles of criminal law, transforming it from an abstract socialist legal system principle to a concrete fundamental principle of criminal law. Despite being subjected to heated debates, this principle was included in the criminal code as it "embodies the basic nature and spirit of the rule of law in criminal justice in China and helps reduce and eliminate the privileges in the application of criminal law in judicial practice". The concretization of the principle of equality before the law to the principle of equality in the application of crime and punishment of the criminal law fully reflects the development track and progressive trend of the cause and theory of socialist human rights with Chinese characteristics; meanwhile, its concept of substantive human rights protection coincides with the ideology of equality proposed by the Western classical thinker Rousseau that "all men are born equal and free", which suggests that the concept of human rights knows no national and temporal borders. In short, the concept showcased by the principle of equality in the application of crime and punishment is worldwide, but its concept as a basic principle of criminal law is unique to China, which is an important embodiment of the socialist rule of law concept in criminal legislation and marks the doctrinal inception of the criminal legislation concept.

3.3.2.3 Proviso

The definition of crime stipulated in Article 13 of China's criminal law has two core concepts: social harmfulness and proviso. Over the 40 years since the reform and opening up was introduced, especially against the backdrop of drawing on the concept of legal interests in German and Japanese criminal law in the recent 20 years, social harmfulness has been castigated in the academic circle but undoubtedly maintains tenacious vitality in the criminal justice in China due to its inextricable relationship with the legal interest concept and the existence before the positive law, spiritualization and abstraction of legal interest concept; most judicial judgments still directly use the theory of social harmfulness as the basis for determining crimes. However, the tenacious vitality of social harmfulness theory might be from the provision of "however, if the circumstances are obviously minor and the harm done is not serious, the act shall not be considered a crime" at the end of Article 13 of the criminal law; this innovative provision is vividly called "proviso". The proviso effectively overcomes the defect in the first half of Article 13 of the crime definition about the inclination toward criminalization based on the convenient social harmfulness concept, and "allows the purposive interpretation of criminal law provisions on the premise of adhering to formal justice, so that those acts with minor social harm are excluded from the crime circle of the criminal law",[17] "which boasts great legislative and judicial value. Legislatively, the proviso tightens the crime circle to satisfy the modest-and-restraint requirement of the criminal law; judicially, it coordinates the sensibility and law to guarantee substantive rationality".[18] The proviso in the crime definition in China's criminal law is identical to the numerous seemingly different concepts such as punishable infringement of legal interests, substantial illegality, punishable illegality and social equivalence, namely criminalization rests on the form while decriminalization on the substance; the embodied principle of human rights protection that is beneficial to the defendant and the modest-and-restraint concept of the criminal law enable a dialogue with the criminal law theoretical systems of different countries in the international community.

The criminal legislation in China has also created many concepts with Chinese characteristics, such as unit crime, criminal injunction and punishment of public surveillance. These concepts created in legislation and theory have promoted the benign cycle of in-depth researches on theories of criminal law and greatly enriched owing to theoretical studies. Without the guidance of criminal legislation, it is impossible to form the concept of socialist criminal law discourse with Chinese characteristics.

However, Chinese criminal jurisprudence still lacks a discourse concept with Chinese characteristics, which can play a leading role and is easy to spread. Administrative reconsideration and administrative licensing in the administrative law[19] are all discourse concepts under the administrative legislation, and the "equilibrium theory" in the administrative law[20] is an academic discourse stemming from studies on the theoretical basis of administrative law. The green principle, as a fundamental principle of the civil law, may facilitate economic development and ecological improvement at the physical level and also meet the needs of life; at the metaphysical sphere, it conforms to the philosophy of "unity of nature and human" espoused by ancestors; in terms of guidelines and policies, it is consistent with the "scientific outlook on development", so the green principle is a civil law discourse with Chinese characteristics that China has exported to the world. The criminal law discourses with Chinese characteristics formed under the guidance of criminal legislation comprise the foregoing combination of leniency and strictness, equality in the application of crime and punishment and provisos, but are still in a small number and can hardly form a discourse system. How to further innovate the criminal law discourse system with Chinese characteristics is an important task facing criminal law scholars.

In the process of forming the criminal law discourse system with Chinese characteristics, "we must continue to forge distinguishing conceptual systems that could accurately convey China's thoughts, culture and mentality on the rule of law, and uses Chinese discourses to communicate Chinese theories and apply Chinese theories to solve Chinese problems". "We should draw on the advantages and learn from the disadvantages of different schools of thought and advocate true academic freedom rather than intimidating people by pinning political labels on them such as subjectivity, nationality or diversity".[21] The innovation of the criminal law discourse system with Chinese characteristics must properly handle the relationship between subjectivity and objectivity, nationality and worldliness, and singularity and pluralism, which should not only respect the practice of the rule of law in

China but also learn from the theoretical achievements of other countries; not only form our own discourse system but also avoid remaining aloof from the world. At the same time, the existing criminal law discourses with Chinese characteristics should be disseminated through various channels such as participation in the legislation of various organizations in the world or the formulation of treaties and conventions, execution of agreements between countries and non-governmental academic exchanges; through dialogues with the criminal law academic circles in other countries in the world, discourse concepts with abundant Chinese cultural elements and characteristics of rule of law in criminal justice such as the combination of leniency and strictness can be brought to the world arena, thus making contributions to enhance the rule of law discourse system of China.

3.4 Development direction: China's legislation should desist from criminalization

The past 24 years since the promulgation of the current criminal law in 1997 mark the most active period of criminal legislation in China, namely the era of "activation of criminal legislation". The 11 amendments to the criminal law are witnesses and products of the activation era; the nearly a hundred charges newly added represent the main content of China's criminal legislation in the activation era – criminalization. Therefore, to make a sober and in-depth analysis of the status quo and future development direction of China's criminal legislation toward either criminalization or decriminalization is a problem that needs to be solved urgently.

3.4.1 Criminalization: Absolute dominant direction of criminal legislation since the promulgation of the current criminal law

Since its promulgation, the criminal law has been pushing forward the process of criminalization in China with in total 11 amendments at the speed of 1 amendment every two years. Except the Amendment (8) that has made a tremendous progress in the mitigation of punishment typically the death penalty, most of the first eight amendments were all drafted to protect the interests of the society and country, continuously restrict civil liberties and add various new crimes to expand the restriction of the state's punishment power on citizens.[22] The Amendment (7) hailed as "looking to combine criminalization and decriminalization and coordinate strictness and leniency to better reflect the criminal policy of combining leniency with strictness" also added nine new charges. The so-called decriminalization just involved the crime of tax evasion; "leniency" was only reflected in commutation of the prescribed penalty against the crime of kidnapping; all other clauses were aimed to create new crimes, lower the inculpation conditions for existing crimes, expand the punishment scope and toughen the punishment. The Amendment (8), which was highly appraised for abolishing the death penalty on a large scale for the first time in Chinese history of criminal legislation, had 50 articles, but half of them were drafted to increase the penalty or add new crimes, such as the crime of dangerous driving, crime of bribing a functionary of a foreign country or an official of an international public organization, crime of falsely issuing invoices, crime of possessing counterfeit invoices, crime of organizing the sale of human organs, crime of refusing to pay labor remuneration and crime of dereliction of duty in food supervision, which are all the product of criminalization.

Throughout the 11 amendments, nearly a hundred new crimes have been created and all of them aim to broaden the state's penal power, shrink or restrict civil liberties. This indicates that the criminal legislation in China is still marching on along the track of instrumentalism and that the concept of state power criminal law is deeply ingrained among legislators while the concept of civil right criminal law is far away from us. Against the backdrop of the rapid social transition and economic development in China, legislators may be able to find many reasons to justify the expansion of penal power but as China is working toward the direction of building a rule of law country, the intensive use of criminalization in these 11 amendments in just 24 years is worthy of deep reflection.

3.4.2 "New crime complex" and possibility of criminalization in future criminal legislation

The continuous criminalization of China's criminal law is not just a matter of the legislators' own concepts, but to a large extent, is an embodiment of the high expectations of Chinese people for criminal law. "All problems arise from and should be tackled by culture".[23] The Chinese legal tradition that emphasizes criminal law over civil law manifested in disguise in current society by superstition and over-reliance on criminal law, and constant creation of new crimes. It is also reflected by the "legislative complex" and "new crime complex" of Chinese people. In the theory and practice of criminal law, "creating a new crime" has always been a hot topic but the name of the new crime is changing steadily; the proposed creation of new crimes in the criminal law is expected to give play to the "all-powerful" effects of the "omnipotent criminal law" imaged by the Chinese people so as to try to deal with all social problems through criminal law.

Based on legislation centrism rather than interpretation centrism, Chinese people have proposed criminalization of many acts. First, for some behaviors that often occur in practice, if the existing laws cannot realize subsumption by interpretations, people would call on creation of new crimes or "expanding" existing crimes to solve the problem. For example, since sexual bribery cannot be subsumed into the scope of "property" in the crime of acceptance of bribes, it has been proposed that sexual bribery be punished as a bribery crime through legislation. Second, criminalization is recommended for some victimless crimes that have been decriminalized in the international community in defiance of the international trend. For example, with the increase in the number of drug addicts in our country, some people will propose to add a crime of drug abuse to the criminal law almost every year on the International Day Against Drug Abuse and Illicit Trafficking. Another example is the crime of accommodating gambling. The international community has decriminalized these victimless crimes since the 1950s, but many people in China turn a deaf ear to the decriminalization theory and practice that the international community has been implementing for a long time regarding such victimless crimes or illegal activities and relentlessly request addition of such crimes as crime of drug abuse and crime of prostitution. Third, in the annual "Two Sessions" proposals meeting, a round of new crimes for the criminal law would be suggested; the legislative proposals of the NPC deputies, to a large extent, seem to have become proposals for the addition of new criminal charges. For example, some deputies suggested that the criminal law add the crime of encroaching on the environment; some deputies suggested adding the crime of child abuse to protect the interests of street children. Fourth, suggestions about new crimes do not consider whether other criminal charges in the criminal law could be applied to and address the behavior concerned. Considering the frauds in the field of civil activities, it has been proposed to add the crime of civil procedure fraud in the criminal law; in light of the frequent abuses of the right of action and use of lawsuits to seek illegitimate interests in the field of civil actions, it has been suggested to add the crime of litigation fraud; believing that the crackdown on crimes of bribery is not effective, some people have proposed that the criminal law "shall stipulate the activity of abetting bribery separately as a crime" "from the prospective of tightening the net of justice and punishing crimes of bribery". It can be easily foreseen from the above proposals or suggestions about addition of new crimes that China's criminal legislation seems to continue moving ahead along the road of criminalization. This potential trend of criminalization is worrisome.

3.4.3 Future development direction of criminal legislation in China: Stop further criminalization

Facing the raging trend of criminalization in China's criminal legislation, should it continuously broaden the crime circle for criminalization or restate and promote the modest-and-restraint principle to desist from criminalization and properly implement decriminalization? In this regard, those in favor of decriminalization propose that the criminal law of China should "establish a correct concept of decriminalization based on an examination of the ideological origin and theoretical basis of decriminalization and further carry out theoretical studies and legislative and judicial practices on decriminalization". However, there are more scholars who seem to endorse further criminalization. They believe that the current trend of criminalization in the international community has not received due attention and reflection, and "compared with decriminalization, the rising trend of criminalization worldwide has not evoked a strong response in China", so "our main task is to push forward criminalization rather than decriminalization".

The important argument for criminalization in China's criminal law is that drawing on the practice of penalizing misdemeanors in German and Japanese criminal laws is conducive to the implementation of the rule of law. "In China, the choice of criminalization mainly requires prescribing a considerable number of misdemeanors", and "tightening the net of justice to enhance people's awareness of norms"; the specific path is "to abolish the reeducation through labor system, formulate the Law on Misdemeanors, incorporate the harmful behaviors stipulated in the Public

Security Management Punishment Law and the regulations on reeducation through labor into the Law on Misdemeanors and lay down the proposed trial procedures; at the same time the rights of the defendant should be fully protected to make sure various criminal acts are tried by the court in accordance with the law. This is the requirement and necessity of building a socialist rule of law country"; "all minor criminal acts should be prescribed by the criminal law and subject to punishments of different sanction degrees granted by the court in accordance with the law", instead of "at the discretion of the administrative organs", "which is the requirement of the law-based governance of the country and an embodiment of social maturity". Obviously, although the reasons of these scholars endorsing criminalization are phrased differently, the essence is the same, that is, in the name of the rule of law, calling for continuous implementation of criminalization as the main task of the current criminal law in China.

The criminal law legislation model of Germany, Japan and other civil law countries is "rigorous but not draconian", while the criminal law legislation model of our country is "draconian but not rigorous". "Draconian but not rigorous" means that the crime circle in China is not as rigorous as those of foreign countries or overseas regions and is relatively small, but the threshold for the establishment of crimes is relatively high in China and an act that is convicted is always given very harsh punishments and the prescribed punishments are indeed too heavy on the whole. "Rigorous but not draconian" indicates that the crime circle set forth by criminal laws and relevant legal provisions of Western countries and regions represented by Germany and Japan is very meticulous and comprises numerous acts, but the threshold for the establishment of crimes is very low and the conviction of an act does not represent very strong denouncement or harsh punishments and the prescribed punishments are generally light. However, scholars in favor of criminalization harbor another concealed but self-evident issue behind their support for penalization of misdemeanors, that is, the criminal legislation model in China can be transferred from one model to the other one. This leads us to the question whether the transformation of the criminal legislation model can truly be realized and petty criminal acts be criminalized in the name of the rule of law.

From the perspective of jurisprudence, the "rigorous but not draconian" legislation model for the German and Japanese criminal laws allows the restriction on personal freedom of the crime perpetrator to be meted out through the court trial, which is more in line with the requirements of the rule of law compared with the ruling on restriction of personal freedom that the administrative organ enters into without due process. However, in terms of practice, the rule of law should not just be practical at the level of jurisprudence but has been and can only be intimately related to the situation of a country. The specific path for the rule of law must be explored in combination with the actual conditions of a country. The huge differences between China and other countries determine that their paths for the rule of law cannot be the same and that criminalization of misdemeanors is infeasible in China.

Judging from China's current actual situation, changing the criminal legislation model means diverting a multitude of administrative violations that are currently handled by public security organs to procuratorial organs and courts. "The purpose of the adoption of criminalization is to reinforce people's awareness of norms by tightening the net of justice rather than imposing harsh penalties on misdemeanors", which is exactly the view of proponents of criminalization and also the main reason why they highly recommend the rigorous but not draconian legislation model. However, for China that is one of the few multi-ethnic major countries, how to maintain the security and solidarity of all ethnic groups has always remained the main political goal of the Chinese government; in addition, China is still in a period of social transformation, characterized by rapid economic development, strong collisions between old and new social concepts, active minds and ever-changing lifestyles, how to balance various social forces to achieve social stability has always been the priority of Chinese government. Therefore, there is a well-known saying in China that "stability overwhelms everything". The political task of safeguarding stability will inevitably require the state to "properly maintain the incentives for the public security organs as the social security control organization, so as not to blunt the edge of their advance and sustain the strong position of the public security organs". The numerous illegal activities should still be handled by the public security organs as administrative violations and punished for public security rather than being treated as crimes in the criminal law, which was, is and even will be an objective existence for a long time in the future. In other words, the politics of maintaining stability has determined the dominant position of the public security organs among the public security, procuratorial, court and judicial organs. The appeal of proponents of criminalization to "punish harmful behaviors by legislation" rather than by administrative means like enactment of the Law on Misdemeanors is at least infeasible in the current China. Otherwise, the governance scope of the public security organs will be greatly shrunk and administrative powers weakened, while the powers of the procuratorial organs and courts will be strengthened. Getting the public security organs to deal with the prodigious number of illegal activities, namely minor criminal acts prescribed in the German and Japanese criminal laws, will indeed "run counter to the constitutional spirit of guaranteeing procedural fairness", but the rule of law inherently has paradoxes. Many practices that seem to violate the rule of law, such as "permitting the private settlement of civil cases and certain criminal reconciliation, seem to undermine but in fact maintain the rule of law". These are not difficult to fathom under the interpretation with various terms such as stability, harmony and judicial costs.

These situations may deviate from the objectiveness goal of the rule of law, but in China, without long-term social stability, the rule of law can only be an extravagant hope. It is practically impossible for the judiciary to handle the enormous minor disputes in China, a major country but still in the developing stage. "In the past few years, it is generally believed in the process of judicial reform that other mechanisms for dispute settlement are less important than the rule of law, but the rule of law is understood merely as the judiciary or court. People file a lawsuit for even a dime and 'fight for rights', so numerous disputes flood into the judicial procedure, resulting in a sharp increase in the pressure on the judiciary. Justice is indeed important but is not the only mechanism for resolving disputes and sometimes may not be the most effective one". In a word, the road to the rule of law in

China must be combined with the situation of China. The "rigorous but not draconian" legislative model that scholars in favor of criminalization yearn for is at least unrealist for China. Forcibly incorporating the Security Management Punishment Law with the criminal law and changing our current legislative model to the "rigorous but draconian" model for the German and Japanese legislation will only distort the original intention of the rule of law; the rule of law must be localized and the so-called global rule of law may work for some economic fields and international cooperation but is neither practical nor possible for the governance of the criminal and civil law.

At present, there are instances of criminal legislation that are leaning toward the "rigorous but not draconian" legislative model, but with unsatisfactory effects. A case in point is that the Amendment (8) criminalizes drunk driving regardless of the circumstances and the prescribed punishment is just "criminal detention and fine", which is light. Therefore, the practice of broadly criminalizing this offense irrespective of its consequences and stipulating a lighter penalty aligns well with the Western criminal legislation model. However, whether this has achieved the intended rule of law effects of the Western criminal legislation model seem not optimistic. On the one hand, what corroborates the criminal legislation model in China is the recognition of the public. The criminal law in the mind of the overwhelming majority of Chinese people is stringent with draconian punishments, while a crime is an act with extremely serious social harmfulness, which is subjected to very harsh penalties. However, the dangerous driving to which such a light penalty is meted out is stipulated as a crime, which is difficult to be accepted by many people in their perception; even if they accept the fact that it is a crime, the people still believe that a crime should be imposed heavy punishments; in the legislative discussion stage of the crime of dangerous driving, "the sentencing provision about criminal detention and a fine have been severely question".

This means that the Chinese people may be able to accept the "draconian but not rigorous" or even "draconian and rigorous" criminal legislation model but may be not ready to accept the "rigorous but not draconian" model. On the other hand, the misdemeanors such as dangerous driving are still investigated by the public security organs. If the public security organs deem, it could be filed, the case would be referred to the procuratorate; if the case could not be filed but can be closed by administrative penalties, it would be handled on their own. In other words, even if misdemeanors in the German and Japanese criminal laws such as dangerous driving are criminalized, the investigation department is still the public security organ that in fact guards the first and the most important pass. This determines that even if minor offenses are criminalized, it won't necessarily generate the practical effects of the rule of law pursued by scholars in favor of criminalization. Therefore, even if the subsumption of an act under the criminal law represents the practice of the "rigorous but not draconian" legislation model in China, whether it could achieve the same effect as the rule of law in Western countries could not be answered by scholars in favor of criminalization.

It can be seen that the realization of the rule of law in a country depends on its own national conditions and history and would by no means be cracked by simple legislative comparisons. In China, one of the few multi-ethnic countries worldwide, how to achieve the rule of law may require more in-depth corroboration and experiments; in this process, how to sustain the social stability is the priority for those pursuing the rule of law. Penalization for misdemeanors is not only difficult to achieve in China today but also may not generate the expected effects of the rule of law. Therefore, considering the actual situation of China and the relentless criminalization process over more than ten years following the implementation of the current criminal law, the author strongly advocates halting the expansion of the regulatory scope of the criminal law and excluding misdemeanors from criminalization while upholding the modest-and-restrained principle!

In addition, some scholars represented by risk criminal law scholars hold that as human beings have entered a risk society, the criminal law should maximally protect abstract and general legal interests at an early stage and subsume some abstract potential damage offenses, environmental crimes, economic crimes and terrorist crimes under its scope, so these scholars claim further criminalization of the criminal law in the future. The author opposes the unreasonable expansion of the boundaries of criminal law on the ground of preventing and controlling social risks; the prevention and governance of risks is more of a social problem; it is a new issue that human beings have to face in a highly developed industrial society and a question in anthropology, sociology and political science that human beings need to reflect on regarding the harmonious co-existence between our own development and nature. It is not only a superstition about criminal law but also an unrealistic assumption that the early intervention of the criminal law can resolve the risks in the risk society. This view and practice of "risk is everywhere" and thus "criminal law is everywhere" is the biggest "risk" in today's "risk society". If we do not maintain sufficient prudence and vigilance in this regard, I am afraid that human beings will take another hit in addition to the "social risks" brought about by industrial society, which is the "rule of law risks". Undoubtedly, that will be a more deadly risk than the risk society! The prevention and control of risks in the risk society should be carried out from the political, economic, social and cultural levels, rather than from the criminal law. Therefore, the idea that the criminal law should be further criminalized on the grounds of preventing risks in a risk society should not only be guarded against but is also strongly opposed by the author. As this issue has been expounded in other articles, the author will not give unnecessary details here.

In short, the author opposes the continual criminalization in China and advocates that the criminal legislation should implement the modest-and-restrained principle to ward off further criminalization and carry out conditional decriminalization.

The current criminal legislation in China should abandon the magnified concept of omnipotence of criminal law; in the face of endless illegal acts, legislators should remain cool-hearted and objective instead of arbitrary criminalization. At present, the number of existing crimes in the criminal law is several times that of the first criminal code of our country. The "jungle of crimes" of nearly 500 charges is not only difficult for ordinary people to understand and familiarize with but also often makes professionals bewildered; the continuous amendments to the criminal law have resulted in people's "aesthetic fatigue" about new crimes; the overlapping crimes have hampered judicial practice, and many charges difficult to apply have been put on the shelf. All these should have propelled legislators to reflect on this excessively fast criminalization process. Concerning the criminal code that should keep authoritative and stable the most, criminal legislators in China should never be "the impatient vanguard in the legislation realm like *Suo Chao*".[24] During the period of social transformation, if it is impossible to accomplish the political, economic and social reform in a relatively ideal way so as to minimize social conflicts, we should not frequently resort to the criminal law when political, economic and administrative means are failing. What's more, there is a tendency of criminalization in criminal justice, so we should be more cautious about the criminalization of criminal legislation and excessive criminalization in criminal legislation will inevitably lead to further expansion of the crime circle. All in all, as the most stringent legal branch, criminal law should follow the Western logic of rights and grant citizens the greatest freedom rather than blindly expanding the crime circle to combat crimes, a practice that has been formed since the founding of New China!

3.5 Conclusion

In recent decades, the criminal legislation of China keeps leaning toward criminalization, and before the judicial organs become accustomed to the new amendment, a newer amendment is promulgated. Lack of rigorous theoretical demonstration and scientific empirical research, the frequent legislation in response to social appeals may not generate satisfactory effects. A thought-provoking phenomenon is that it is not criminal law dogmatics that guides legislation but the criminal law theory endorses the legislation after being promulgated. There is no doubt that the criminal law dogmatics should serve as the basis for criminal legislation but excessively rapid criminal legislation would also hinder the real sedimentary accretion of legal dogmatics. Reflecting on the current criminal legislation, perhaps we should suspend criminalization and focus on the theory of decriminalization that is theoretically based on the modest-and-restraint principle and takes the human rights protection as the foothold. The criminal legislation should be guided by the legal dogmatics of the theory of decriminalization to realize the benign balance between criminalization and decriminalization.

Notes

1 Liu Yanhong: Source, Function and Significance of Formal and Substantive Interpretation of Criminal Law, *Science of Law*, 2015(5).
2 Liu Yanhong: Damage of Symbolic Legislation to the Function of Criminal Law, *Political Science and Law*, 2017(3).
3 Liu Yanhong: Evaluation and Reflection on the Value of Criminal Legislation for Terrorist Crimes in the Past 20 Years, *Peking University Law Journal*, 2018(1).
4 Liu Yanhong: Strategic Transformation of China's Anti-Corruption Legislation and Its Systematic Construction, *China Legal Science*, 2016(4).

5 The Fourth Plenary Session of the Eighteenth Central Committee of the Communist Party of China: Decisions of the Central Committee of the Communist Party of China on Several Major Issues Concerning Comprehensively Promoting the Rule of Law, *People's Daily*, October 24, 2014, p. 1.
6 Xi Jinping: Strengthen the Party's Centralized and Unified Leadership for the Law-based Governance on All Fronts, and Better Harness the Role of the Rule of Law in Solidifying the Foundation, Keeping the Expectation Stable and Seeking Long-term Benefits, *People's Daily*, August 25, 2018, p. 1.
7 Xi Jinping: Improve the Rule of Law Construction Plan to Increase the Quality and Efficiency of Legislative Work and Foster a Good Legal Environment for Promoting Reform, Development and Stability, *People's Daily*, February 25, 2018, p. 1.
8 Xi Jinping: Improve the Rule of Law Construction Plan to Increase the Quality and Efficiency of Legislative Work and Foster a Good Legal Environment for Promoting Reform, Development and Stability, *People's Daily*, February 26, 2019, p. 1.
9 Liu Yanhong: Misconceptions and Obstacles to Application: General Comments on Judicial Interpretations since the Promulgation of the New Criminal Law. *Peaking University Law Journal*, 2002(5).
10 See (2013) X.S.C.Z.No.580.
11 See (2018) J. 0108. X.C. No.1789.
12 Zhang Wenxian: Views on Innovating and Developing the Theory of Socialist Rule of Law with Chinese Characteristics, *Legal Daily*, May 9, 2018, p. 13.
13 Xi Jinping: Speech at the National Party School Work Conference, *Qiushi*, 2016(9).
14 Zhou Youyong: New Tasks for Chinese Legal Research and Disciplinary Development in the New Era, *Journal of Wuhan University (Philosophy and Social Science Edition)*, 2019(2).
15 Xi Jinping: Secure a Decisive Victory in Building a Moderately Prosperous Society in All Respects and Win a Great Victory of Socialism with Chinese Characteristics in the New Era, *People's Daily*, October 28, 2017, p. 1.
16 See Zhou Youyong: Five Development Concepts and Rule of Law China Construction, *Law and Social Development*, 2018(3).
17 Liu Yanhong: Study on the Theory of Social Harmfulness, *China Legal Science*, 2002(2).
18 Chu Huaizhi, Zhang Yonghong: The Value Connotation of the Proviso to Article 13 of the Criminal Law, *Journal of Jiangsu Police Academy*, 2003(2).
19 See Zhou Youyong: *Principles of Administrative Law*, 3rd Edition, Peking University Press, 2018, p. 258, 358.
20 See Zhou Youyong: *Principles of Administrative Law*, 3rd Edition, Peking University Press, 2018, p. 83.
21 Liu Yanhong: The Development Direction of Criminal Law under the Formation of Schools of Chinese Jurisprudence: Doctrinalization, *Politics and Law*, 2018(7).
22 For detailed analysis, see Liu Yanhong: Three Major Characteristics of the Amendment (8) – A Comparison with the First Seven Amendments, *Legal Forum*, 2011(3).
23 Qian Mu: *General Introduction to Cultural Studies*, Zhengzhong Book Company, 1981, p. 3.
24 An simile used by the author. Suo Chao is a character in the Chinese novel *Water Margin* (*Shuihu Zhuan*). As he is impatient in battles, often charging ahead of his men, he is nicknamed "impatient vanguard".

4 Intrinsic Basis of Legal Dogmatics of Decriminalization Theory

Concept of Crime

The concept of crime stipulated in Article 13 of the Criminal Law of China is a mixed concept which has both exculpation and inculpation functions, but its exculpation function is obviously weaker in consideration of the principle of *nulla poena sine lege* and the four elements of a crime, which is even reduced to policy-oriented appendage in many circumstances. Against the backdrop of building a country of legal protection of human rights, the mixed concept of crime in the criminal law should transform from the current dual functions to sole decriminalization function, and meanwhile such transformation should not just be confined to the "proviso" of Article 13 of the criminal law[1] but should also be manifested in the overall concept of crime. The principle of *nulla poena sine lege* of the criminal law of China has both the function of human right protection and social protection, and the "ground for exclusion of criminality" has an ambiguous position in the four elements of a crime, so the criminalization and decriminalization functions of the crime concept would inevitably be inclined to the former under the value orientation of "human rights under order". Therefore, since the criminal code of China is unable to establish a formal concept of crime and the crime theory can hardly undergo substantive changes, the functional transformation of the crime concept in the criminal law to effectively protect human rights is an alternative plan to advance the process of rule of law in criminal justice.

4.1 Dualization of criminalization and decriminalization functions in the mixed concept of crime

Despite stated differently in extraterritorial criminal law doctrines and legislation examples, the concept of crime is roughly categorized into the formal crime concept, substantive crime concept and mixed crime concept. There is no dispute in the field of criminal law that "the definition of crime in the criminal law of China is the unity of the substantive conception and formal conception of crime". In other words, the definition of crime in Article 13 of the criminal law of China is a mixed one.

In contrast, the interpretation about the concept of crime in the field of criminal law in China has a unique dual structure, namely serious social harm, criminal illegality and punishability (three characteristics) which are basic attributes of crime,

DOI: 10.4324/9781003456773-5

and four elements constituting a crime which are specific characteristics of crime. This dual structure and their intertwined relationship have profoundly affected the function of the concept of crime in China which combines the criminalization and decriminalization functions; considering the history of the formation of the principle of *nulla poena sine lege,* the dual functions are more prominent.

4.1.1 Criminalization function of the mixed crime concept

The concept of crime in the criminal law of China comprises two parts: establishment of crime and exclusion of crime, with the former called "non-proviso" and the latter called "proviso". Before the principle of *nulla poena sine lege* was elaborated in the criminal code, the "non-proviso" section had both criminalization and decriminalization functions but the decriminalization function was relatively weak, although the legislative purpose of the clause "for acts that are explicitly defined as criminal acts in law, the offenders shall be convicted and punished in accordance with law" (positive side) in Article 3 of the criminal law is interpreted as "only an act that is explicitly defined as a crime in law could be convicted and sentenced and the conviction and sentencing must be carried out in accordance with legal provisions". It actually emphasizes "in accordance with law" and poses restraints on the judiciary. However, this is doubtful in terms of the formation process of the principle of *nulla poena sine lege* in the criminal law; after all, it is worth pondering whether it is necessary to limit the judiciary through the much-criticized positive side of the principle of *nulla poena sine lege.* Article 28 of the current Constitution proclaims, "the State maintains public order and suppresses treasonable and other criminal activities that endanger State security; it penalizes criminal activities that endanger public security and disrupt the socialist economy as well as other criminal activities; and it punishes and reforms criminals". Therefore, the clause "for acts that are explicitly defined as criminal acts in law, the offenders shall be convicted and punished in accordance with law" is unquestionable under the purpose and tasks set out in the criminal law of China (Article 1 and 2 of the criminal law), and repetitive expression about the positive side is indeed unnecessary. Even if there are arbitrary judicial powers or extrajudicial sanctions in practice, they should not be simply attributed to the ills implicated by the principle of *nulla poena sine lege* with a purely negative side, so the so-called arbitrary judicial powers or extrajudicial sanctions are probably the deviation or heterization due to ineffective implementation of relevant legal provisions. Nevertheless, echoing the interpretation of restricting the judiciary is that the human rights protection function of the principle of *nulla poena sine lege i*s receiving increasing attention, which should be acknowledged.

4.1.2 Decriminalization function of the mixed crime concept

The attribute of serious social harmfulness of the crime concept not only has the function of incrimination under the pursuit of order value but could also realize the function of decriminalization under the human rights value or "human rights under order" while turning to four elements of a crime; the "proviso" of the crime concept also realizes the function of decriminalization by negating the serious social harmfulness of "obviously minor circumstances without serious harm". To put it bluntly, the crime concept in China includes the following two decriminalization functions:

First, negative decriminalization function. "This feature also shows whether a certain behavior is socially harmful and the degree of such harm are major indicators to distinguish crime from non-crime". Before the principle of *nulla poena sine lege* was narrated in the criminal code, the criminal policy of "combination of punishment and leniency" with a clear political complexion served as a stabilizer for the overall or regional social security, despite its obvious hidden disadvantages. Since its essence is differential treatment, the criminal policy of "combination of punishment and leniency" is inevitably subjected to criticism like "unconventional 'criminal law overload' against so-called felonies and 'statutory judicial malpractice' against so-called non-felony part". This high-risk legal policy is nothing more than a footnote that political decision makers make resignedly or indulgently under the principle of *nulla poena sine lege* out of concerns about the overall or regional social security. Therefore, as the criminal code has portrayed the outline of the principle of *nulla poena sine lege,* the decriminalization function of the crime concept in China is manifested in the security sustained by "special rectification campaigns" that replace the unified positional warfare-like "crackdown", and in the hollow, loose and mitigated punishments against "non-felonies" due to saving manpower, material and financial resources to more severely punish "felony offenders". Its benefits can be interpreted as a restricted release of the pent-up human rights protection function of the principle of *nulla poena sine lege* and also moderate correction of the principle of *nulla poena sine lege* that has been distorted from time to time. Perhaps, it was in this sense that Lister, who belonged to the new school of criminal law, uncharacteristically uttered the thought-provoking maxim: the principle of *nulla poena sine lege* is an insurmountable barrier for criminal policy! Therefore, the negative decriminalization function of the crime concept is relatively obvious at the lenient end of the criminal policy.

Second, positive decriminalization function. The positive decriminalization function espoused in the crime concept in China is roughly reflected in the "proviso". Whether the "proviso" has the decriminalization function has been debated for a long time in the criminal law theory in China, where the proponents are basically in a superior position but are also divided in opinions. The recent trend is to establish the substantive interpretation role of the "proviso" in the constitution of crime on the basis of maintaining the monistic crime constitution to internalize the decriminalization function of the "proviso". In addition, under the four-element crime constitution model, the monistic standard for crime constitution has to be established for conviction in order to meet the formal requirements of the principle of *nulla poena sine lege,* while the social harmfulness is reflected comprehensively and holistically via the four elements of crime, so it is inevitable to resort to substantive interpretation to sustain the positive decriminalization function of the crime concept. Accordingly, the "proviso" of the crime concept is manifested in different forms during the judicial process, such as refusal to file a case by the public security organ, refusal to prosecute or withdraw the prosecution by the procuratorate, or acquittal by the court.

4.2 Disadvantages of the dual function of the mixed crime concept

The concurrent mixed crime concept in China is built on Article 10 of the 1979 criminal law and could be traced back as early as to the concept in the criminal code of Russia. It is known that the crime concept with substantive contents in the criminal code of Russia was given birth to and grew on the basis of criticizing the capitalistic crime concept and is strongly ideological. The crime concept in China basically inherited this feature but the ideological hue gradually fades after the principle of *nulla poena sine lege* has been explicitly indicated and tends to be replaced by the value orientation of "human rights under order". Nevertheless, the remnants of ideology and the value orientation of "human rights under order" endow the dual function of the mixed concept of crime in China with many disadvantages.

4.2.1 Heterization of the principle of nulla poena sine lege

In combination with relevant analysis in foregoing sections, the author holds that the basic attributes of social harmfulness and criminal illegality that the mixed crime concept in China has are objectively contradicted against the principle of *nulla poena sine lege,* and the decriminalization and criminalization function of the social harmfulness attribute confers the decriminalization function with a superior or overwhelming position under the value orientation of "human rights under order" (particularly under policies aiming to safeguard social security and stability). Together with the principle of *nulla poena sine lege* with Chinese characteristics, this renders the criminalization function at greater risks of expansion. Consequentially, the social protection function of the principle of *nulla poena sine lege* will increasingly compress its human right protection function, with the principle itself in danger of heterization.

Despite that "the conventional purposeful basis of the principle of *nulla poena sine lege* (safeguarding freedom via power division) has not been lost due to modern legal theories or social science knowledge but only been revised", the principle of *nulla poena sine lege* implies the human right protection function as well as social protection function, which has deep roots in history. After the principle of *nulla poena sine lege,* the quintessence of the rule of law carries "Chinese characteristics", its social protection function can easily take precedence over the human right protection function either in form or substance; thus even if the positive side of the principle of *nulla poena sine lege* is originally intended to "restrict the judiciary", it would also be forced by the order value to undertake additionally the social protection function, which is even prominent against the policy requirement of safeguarding social order and stability. Therefore, the social protection function and human right protection function of the principle of *nulla poena sine lege* in China can fully accord with the criminalization/decriminalization functions of the mixed crime concept; in light of the value orientation of "human rights under order" and policies aimed at safeguarding social order and stability, it is not difficult for the social harmfulness criteria of the crime concept to break the formal rationality requirement contained in the principle of *nulla poena sine lege* so as to broaden the criminalization function. This will undoubtedly exert an immeasurable negative impact on the rule of law in criminal justice in China, which is worthy of vigilance.

4.2.2 Interference in crime constitution

Are the four constituent elements of a crime self-sufficient in conviction and the sole and final standard in conviction, namely is the conviction standard in China monastic? This issue has been acutely controversial for a long time. The dispute mainly revolves around following two questions: the relationship between the decriminalization of the "proviso" of crime concept and constitution of crime; relationship between the ground for elimination of crime and constitution of crime. It can be seen that the crux still boils down to the relationship between crime concept and crime constitution.

Regarding the former, one view is that the "proviso" in the crime concept breaks through the principle of *nulla poena sine lege* as an act with criminal illegality may not constitute a crime. Such crimes are convicted in two steps: Step one, whether there are constituent elements of a crime, if no, the act is directly excluded from criminality (formal judgment); Step two, if there are constituent elements of a crime, then evaluate whether the circumstances are minor and the harm done is not serious, if yes, the act is acquitted, otherwise the act is convicted (substantive judgment).[2] That is, the social harmfulness standard of the crime concept takes precedence over the social harmfulness standard contained in the crime constitution. Its logic inference is: the crime concept can act as the direct basis for conviction. As a result, the conviction standard is undoubtedly binary with crime concept and crime constitution. As mentioned before, the crime concept in China has both the criminalization and decriminalization functions. If the interference is for decriminalization and does not contravene the basic value of justice, it is still one of the means to protect human rights in nature despite of possible criticisms. After all, the degree of protection is a matter of competence and the least efficient means of guarantee still deserves exploration, while the protection of human rights matters the attitude and marks dividing line between exploration and criticism. However, the problem is that the game between the functions of incrimination and exoneration in the concept of crime in China under the value orientation of "human rights under order" (especially under the policy of maintaining social security and stability) will only give the criminalization function a superior or overwhelming position over the decriminalization, which implies a huge risk at the expense of delaying the process of rule of law in criminal justice. However, in judicial practice, the "proviso" of the concept of crime is seldom applied and will cause an imbalance in standards. For example, a person acquitted of a crime may be subjected to reeducation through labor that is even more harsh than the punishment of a crime, so in the absence of an effective connection with the punishment measures of the administrative law, the decriminalization prescribed in the "proviso" are no good tidings. Therefore, the binary conviction standard is not advisable considering the pros and cons.

Moreover, although "in fact, the judiciary will always consider the reasons for excluding a crime when judging the compliance of a certain element of a crime; rather than after the compliance of all elements of a crime is evaluated", the four-element crime constitution theory, which originated in Soviet Russia and has long occupied a common position, does not incorporate justifiable reasons such as self-defense and emergency avoidance into the crime constitution. In this way, "the circumstances that do not constitute a crime (justifiable defense, emergency avoidance, etc.), as exceptions, should not be considered in the constitution of a crime, but should be studied outside the constitution of a crime as a justifiable causes". In essence, this kind of view is also tolerating the binary conviction standard and cannot get rid of the predicament mentioned above.

4.2.3 Rejection of supra-law grounds for eliminating a crime

The so-called supra-law grounds for eliminating a crime refer to grounds not expressly stipulated in the criminal law. "A behavior that should constitute the elements and does not meet the ground for eliminating a crime expressly stipulated in the criminal law, shall be a reason for negating illegality if it conforms to the overall legal order". The behaviors mainly include self-rescue, conflict of obligations (used to negate the crime of omission) and victim's commitment.

It has been explained before that the social harmfulness and criminal illegality, which are the basic attributes of the concept of crime in China, overlap with each other. This endows the substantive illegality with different positions in the crime theory inside and outside the territory, which leads to the very different status and destiny of the supra-law ground for eliminating misfeasance in the criminal theory and practice. In the extraterritorial hierarchical crime theory, the supra-law ground for eliminating misfeasance is generally interpreted in the illegality hierarchy and corresponds to the substantive illegality; in China, since the illegality is unrolled in the criminal illegality attribute of the crime concept, the supra-law ground for eliminating misfeasance can hardly earn a justifiable and clear position in the four constituent elements of crime under the framework of upholding monastic conviction standard based on four constituent elements. However, in the judicial practice of our country, the victim's promise, presumed promise, self-injurious behavior, conflict of obligations and other supra-law grounds for eliminating misfeasance actually exist. Therefore, the criminal theory must present a corresponding "reasonable" interpretation, which is exactly the reason and motivation of the traditional general theory to add "exclusion of criminal behavior" in a special chapter in addition to the four elements of crime.

After all, even if it is considered that substantive illegality is carried out by the criminal object or the criminal object and all or some other elements in the four-element crime constitution, in fact, the supra-law ground for eliminating misfeasance "at least involves two elements (objective and subjective)",[3] but interpreting it in any element of the crime constitution is not logically or systematically sound and is also suspected of disrupting the judgment of illegality. However, the bigger problem that arises from the interpretation in a special chapter outside the crime constitution system is that the supra-law ground for eliminating misfeasance and the four constituent elements of crime are roughly at the same level, which acquiesces to the binary conviction standard. In other words, the detached position of the supra-law ground for eliminating misfeasance in the crime theory is attained at the cost of the monastic conviction standard.

In fact, the concept of crime exerts the function of decriminalization by means of supra-law ground for eliminating misfeasance. When the position of the supra-law ground for eliminating misfeasance is not clear and difficult to define in the system of four constituent elements of crime, the foregoing decriminalization function is extremely likely to be reduced to appendage of the order value or social security and stability. Besides, the supra-law ground for eliminating misfeasance is also applied with great caution in extraterritorial trial practice, and based on their own risk considerations, judges reject the supra-law ground for eliminating misfeasance within the scope of discretion, causing the decriminalization function of the crime concept to conceivably give way to the criminalization function.

4.3 Criminalization/decriminalization→decriminalization: Conversion from binary to monastic function of the crime concept

The mixed crime concept established in Article 13 of the criminal law of China has both decriminalization and criminalization functions, while the social harmfulness, one of the basic attributes of the crime concept, could help explain the four constituent elements of crime and may realize improper incrimination by virtue of expanded interpretations allowed by modern criminal law under the order value, thus making the criminalization function of the crime concept superior to the decriminalization effect, which are at a huge risk of infringing upon human rights. Accordingly, the mixed concept of crime in our country should be transformed from the functions of criminalization and decriminalization to the function of decriminalization. In other words, as the concept of crime in China with the attribute of social harmfulness has the functions of criminalization and decriminalization that both have a say in theory and practice, it is necessary to strengthen the decriminalization function of the crime concept and void the criminalization function to transfer the dual functions to single decriminalization function so as to highlight human right protection. This generally involves three aspects:

First, strengthen the human right protection function of the principle of *nulla poena sine lege* to provide a guarantee for the conversion of the dual criminalization/decriminalization functions to single decriminalization function.

Based on the previous analysis, the principle of *nulla poena sine lege* stipulated in Article 3 of the criminal law of China has both the social protection function and the human rights protection function. In order to realize the single decriminalization function, the crime concept should be more restricted by the human rights protection function of the principle of *nulla poena sine lege* which needs to compress or reduce its social protection function. After all, what is lacking in the process of rule of law in criminal justice in China is not the emphasis on the value of order, but how to demonstrate the value of human rights under the order value. The principle of *nulla poena sine lege* in China gives more prominence to the social protection function that prohibits decriminalization or can be deemed that the positive side is no different from the principle of criminalization. This would to some extent inevitably shrink its own human rights protection function and departs from the original principle of *nulla poena sine lege* that takes innate rights of man as the logical starting point, restricting the state's penalty power as the content and maintaining individual freedom rights as the primary or main goal.

In fact, the function of social protection is not completely or mainly undertaken by the principle of *nulla poena sine lege* in other countries. When the 1979 criminal law did not stipulate the principle of *nulla poena sine lege,* the social protection function was more borne by the tasks of the criminal law, the concept of crime and the constitution of crime. The revised criminal law clarifies the principle of *nulla poena sine lege* that includes a positive side, highlighting the social protection function of the principle of *nulla poena sine lege.* To strengthen the human rights protection function of the principle of *nulla poena sine lege,* there are two alternatives: first, "legislative centrism", where the positive side of the principle of *nulla poena sine lege* is deleted or omitted; second, "interpretation centrism", where an interpretation in favor of the defendant is made in the form of "supplementary interpretation", namely the positive side is aimed to prohibit the arbitrary exercise of judicial power and prevent improper criminalization so as to maximally neutralize the negative effects. Obviously, the former solves the issue from the root, while the latter is a temporary expedient.

Second, the constituent elements of crime are the sole and final criteria for conviction that should be strictly upheld, and the absolute status of the decriminalization function of the crime concept in interpreting the constitution of crime should be established, and the role of the criminalization function should be voided and even denied.

As it is difficult to diffuse its embarrassing position of the ground for eliminating misfeasance in the four constituent elements of crime, the crime concept exerts the decriminalization function by virtue of the ground for eliminating misfeasance, which is still one of the ways to highlight human rights although this may not be circumspect logically or systematically and could acquiesce to the binary conviction standard of crime concept and crime constitution; it can only be an improvised makeshift before a more efficient solution is identified. In fact, it is undoubtedly a dangerous and misguided path to sacrifice the protection of human rights to realize the extension of the crime system, while implementing the value concept of human rights protection at the expense of the extension of the crime system may draw many criticisms under the "human rights under order", but is not an entirely unacceptable heresy. Therefore, that the constituent elements of crime are the sole and final criteria for conviction should be strictly upheld, and the role of the criminalization function in interpreting the constitution of crime should be voided and even denied to narrow the crime circle; meanwhile, the absolute status of the decriminalization function of the crime concept in interpreting the constitution of crime should be established to highlight human rights; efforts should be made to identify a breakthrough in the extension of interpretation and a possible fundamental solution, and make substantive adjustments when the time is ripe for theory and practice.

In this way, the remaining problem is how to prevent the decriminalization function of the concept of crime from being reduced to be an appendage of order value or social security and stability. As has been analyzed above, the criminalization and decriminalization functions of the crime concept in China can be manifested in their role in guiding judges to understand and apply the interpretation of the constitution of crimes. Therefore, the argument denying that the four constituent elements of crime have the function of decriminalization is indeed inappropriate, but ignoring the criminalization/decriminalization function of the crime concept on the grounds that the existing crime constitution has the decriminalization mechanism would inevitably be mired in a predicament that the criminalization function gains superiority under the value orientation of "human rights under order" (especially under the policy of maintaining social security and stability). If the crime constitution sticks to the beaten track or does not undergo substantive improvements, its prospect is bound to be bleak.

Therefore, one of the possible solutions to the above-mentioned problem is, the human rights protection function of the principle of *nulla poena sine lege* should be strengthened and act as the general guideline of the criminal policy of "combining leniency with strictness"; it is resolutely prohibited that the criminal policy oversteps or goes beyond in disguised form the restraint of the principle of *nulla poena sine lege* and as a bellwether of the overall or regional social security, the "leniency" and "strictness" of the criminal policy only play a macro-guidance role in the punishment of crimes instead of specific regulation on individual cases so as to eliminate policy-related risks. We should resolutely oppose the "excessive penalty" or disguised "excessive penalty" to carry the punishment purpose of "education" or "improvement" based on concerns about social security conditions or the leniency and strictness of the criminal policy, clarify the level and hierarchy of the punishment retribution and correction purposes and prevent "criminal law overloading" and "statutory judicial malpractice". In the handling of specific cases, the constitution of crime is the sole basis for inculpation, but tolerance is made to interpretation about the crime constitution by the decriminalization function of the crime concept under the principle of *nulla poena sine lege* that has restored the human right protection function to redress the predominance of the incriminating function over the exculpatory function of the concept of crime, thus transforming the dual criminalization/decriminalization functions to substantive single decriminalization function.

Third, considering the overlapping between the social harmfulness and criminal illegality in the concept of crime, it is necessary to explore and innovate the existing theory of social harmfulness and criminal illegality to reduce the dependence on the dual structure of basic attributes and specific features of the crime concept.

On this basis, the relationship between the concept of crime and the constitution of crime should be gradually sorted out to establish the constitution of crime as the sole standard for conviction while highlighting human rights.

Regarding the above-mentioned overlapping, it is urgent to seek a solution in terms of interpretation, and start to explore a thorough solution to get rid of the reliance of the criminal theory and judicial practice on the dual structure of the crime concept, in order to substantively ascertain the relationship between the crime concept and crime constitution and endow the criminal code of China with the characteristics of "Magna Carta" for criminals. However, the subsequent exploration is still arduous and calls for unremitting efforts both in criminal theory and practice.

Naturally, the confounding relationship between the social harmfulness and criminal illegality of the mixed concept of crime stems from specific historical reasons, and the resulting shortcoming is difficult to eliminate in a short period of time since the mixed concept of crime still has a solid foundation in China even nowadays. Therefore, the attempt to abolish the mixed concept of crime in our criminal code and replace it with a formal concept of crime is nothing more than the wishful thinking of criminal law scholars. After a correct understanding about the objective situation of the rule of law in criminal justice in China, the logical approach seems to be: on the basis of acknowledging the established fact of the mixed concept, transform the dual criminalization/decriminalization functions of the crime concept to single decriminalization function and gradually improve the crime system to realize monastic conviction standard while highlighting human rights, so as to blur the decriminalization interpretation function of the substantive crime concept and ultimately put in place a formal crime concept.

All in all, the overlapping between social harmfulness and criminal illegality should be first eliminated. Only the decriminalization function of the crime concept is affirmed able to interpret the four constituent elements of crime and the corresponding criminalization function of the crime concept should be voided and denied. Then, the relationship between the concept of crime and the constitution of crime should be explored to seek breakthroughs in interpretation theory or related theories, to eliminate the dependence of theory and practice on the dual structure of the mixed concept of crime and to establish clear and definite position and hierarchy of the substantive illegality in the crime theory, thus completely realizing the monastic conviction standard and attenuating the decriminalization function of the crime concept. At last, the formal crime concept should be gradually formed under the framework of the principle of *nulla poena sine lege* that restores the human rights protection function, so as to build the crime system in line with the objective situation of our country that can effectively protect human rights.

4.4 Interpretation principle for substantive decriminalization theory in legal dogmatics

The interpretation principle of criminal law is an ultimate issue that bears on the overall situation and governs other aspects of criminal law interpretation. The decriminalization interpretation and criminalization interpretation are juxtaposed, and the decriminalization interpretation is aimed to acquit a behavior without the rationality and necessity of punishment and naturally should also abide by the interpretation principle of criminal law.

4.4.1 Establishment and basic requirements of decriminalization interpretation principles of criminal law

The decriminalization interpretation principles of criminal law refer to the criteria that run through the decriminalization process of criminal law, guide and restrict the decriminalization interpretation and embody the fundamental spirit of criminal law. Fundamentally, the following matters should be noted in fleshing out the interpretation principles.

First, the standards and reasons for these principles should be clarified while establishing the decriminalization interpretation principles of criminal law. Otherwise, the established decriminalization interpretation principles of criminal law will become a non-existent.

Second, the word "principle" must always be borne in mind while establishing the decriminalization interpretation principles of criminal law. The decriminalization interpretation principles of criminal law are rules and criteria that penetrate and guide all kinds of decriminalization interpretations, including authoritative interpretation and non-authoritative interpretation, and also including decriminalization interpretations based on various methods and purposes. Therefore, when establishing the reasons for the decriminalization interpretation principles of criminal law, attention must be paid to their overarching and global guidance features, otherwise the decriminalization interpretation principles of criminal law cannot be truly created.

Third, the decriminalization interpretation principles of criminal law and decriminalization interpretation purpose be must differentiated while establishing the decriminalization interpretation principles of criminal law. They are closely interconnected and the purpose of interpretation will decide the interpretation principles, but they are two different propositions and cannot be equated or confused.

Fourth, policy factors must be excluded while establishing the decriminalization interpretation principles of criminal law.

Fifth, the requirements of criminal law interpretation itself for interpretation techniques must be taken into account while establishing the decriminalization interpretation principles of criminal law. Decriminalization interpretations of criminal law are actually a reflection on written criminal law norms and a reintegration of criminal law norms based on the reflection, thus ensuring the rational and scientific existence of the intrinsic effect of criminal law norms in reality. Otherwise, it is impossible to explain why the criminal law decriminalization hermeneutics can still exist under the principle of *nulla poena sine lege*. Then, for such an activity where subjective human beings act as the subject of reflection, the interpretation itself will inevitably be subjective. In order to eliminate the subjective color in the reflection of criminal law interpretation and achieve the expected goal of making the effectiveness of criminal law norms more reasonable and scientific, only by establishing objective technical elements between the raw materials of interpretation and the operators of interpretation can high-quality results be produced. Moreover, this kind of emphasis and requirement on technology should always go along with the decriminalization interpretation activity itself. Then the contents of decriminalization interpretation principles must conform to the foregoing requirement of the decriminalization interpretation activity. Therefore, technical orientation should be seen as one of the decriminalization interpretation principles. The principle of wholeness is only a specific connotation of technical orientation and cannot fully express the technical requirements of criminal law decriminalization interpretation.

To sum up, the decriminalization interpretation principles of criminal law should comprise legality, rationality and technical orientation.

4.4.2 Specific contents of the decriminalization interpretation principles of criminal law

Since the decriminalization interpretation principles of criminal law should comprise legality, rationality and technical orientation, how to understand these three principles needs to be further elaborated.

First, the principle of legality. "The principle of legality means that the interpretation of criminal law must conform to the requirements of the Constitution and the law".[4] In other words, no matter who interprets the criminal law by which methods, the provisions, spirit and value of the Constitution must be taken as the paramount index of interpretation. At the same time, if interpretation results with multiple meanings coexist, the interpretation result that is consistent with the provisions of the Constitution and its spirit should be first selected. This is also the minimum requirement for all legal interpretation activities in a country ruled by law, and also the adherence to the formal justice of the principle of *nulla poena sine lege*. Therefore, any interpretation result should not only abide by the provisions and spirit of the Constitution but must also conform to the constraints imposed by the principle of *nulla poena sine lege* on the decriminalization interpretation of criminal law, that is, the decriminalization interpretation of criminal law should also satisfy the formal requirement of the principle of *nulla poena sine lege* and respond to the value appeal of formal justice. The decriminalization interpretation of criminal law must be grounded on the literal content of the written criminal law norms rather than on subjective and arbitrary conjectures; the content of decriminalization interpretation of criminal law cannot exceed the possible scope prescribed by the criminal law and the results of interpretation must also conform to the possible intentions of legislators. In this sense, the principle of legality is the implementation and embodiment of the principle of clarity, one of the derived principles of the principle of *nulla poena sine lege.*

Second, the principle of rationality. The principle of rationality means that the interpretation of criminal law must meet the requirements of substantive legitimacy. In other words, no matter who interprets the criminal law by which methods, in addition to conformity with the above principle of legality, they should also follow the requirements of the substantive justice of the rule of law principle and the substantive appropriateness of the principle of *nulla poena sine lege.* Otherwise, the interpretation conclusion drawn is unreasonable. The realization of the stability of the criminal law does not mean that the interpreters of the criminal law can bypass all conflicts and freely interpret the criminal law norms. The principle of legality only creates a harmony of the external environment of the interpretation. When delving into the interior of the norms and the specific internal context of the interpretation, we may find that the internal contradictions and conflicts of the criminal law norms are everywhere. This is because, first of all, the history of human society, especially the history of law, is the history of reason. The connotation of the word "reason" is like the origin, but its extension is too numerous to enumerate. But the most essential requirement is that moral discourses such as justice, equality and conscience, and natural regularity, rationality and reasonableness are realized in human cognition, understanding and practical activities. Therefore, the rationality of the interpretation subject would inevitably clash with the already stable legal provisions and the legal morality determined by the legal provisions. Secondly, once coming into contact with the real life, the stable legal provisions and the spirit embodied in them would immediately reveal their insularism and conservatism. Therefore, contradictions would be unavoidable when the interpreter faces the quiet laws. These inherent contradictions are particularly prominent when interpreting the criminal law that contains the principle of *nulla poena sine lege.*

Therefore, in order to resolve the inherent contradictions and conflicts of these criminal law norms, another principle for criminal law decriminalization interpretation must be introduced – principle of rationality. It is generally held that rationality and legality are conflicting and contradictory, because the former tackles substantive justice, while the latter addresses formal justice. However, the author believes that rationality and legality are not contradictory, and what really conflict are the legality and the real world while rationality is precisely a powerful weapon to dissolve contradictions and conflicts. In this sense, the principle of rationality is the necessary supplement to the principle of legality. What is the principle of rationality, that is, what is its content? Some scholars believe that "the principle of rationality means that the interpretation of criminal law must conform to legal principles, common sense of human relations and the needs of social development". This view is not entirely reasonable. First, the scholars who explained the content of the principle of rationality as above believe that "the interpretation of criminal law must conform to the axioms of criminal law. The so-called axioms of criminal law refer to the basic theoretical propositions of criminal law that have been generally accepted by the criminal law circles in China for a long time. These theoretical propositions of criminal law are like mathematical formulas, whose correctness has been recognized, so they must be observed by decriminalization interpretation of criminal law".[5] However, the basic theoretical propositions of criminal law are by no means universally recognized like mathematical axioms and logical formulas. Second, the concept of human ethics and common sense still stays at the level of "human feelings" and "rituals" in the traditional concept, which is extremely unstable. For example, the first "marital rape" judicial precedent in our country reflects the huge changes in modern society's ethical concepts such as marriage and women's status. Third, the need of social requirement is out of question, but it is not the content but the cause of rationality.

The author believes that the principle of rationality means that the decriminalization interpretation of criminal law should reflect the basic concepts of criminal law, that is, the concepts of equality, fairness and justice of criminal law. First, the decriminalization interpretation of criminal law should reflect equality. This requires that of the decriminalization interpretations of criminal law, particularly targeted at specific cases, the interpretation about one criminal law norm should be uniformly applied to all the same situations, and different interpretations cannot be made at any time. In this sense, rationality and legality are not decisively separated, but closely related. Second, the decriminalization interpretation of criminal law should be fair and not biased or contradictory. The interpretation effect reflected in the criminal law norms is that the punishment should be commensurate with the crime, the scope of punishment is appropriate, and the provisions of the criminal law must be coordinated without contradiction. Third, the decriminalization interpretation of criminal law should always pay attention to the requirements of justice. In the interpretation, we should not only dare to explain the huge changes in the real society within the scope of the adjustment of criminal law norms according to the requirements of justice but also resolutely oppose ramming all social changes and developments into criminal law norms without evaluating the justice value.

Last, the principle of technical orientation. Although a decriminalization interpretation of criminal law satisfies the principles of legality and rationality, there are still multiple interpretation conclusions to choose from so it is necessary to use multiple interpretation methods to deduce and identify the most effective one by scientific techniques. Once the legality and rationality are met by the criminal law interpretation, it will not only provide the interpretation subjects with an external harmonious environment and favorable conditions for the dissolution of internal contradictions but also offer them a scientific guarantee for the interpretation result. The crux of the problem lies in how the interpreter achieves the legality and rationality of an interpretation in actual operations. This answer is orientation toward scientific techniques. The principle of technical orientation is proposed to serve as the neutral bridge and medium to achieve the principles of legality and rationality. In addition, it should also be noted that meeting the requirements of technical orientation not only guarantees that the interpreter can fully cope with the interpretation activities, but also ensures to prevent the mutual conflict and exclusion of legality and rationality nicknamed "chameleon" effect by Posner, which is incurred due to the need of concurrent satisfaction with the legality and rationality principles in the limited maneuverable space of interpretation.

It can be said that various methods of criminal law decriminalization interpretation are repeatedly studied and discussed by legal interpretation theorists to meet the technical orientation principle. However, some available methods are not necessarily highly scientific techniques. To this end, it is necessary to clarify the points of the general technical orientation that coordinate various means. First, a practical and sophisticated decriminalization interpretation is not an overfastidious analysis of individual provisions but should always focus on ascertaining the logical consistency of the overall system of criminal law norms and the relevance of various norms. Decriminalization interpreters should find out the most basic thoughts or wills of the legislators behind the text, and should not take the diction of each article of criminal law as the ultimate platform but should detect the meaning behind the words from overall relationship of criminal law language. Second, legal and rational criminal law decriminalization interpretation must focus on deliberation and comprehensive operation of the reasonable meaning of criminal law norms. Third, the decriminalization interpretation of criminal law must always pay attention to the reconciliation function of formal logic syllogism and the integration function of dialectical logic. In order to achieve well-reasoned and rigorous interpretation result, it is necessary to discover the logical relationship throughout the criminal law norms; only by syllogistic reasoning with the foregoing detected logical relationship can the overall meaning of the criminal law norms be attained; only by boldly using dialectical logical reasoning can the scattered meanings in criminal law norms be integrated into scientific interpretations. Fourth, an intelligent criminal law decriminalization interpretation must dare to use innovative theories as a reference. Innovative criminal law theory has the effect of cultivating the spirit of justice and promoting system innovation. With reference to these theories, the result of criminal law decriminalization interpretation crackles with wisdom and the interpreter can be called a wise man.

4.5 Conclusion

The mixed concept of crime stipulated in Article 13 of the criminal law of China has its profound roots in the times, and the conditions on which the concept of crime depends still exist at present and can hardly be eliminated in a short period of time. Therefore, the argument of establishing the formal crime concept in the criminal code of China and then forging the crime system oriented toward human rights protection distinctly goes against the objective situation of the rule of law in criminal justice in our country and is strongly subjective. Although the author does not deny that the formal concept of crime and the crime system need to undergo substantial changes (even including the stratification of the crime system), which can and should at least become one of the directions of criminal law theory and practice exploration, putting it into practice in an "explosive" manner while ignoring the objective constraints of the rule of law would generate side effects that are self-evident and even unexpectedly destructive.

Under the situation that the reality of the mixed crime concept in criminal law is difficult to be effectively changed for a while, it is undoubtedly more rational and realistic to continue strengthening its decriminalization function and attenuating the criminalization function to transform the dual functions of the mixed crime concept to single decriminalization function and guide the current criminal judicial practice, thus implementing the concept of human rights protection and transitioning to formal crime concept and substantive changes to the crime system. Of course, the transformation of the dual functions of the crime concept to the single decriminalization function is not without cost but also has the disadvantage of sacrificing the monastic conviction standard of four constituent elements of crime. In other words, when the concept of crime exerts the function of decriminalization, it is difficult to clarify the status of legitimate defense, emergency avoidance and supra-law grounds for eliminating misfeasance in the four constituent elements of crime, which essentially tolerates the binary conviction standard of crime constitution and crime concept. In addition, accompanying this transformation is to make necessary correction of the human rights protection function of the principle of *nulla poena sine lege*, and establish a substantial connection between this principle and the constitution of crimes, so as to speed up the process of criminal law taking into account the protection of criminals' human rights; reduce or even dispel the interference of criminal policies that deviate from restraints of the principle of *nulla poena sine lege* to conviction and mitigate policy-related risks of criminal justice; actively promote the innovation of basic criminal law theories such as social harm theory, illegality theory and crime constitution theory so as to provide indispensable and optional useful materials for the improvement of the crime system along with the contention of doctrines.

Decriminalization interpretation is a crucial part of criminal law interpretation, which not only reflects the normative nature of criminal law semantics but also highlights the initiative of the process of criminal law interpretation. Since different criminal law norms have different purposes, and various criminal law interpretation methods have different characteristics and application conditions, to summarize the basic rules that all criminal law decriminalization interpretation activities must abide by according to the characteristics of legal interpretation in the field of criminal law should be of great benefit to standardize the interpretation of criminal law, especially to implement the human rights protection thought of the principle of *nulla poena sine lege*. Establishing the principles of criminal law decriminalization interpretation is to better apply the criminal law norms and different from criminal law decriminalization interpretation methods are the basic rule guiding the application of the various decriminalization interpretation methods and intended to afford governing rules for them so as to prevent the criminal law interpretation from following technical fragments and forgetting the cardinal rule. Among the three principles of legality, rationality and technical orientation, the principle of legality is the premise. If an interpretation is reasonable but illegal, then the interpretation may be directly declared invalid without discussion; if an interpretation is legal but unreasonable, or legal and reasonable but with many alternative interpretation conclusions, it is necessary to use the technical orientation principle to discriminate. From this point of view, the technical orientation principle plays a vital role in resolving conflicts and contradictions. However, which criteria should be employed for discriminating the final interpretation conclusion must be determined based on the criminal law norms to be interpreted and the nature of the case reality rather than predetermined legal interest protection purpose or original legislative intention. Meanwhile, judges can creatively use the interpretative principle of criminal law while applying to individual cases, but the principle of legality must be upheld upon inculpation; otherwise, it will run counter to the human rights protection function of the principle of *nulla poena sine lege*.

Notes

1 See Liu Yanhong: Study on the Theory of Social Harm, *China Legal Science*, 2002(2); Liu Yanhong: Self-Consistency of the Two-Hierarchy System of Purpose and the "Proviso" Decriminalization Function, *Law Review*, 2002(6).
2 Chu Huaizhi: *Criminal Integration*, Law Press, 2004, p. 485–486.
3 Feng Yadong: Study on the relationship between crime constitution and its various forms, *Chinese Journal of Law*, 2009(5).
4 Zhang Zhiming: *Operational Analysis of Legal Interpretation*, China University of Political Science and Law Press, 1999, p. 238.
5 See Li Xihui: *On the Interpretation of Criminal Law*, People's Public Security University Press, 1995, p. 89.

5 Non-Conformity of Constituent Elements

Decriminalization Interpretation of Constituent Elements

5.1 Decriminalization interpretation of constituent elements and doctrine of *nulla poena sine lege*

Each crime has its own independent constituent elements and the constituent element theory is significant for providing standards for distinguishing different types of crimes. Judgment of the conformity of constituent elements is on an organic combination of constituent elements of a specific crime, and since each element is relatively independent, the conformity of constituent elements still hinges on whether each element of the crime is satisfied. The constituent elements have the function of the principle of *nulla poena sine lege,* that is, the judgment of the constitutive elements conformity "is to exclude the behavior that does not satisfy the legal punishment provisions from the criminal object, so as to guarantee the principle of *nulla poena sine lege*". However, not all criminal law provisions are complete criminal law norms and may be left blank. For example, provisions about the constitution of the crime of selling or presenting as a gift to a foreigner without authorization any valuable cultural relic in Article 325 of the criminal law require, "in violation of the laws or regulations on protection of cultural relics…", and the "laws or regulations on protection of cultural relics" here obviously refer to the Cultural Relics Protection Law, Cultural Relics Protection Law Implementation Regulations and other relevant regulations. If we only search for the constituent elements of a crime based on the criminal law norms, we may not be able to piece together the complete elements of a crime and naturally cannot guarantee the realization of the doctrine of *nulla poena sine lege.* It can be seen that the judgment of the conformity of constituent elements is the most direct embodiment of the principle of *nulla poena sine lege.*

The decriminalization interpretation of the constituent elements is the embodiment of the doctrine of *nulla poena sine lege* and is one of the conclusions of transforming the norms of criminal law into the constituent elements. In face of a case, converting the case facts into the theoretical language of criminal law, namely constituent elements, could give rise to two conclusions: conformity of constituent elements and non-conformity of constituent elements. Obviously, the former is the most normal phenomenon and can be drawn in most cases. However, it is

DOI: 10.4324/9781003456773-6

undeniable that in some cases, the conclusion of non-conformity of constituent elements could also be reached, such as normative elements and unwritten elements. Conformity of constituent elements is, after all, the theoretical language of criminal law. Although it has been demonstrated by categories as much as possible, the circumstances of individual cases are always complicated. In addition, the judgment of the conformity of the constituent elements may not be able to achieve value neutrality, which therefore carries the risk of misjudgment. Therefore, the theory of constituent elements also needs to be amended in some way, while the decriminalization interpretation of constituent elements is just an important means of self-correction from the perspective of legal dogmatics. Decriminalization interpretation of behaviors that do not comply with constituent elements is to maintain the principle of *nulla poena sine lege* since such behaviors do not meet the constituent requirements stipulated in the criminal law in essence and are not categorized as criminal acts.

5.2 Formal criminalization: The interpretation of the constituent elements should adhere to the bottom line of the rule of law

In addition to conformity of the constituent elements, a crime can be established after the judgment of illegality and responsibility. However, although the concept of substantive criminal law advocates the substantive interpretation of the constituent elements, and the constituent elements have the function of identifying the punishable violations of legal interests, "for behaviors that are not regulated by the law and are seriously harmful to society", we "must uphold the general justice at the expense of individual case justice",[1] and adhere to the principle of criminalization in form and decriminalization in substance, so as to achieve the inculpation in compliance with formal *nulla poena sine lege principle* and the substantive aspect implied by this principle, namely rational punishment scope. Formal interpretation must be followed by inculpation, and only when the law has express provisions can conviction and sentencing be granted. Substantive interpretation is limited to exculpation; The theory of substantive crime is limited to decriminalization interpretation and by advocating this, a decriminalization mechanism of "offence does not necessarily have to be punished", so as to "exclude from the scope of criminal law punishment the behaviors that are expressly stipulated in the law but the regulations themselves are unreasonable, those that cannot be punished because they are not expressly stipulated in the law".[2] The principle of *nulla poena sine lege* is the bottom line of the rule of law that must be followed in the interpretation of the constituent elements.

Taking unit offenses that have no express provisions in the law as an example, the view of conviction held by some scholars in the field of criminal law goes against the basic requirements of formal criminalization; the interpretation of constituent elements of specific crimes such as fraudulent fund-raising and credit card fraud breaks the principle of *nulla poena sine lege* and criminalizes the misconduct of unit crime subjects.

Article 30 of the criminal law of China expressly stipulates that "if an act is prescribed by law as a crime committed by a unit, the unit shall bear criminal responsibility". The crime where units can be established as the subject of the crime is called the unit crime; for other crimes that only natural persons could be established as the subject of the crime not units as prescribed by the criminal law, if an unit commits such a crime in judicial practice, such as the crime of theft and credit card fraud, they are called unit crimes not expressly stipulated by the law. For the sake of brevity, the crimes that are not clearly stipulated in the law but committed by units in judicial practice are referred to as non-unit crimes. Where necessary, the reference to unit crimes not expressly stipulated by the law is still used. However, in recent years, regarding the numerous non-unit crimes committed by units in judicial practice, the supreme judicial organ also promulgated a series of judicial interpretations, which are plentiful in number but inconsistent in position, so it leads to many new issues while solving old ones. Reflecting on it may be a respect for the cause of legal dogmatics in our country.

5.2.1 "Norm retirement theory" and "counter-doctrinalization": Closely related topic

The status quo of inculpation irrespective of no express provisions in the law is "norm retirement" and "counter-doctrinalization". It not only dispels the norms of criminal law but also violates the tenet of criminal dogmatics, which regards the current norms as the standard, destroys the stability of the formal rule of law, accommodates utilitarianism but abandons criminal law norms and rules, and satisfies pragmatism but violates legal positivism and dogmatic principles.

1 What is the "norm retirement theory"? What is "counter-doctrinalization"?

In recent years, with the development of Chinese criminal law interpretation theory and skills, in some criminal law interpretation occasions, the interpreter seems to be interpreting the criminal law norms, but in fact is making "interpretive legislation", who actually enacts laws in the name of interpretation. On these occasions, the object of interpretation, that is, criminal law norms, seems to be very important, but their actual functions are weakening and receding, which is called norm retirement. With the declining of the normative role of law, law has become an object that can be "manipulated" by legal researchers at any time. "Creativity has become the essence of legal interpretation, and loyalty to law is rarely mentioned. The normative and restrictive effect of law is getting weaker". The authority of legal norms has been questioned, and criminal law interpretations under various banners, such as objective interpretation and substantive interpretation, have been advocated. "The retirement of the normative effect of law has achieved a 'soft landing' in legal studies, and become a prominent feature of trendy jurisprudence", while the "rule of provisions has actually fallen into disuse". The retirement of legal norms means that creative legal interpretations are highlighted and the role of the object of legal interpretation, that is, legal norms, is reduced, and that the interpreters' subjectivity is playing an increasingly important role in legal interpretation, with the authority of law abated.

The increasing development of criminal dogmatics enriches the theory of criminal law, especially the interpretation of criminal law. However, this phenomenon also exacerbates the phenomenon of norm retirement to some extent, which is probably beyond the expectation of scholars of legal dogmatics. If there was a list of top trending searches, then its headline would undoubtedly be legal dogmatics, which is the most popular legal research paradigm among Chinese jurists. In the view of scholars of criminal dogmatics, criminal dogmatics is equivalent to criminal law hermeneutics, because "historically, the authority of law is not based on rational study, but by means of political coercion". Therefore, researches on law by traditional jurisprudence are basically built on an invincible faith in it and seldom have criticisms. "Legal hermeneutics is therefore called dictatorial interpretation".[3] This determines the close connection between legal dogmatics and legal hermeneutics from the very beginning and is the reason why Chinese scholars equate criminal law dogmatics with criminal law hermeneutics. Since the criminal dogmatics emphasizes the understanding of "exact concepts, to produce justifiable judgments", namely interpretation of criminal law norms and systematizing on its basis, scholars of criminal dogmatics consequently believe that interpreting bad laws as good laws is their highest pursuit, which leads to the loss of the rule of law and interpretative dissolution of legal norms and gives rise to the "interpretation omnipotence theory" with rich interpretation skills, powerful interpretation functions and even all-powerful while neglecting that the legality of interpretation depends on compliance to legal norms rather than overstepping. Therefore, under the influence of the criminal law motto, "the law is not a laughing stock" that has been chanted all the time, scholars of criminal dogmatics are all devoted to making interpretations about criminal law norms based on interpretation centrism and, along with increasingly powerful interpretation function, enable interpretations to surpass norms; the interpretation increasingly becomes the embodiment of the interpreter's personal will, rather than the faithful interpretation of legal norms. The interpretation function of legal dogmatics is developing into a quasi-legislative function and criminal law scholars seem to be dissolving dogmatics in the name of dogmatics. As a result, the criminal law in China has also slipped into "counter-doctrinalization".

2 Integrated relationship between "norm retirement theory" and "counter-doctrinalization"

The "norm retirement theory" and "counter-doctrinalization" are the same. "Normativeness and legal effect are the research objects of legal dogmatics", and "legal dogmatics is the link that connects statues and judges", so legal dogmatics regards the current criminal law norms sacred and does not allow arbitrary criticism but advocates interpretations in strict accordance with legal norms; its boundary is dealing with criminal law norms rather than legal facts. The interpretation of criminal law norms should not base on anything other than legal norms, so it is asserted that "legal dogmatics demonstrates respect for legal provisions". In short, legal dogmatics takes legal norms as the core, legal interpretation as the method, dogmatic development and system construction as the theoretical purpose, and serving judicial practice as the practical purpose. As mentioned above, legal dogmatics is a dictatorial interpretation. According to Kant, "dogmatics is 'the arbitrary process of pure reason without prior criticism of its own abilities and usually metes out punishments on presuppositions that are deemed real without examinations. Scholars of legal dogmatics do not ask what law is, and under what circumstances, within what scope, and in what way legal cognition exists". Dictatorial interpretation has a deep relationship with subjective interpretation, and means acknowledging the legislators' intention, which advocates the use of subjective interpretation of legal norms to explore the legislative purpose of legal norms. Clearly, legal dogmatics is the very same to formal rule of law and subjective interpretation. All foregoing interpretation cases that result in retirement of criminal law norms all adopt objective interpretation and are extreme objective interpretations. If general objective interpretations are only to enrich the meaning of legal norms, extreme objective interpretations are legislation, which makes interpretation conclusions far deviate from existing legal norms; norms are no longer important, and new norms created by interpretation conclusions are the goal. "In the judicial process and legal interpretation, seeking the original meaning of the law seems to have become a laughingstock. People forget that arbitrariness of law is related to the exploratory nature of legal interpretation, and are only looking for meaning in an exploratory way". At present, the interpreter considers too many factors such as the background of the times, the need for combat, and the balance of interests, so that the meaning of the criminal law norm is not explored but created; the criminal law norm is nothing but the clay sculpture of the interpreter. In the name of the objective needs of the era, various realistic needs based on fighting crime have repeatedly challenged the authority of legal norms. If legal dogmatics is divorced from norms, it may evolve into social science jurisprudence, or political jurisprudence, but certainly not legal dogmatics. Doctrines in legal dogmatics are formed by explaining and developing norms, and norms further solidify the status and function of doctrines. For example, the theory of crime constitution in the criminal law tackles issues of crime and innocence, this crime and that crime by interpreting each crime and punishment norm in the specific provisions of the criminal law, and gives rise to different exquisite interpretation theories such as subjective and objective imputation, behavior and result valuelessness by docking of criminal law norms and the facts of various cases; meanwhile, through provisions about constituent elements in the general provisions and specific provisions, criminal law norms further maintain and develop the theory of crime constitution. Without norms, legal dogmatics has no object of interpretation, thus impossible to form "doctrines". At present, there is an upsurge of doctrinalization in Chinese legal science, and the research on doctrinal studies has achieved remarkable results. However, under the guise of dogmatics, many scholars are deconstructing norms and annihilating doctrines. When all kinds of criminal law interpretations seem to revolve around criminal law norms, but actually violate or even abandon norms, it not only represents the retirement of criminal law norms but also departure from and violation of legal dogmatics, since this gets farther away from legal dogmatics that takes norms as the core.

The common harm of the retirement of norms and counter-doctrinalization is the damage to the formal rule of law. The ideal rule of law is the unity of the formal rule of law and the substantive rule of law, and the Achilles heel of the rule of law is the formal rule of law; the substantive rule of law has value only in the sense of realizing the formal rule of law. The substantive rule of law that breaks through the formal rule of law is anti-rule of law. Legal norms are the embodiment of the formal rule of law and the carrier of the rule of law. In the process of realizing the inherent substantive rule of law concepts such as legality and rationality, the bottom line of the formal rule of law must be adhered to. Legal norms represent the important values of formal rule of law such as the security, stability and predictability of law, so the respect for legal norms is the corollary of upholding the formal rule of. The popularity of legal dogmatics is precisely due to its natural characteristics of formal rule of law. An important manifestation of the legal circle's understanding and acceptance of the concept of formal rule of law is the "emergence of various legal dogmatic propositions in various legal disciplines", such as "the discipline of criminal law diverts its focus from multiple perspectives such as criminal law philosophy and criminal policy to criminal dogmatics", since "legal dogmatics is just a set of basic tools to restrain legal judgments, avoid arbitrariness, prevent the influence of extra-legal factors on legal judgments, and ensure formal justice".[4] Therefore, when Chinese criminal law scholars criticize the traditional Soviet Russian criminal law, criminal dogmatics has become a new tool to replace the Soviet Russian criminal law theory, so as to eliminate political arbitrariness and other incompatibilities with the construction of the rule of law. For this reason, in the recent 20 years, the study of criminal law in our country has been advancing along the road of criminal dogmatics. That being the case, the bottom line of the formal rule of law required by criminal dogmatics cannot be ignored when interpreting criminal law. "The core content of criminal law is criminal dogmatics and its foundation and boundaries come from criminal law norms". The degree of compliance with criminal law norms determines the realization of the formal rule of law. The formal side of the principle of *nulla poena sine lege* also requires strict observance of criminal law norms, and effectively constrains the interpretation of criminal dogmatics, so the interpretation of criminal dogmatics should be carried out within the scope of the principle of legality, and legal dogmatics cannot break through formal legality; only by compliance with the current criminal law norms can the formal legality of interpretation conclusions be guaranteed. Behind the retreat of legal norms is a violation of the characteristics of legal dogmatics, such as norms as the core and formal rule of law as the bottom line, and "expansion of the state's powers and damage of the rights of the subject at the cost of freedom and extensive violation of legal principles by broadening exceptions", which eventually leads to "the reduction of the normative role promoted by the formal rule of law" and in turn results in the damage of the formal rule of law. If the interpretation of the criminal law does not strengthen the role of the criminal law norms in restricting state power, but generalizes its function to render it an ambiguous law that can be used as needed, there will be no boundaries, which would greatly weaken the authority and seriousness of the criminal law norms and make it difficult to achieve the goal of rule of law in criminal justice.

Only by defending the normative thinking of legal dogmatics can (criminal) legal dogmatics be established. Legal dogmatics is characterized by emphasis and reliance on norms, and its primary task is to interpret norms and build a system and even develop doctrines. The characteristic of normative thinking is that what is right or wrong is straightforward. Unit crimes that are not expressly stipulated in the law are crimes beyond *nulla poena sine lege*, which therefore are not crimes in the sense of criminal law, but at most crimes in the sense of criminology. The interpretation shall not make up provisions out of thin air. The advantage of normative thinking lies in that it implements the formal rule of law of legal dogmatics to the greatest extent, and only considers whether there are norms and whether there is a crime, instead of deciding the conviction based on the substantive legitimacy of punishment, that is, the serious consequences of non-unit crimes committed by units. The inculpation must strictly conform to normative justice; otherwise, the principle of *nulla poena sine lege* would lose its rule of law significance. The substantive judgment is based on the premise of the existing formal norms and constitutes the value expansion of the actual norms. No matter how serious the harmful consequences of a certain behavior, it cannot be criminalized by having substance to surpass form and consequences to replace norms. Failure to defend the normative thinking of legal dogmatics contravenes dogmatics and criminal dogmatics will never be forged.

5.2.2 Handling of unit criminal behaviors not stipulated by legal norms: Innocent or guilty

Although people have long been familiar with the principle of *nulla poena sine lege*, they still intentionally or unintentionally ignore the absence of express provisions in the law about constituent elements or regard the constituent elements of one crime as those of another crime. The unit criminal behaviors not expressly stipulated by the law are basically convicted in the current legislation, judicial interpretation and even criminal law theory.

1 Unit theft: establishment of guilt theory in three judicial interpretations

In the early 1990s, with the gradual advancement of the reform and opening up and the market economy, the production and operation activities of enterprises became increasingly frequent and correspondingly many cases of electricity theft by units were reported. Since the 1979 criminal code did not stipulate crimes committed by units, whether and how to deal with cases of electricity theft by units has become a major problem for judicial organs. For this end, the Supreme People's Procuratorate stipulates: "Where the unit organizes theft and the acquired property is owned by the unit, if the amount is huge or there are serious circumstances, the directly responsible person-in-charge and other main directly responsible personnel shall be arrested and prosecuted in line with the crime of theft according to law".

After the implementation of the current criminal law, cases of units stealing various energy sources represented by theft of electricity by unit constantly spring up, but according to the principle of nulla poena sine lege, the units are not the subject of the crime of theft, who therefore shall not be investigated for criminal liability; therefore, the Supreme People's Procuratorate reiterated "where the relevant personnel of the unit organize theft for the benefit of the unit, if the circumstances are serious, the directly responsible personnel shall be investigated for criminal liability in line with the crime of theft as prescribed in Article 264 of the criminal law". This interpretation continues the above-mentioned position and content and confirms that the theft should be punished; acknowledges that units that carry out non-unit crimes (such as crime of theft) shall be deemed guilty, but the natural person rather than the unit shall be investigated for criminal liability. This stance is tentatively called "guilt theory".

More than ten years later, the crime of theft has undergone many changes, both in terms of amount and manifestation. As far as unit theft is concerned, many units are found organizing and instigating the crime of theft, but not necessarily for the benefit of the unit, and possible for the benefit of other units or the organizer himself, and who are "relevant personnel of the unit" also arouse many debates. For this reason, the Supreme People's Court and the Supreme People's Procuratorate pointed out in the relevant regulations: "Where a unit organizes or instigates theft, which complies with Article 264 of the Criminal Law and the relevant provisions of this Interpretation, the organizer, instigator, and direct implementer shall be investigated for criminal liability for the crime of theft". This interpretation further clarifies and strengthens the position of guilt and the conditions for pursuing criminal responsibility, so that circumstances that do not seek interests for the unit may also be investigated for criminal liability which expands the scope of criminal responsibility for the crime of theft committed by the unit.

2 Other non-unit crimes committed by the unit: continuation of the guilt theory and appearance of the innocence theory

In the past two decades, there have been four judicial interpretations related to other non-unit crimes implemented by relevant units in our country, three of which continued the guilt position about unit theft in judicial interpretation and one reflected the innocence position. The three judicial interpretations embodying the position of guilt were promulgated respectively for the crime of refusal to execute judgments and orders, computer-related crime and the crime of illegally crossing the national border and the contents are basically identical to judicial interpretation about the crime of theft, which will not be repeated here. The one judicial interpretation with "innocence" position was promulgated against the crime of loan fraud by the unit, which explicitly proclaims, "The act of an unit cannot constitute the crime of loan fraud… the act of loan fraud carried out by the unit cannot be convicted or punished as the crime of loan fraud, and its directly responsible person-in-charge and other directly responsible personnel may not be investigated for criminal liability in line with the crime of loan fraud. However, in the judicial practice, units that defraud a bank or any other financial institution of loans by signing and implementing the loan contract clearly for the purpose of illegal possession, which conform to the constituent elements of the crime of contract fraud prescribed in Article 224 of the criminal law, shall be convicted and punished in line with the crime of contract fraud". The crime of loan fraud set out in Article 193 of the criminal law is a crime that can only be committed by natural persons; when a unit commits a loan fraud, neither the unit nor the directly responsible natural person can be investigated for criminal responsibility. Although the Minutes stipulate that sometimes loan fraud can be dealt with as the crime of contract fraud, that is due to concurrence of legal articles between the crime of loan fraud and crime of contract fraud, while the crime of contract fraud can be committed both by the unit or natural person; when a unit carries out loan fraud that also conforms to the crime of contract fraud, it is convicted of the crime of contract fraud due to concurrence of legal articles. This should be the case in theory and practice even if there is no provision in the Minutes. It can be seen that the interpretation adopts the stance of "innocence" for the unit that commits the non-unit crime, namely the crime of loan fraud; when a unit carries out the loan fraud, neither the unit nor the natural person can be held criminally responsible.

3 Termination of innocence theory by guilt theory: legislative interpretation about non-unit crimes committed by the unit

In order to solve the contradictions and inconsistencies in the above judicial interpretations, and to prevent the phenomenon of no legal basis for other non-unit crimes committed by the unit in the future, the Standing Committee of the National People's Congress issued a legislative interpretation, clearly stipulating that "where companies, enterprises, public organs, government agencies, groups and other units that carry out socially harmful acts prescribed by the criminal law, if the specific provisions of the criminal law and other laws do not stipulate investigating the unit for criminal liability, the person that organizes, plans and carries out the act that endangers society should be investigated for criminal liability in accordance with the law". Compared with the judicial interpretation of unit crimes, this legislative interpretation is undoubtedly universally applicable, and clearly define that when a unit carries out the non-unit crime, it shall be dealt with as crimes, and the natural person shall be investigated for criminal liability, which, to a great extent, resolves the contradictory stances among previous judicial interpretations about unit crimes and declares the end of "innocence" position to unify and clarify the determination of criminal liability for units that carry out non-unit crimes.

5.3 Substantive decriminalization: Adherence to normative theory and doctrinalization

The decriminalization interpretation of constituent elements is an inevitable requirement of criminal law norms and formal rule of law. The overall victory of the theory about unit offenses not expressly stipulated by the law means the retreat of criminal law norms and damage of legal dogmatics. The guilt theory is fundamentally against normativeness and doctrinalization and dissolves the criminal law norms and even the formal rule of law in the name of such utilitarianism and pragmatism as substantive rule of law like rationality of punishment and need to combat unit crimes, which should be watched out for and reflected.

5.3.1 Dissolution of the formal rule of law by the guilt theory about unit crimes not expressly stipulated in the law: "norm retirement"

The guilt theory about unit crimes not expressly stipulated in the law is by far the most typical representative of "norm retirement" in the field of criminal law. Disregarding Article 30 of the criminal law, the guilt theory creates substantively new provisions about unit crimes through criminal theoretical interpretation, judicial interpretation and even the final legislative interpretation, causing the original provisions of Article 30 and the principle of *nulla poena sine lege* in Article 3 of the criminal law to entirely retire and even be dissolved. The guilt theory focuses on social effects rather than legal effects and "overthrows the law with the job in law", which is a manifestation of the retreat and dissolution of criminal law norms.

Article 30 of the 1997 criminal law stipulates, "any company, enterprise, institution, State organ, or organization that commits an act that endangers society, which is prescribed by law as a crime committed by a unit, shall bear criminal responsibility". In the criminal law of China, the unit crime is subject to the principle of legality, and only crimes for which units are the subjects as expressly stipulated in the specific provisions of the criminal law can be called unit crimes. Meanwhile, Article 3 of the criminal law stipulates the principle of *nulla poena sine lege*, where "for acts that are not explicitly defined as criminal acts in law, they shall not be convicted or punished". In this context, the guilty theory is obviously intended to exert the effect of criminal law in the crackdown on crimes and social governance and is a pragmatic and convenient stance. This allows the criminal law to achieve the social governance purpose of making a clean sweep of all unit crimes and renders Article 30 an ornament with its normative significance and effects completely impracticable. A country ruled by law should follow the rule of utilitarianism; the supremacy of rules suggests the principle of rule of law and the rule of law cannot be achieved without the rule of utilitarianism. The consequences of norm retirement are the impairment of the authority of the criminal law and a breakthrough of substantive rule of law to formal rule of law. Here, one does not see norms but reality; does not acknowledge the form but the substance; does not accept the principle of *nulla poena sine lege* but criminalization, which deal a great impact on the theory of unit crimes, the principle of *nulla poena sine lege* and even the cause of rule of law in criminal justice.

5.3.2 Dissolution of the formal rule of law by the guilt theory about unit crimes not expressly stipulated in the law: "counter-doctrinalization"

The guilt theory about unit crimes not expressly stipulated by the law is the most obvious "counter-doctrinalization" in the doctrinalization process of the criminal law of China in recent years. The guilt theory does not take criminal law norms as the core, and does not solve the actual needs of the crackdown on units through the dogmatic process of logical analysis of norms and elevating it to a system, but roughly modifies the original norms through authoritative interpretations and undermines the stability of legal dogmatics. The guilt theory does not use the tool of criminal dogmatics but is indeed endorsed by scholars in this area; it disintegrates legal norms under the guise of interpretation of legal norms by legal dogmatics and ultimately overthrows the legal dogmatics in its name.

Why did jurisprudence take the road of dogmatics? This issue needs to be deliberated. When Kirchmann put forward the proposition "the worthlessness of jurisprudence as a science", Jhering responded with "is jurisprudence a science?" and Larenz made great endeavors to publish the paper "On the Indispensability of Jurisprudence as a Science" which turn out lackluster in front of Kirchmann's flamboyant speech, all these show that the development of legal dogmatics is to save law itself to a large extent and is technical efforts to make the law look like or closer to science and eventually develop into a science. Traditional legal dogmatics puts great emphasis on the value orientation of formalism and logical system. Although modern dogmatics is open under the impetus of the free law movement, the foundation of legal dogmatics has never changed, that is, "to bring calculable and predictable rationalism to the law through dogmatics of conceptual formalism" and to promote the formation of legal dogmatics through interpretation of norms and systematic construction so as to integrate norms and justice. Therefore, legal dogmatics could work to materialize and strengthen the stability value of the law.

Nevertheless, the guilt theory about unit crimes not expressly stipulated by the law just damages the formalism and ruleism. With the promulgation of a series of judicial and legislative interpretations for non-unit crimes carried by units, the principle of legality for unit crimes has been repeatedly impacted by utilitarianism and pragmatism. On the premise that the current criminal law has both the principle of *nulla poena sine lege* and implements the principle of legality for unit crimes, the expedient measure of only pursuing the criminal responsibility of natural persons in response to unit crimes before the current criminal law is extended to all circumstances of non-unit crimes carried out by units under the background of the current criminal law, which is undoubtedly a mockery of the principle of *nulla poena sine lege* and the principle of legality for unit crimes. Instead of a simple question of whether natural persons should be held criminally responsible, the essential issue of whether a unit should be investigated for criminal liability matters how to view the principle of *nulla poena sine lege,* how to address the relationship between the principle of legality of unit crimes and utilitarianism and how to implement accountability in dealing with unit crimes.

The principle of *nulla poena sine lege* is the engine and general embodiment of ruleism, formalism and rationalism of criminal law. In today's world, "a country that holds either a positive or negative attitude towards crimes by legal persons, has an ambivalent attitude towards criminal regulation of legal person activities, and hesitates between the utilitarian considerations that the so-called corporate crime must be regulated by means of criminal law and how to adhere to the principle of accountability, one of the basic principles of modern criminal law". Simply using the effectiveness of legislative interpretation to enforce the theory of guilt cannot directly answer the fundamental question of why the illegal and criminal acts of units that are not clearly stipulated in the law should be dealt with, which involves the principle *nulla poena sine leg;* as a result, the stability value of criminal dogmatics is directly undermined.

"If someone tries to deviate from the existing doctrinal rules based on political, ethical or social effect factors, he must bear the corresponding burden of proof". The theory of guilt holds that when a unit carries out the non-unit crime, it means a natural person is committing the crime. Therefore, if the unit is not investigated for criminal liability, the natural person such as the person who is directly responsible should be held criminally liable.[5] Scholars in favor this viewpoint believe that the innocence theory would cause unimaginable consequences if established,[6] but this argument is not irrefutable. Since no matter in "the criminal laws of a few continental European countries such as Germany that do not recognize legal person crimes" or "in the criminal laws of common law countries that recognize legal person crimes", "there is no such thing as no punishment against employees of legal persons that commit pure natural person crimes. The employees of legal persons must bear criminal responsibility as long as they commit a crime", which is not controversial in criminal law theory and judicial practice.[7] In other words, there is no difficulty in dealing with the homicide that is committed by the personnel assigned under the collective decision of the unit as a natural person crime in terms of criminal law techniques, since homicide is an extreme crime and can be carried out by individuals; here, the will of the unit is more similar to actio libera in causa that a person is persuaded to drink and then drive and have an accident; employees can choose to kill or not to kill which is incomparable to property and economic crimes such as unit theft. Therefore, the crimes like intentional homicide, robbery and rape, even if they are committed by the personnel assigned under the decision of the unit, belong to acts of identity, that is, criminal acts that can only be carried by individuals in person; as the personnel is fully aware of the nature and significance of such acts but still carries them out, holding the said personnel criminally responsible conforms to the principle of *nulla poena sine leg* in accordance with the crime constitution theory of criminal law, regardless of whether the unit constitutes a crime. Personal crimes cannot be carried out directly by units rather must be by individuals; property and economic crimes can be conducted directly by units and groups which may produce better results. The reason why the person in charge of the unit is punished for unit crimes is that the unit as a whole "has no reprehensible soul or body" as articulated by criminal jurist Coffey; when a unit sends an employee to carry out homicide, the employees themselves have both reprehensible soul and body, and punishment for homicide by the employee as pure natural person crime fully complies with the criminal culpability principle of bearing responsibility solely for one's own crime. This means that regardless of the availability of judicial interpretation or legislative interpretation, there is no need to discuss the issue of punishment for these personal crimes committed in the name of the unit; otherwise, it is forcibly seeking sameness from difference and confuse the "normative justice" in Article 30 of the criminal law with the "individual justice" in Article 232. This kind of argument itself is not dogmatic and on this basis, criminalization of all unit criminal acts not expressly stipulated in the law is obviously untenable. That being the case, the arbitrariness of the theory of guilt, its destructiveness to the unified legal norms and the transgression of the bottom line of the formal rule of law will all attract inescapable criticisms. "From the perspective of form, criminal law is primarily an element of the principle of the rule of law that guarantees the stability of the law. Since criminal law may exercise the most severe interference with the personal liberty of citizens, special precautions are particularly necessary to prevent its abuse". In the face of unit crimes that are not clearly stipulated in the law, utilitarianism and pragmatism should not break through the borders of ruleism and should not abuse criminal law punishment. Utilitarianism, which gets free from the constraints of rules, is full of thoughts about the expansion of punishment in the society, and "Utilitarian interpretations often strive to get rid of the shackles of the law and break through the boundaries of basic human rights, which are more likely to 'bleed dry' legal articles and make people drop off the necessary precautions and vigilance that the criminal law may become 'evil'".[8] The theory of guilt makes it possible to pursue criminal responsibility for all unit crimes not clearly stipulated in the law, and makes the provisions of Article 30 of the criminal law impracticable, so that the punishment of unit crimes that are not clearly stipulated in the law is not subject to the value constraints of the formal rule of law and the principle of legality of unit crimes becomes universalism. Here, it is not legal norms or rule of law logic but life value and actual need of crime governance that takes precedence. The method of legal interpretation advocated by legal dogmatics requires "expression of precisely transmitted rules" rather than interpretative legislation. The theory of guilt is exactly interpretative legislation that undermines formalism.

The conclusions that conform to legal norms and interpretation rules have the explanatory power of criminal dogmatics. The theory of guilt about unit crimes not expressly stipulated in the law lacks interpretative power in criminal dogmatics. Article 30 of the criminal law is consistent with articles in the specific provisions that provide for unit crimes, with the latter being the embodiment of the former, and the former being the constraint of the latter, which mutually form a coordinated legal system; but the theory of guilt breaks the coordination of the system. "If the dogmatic theory gets stuck in value contradictions, clearly violates the meaning of words, ignores systematic connections, or draws conclusions that flagrantly disregard the purpose of norms, we can easily judge that this dogmatic theory cannot hold up".[9] Therefore, if the theory clashes with the current legal norms, then the interpretative power of the theory will be weakened or even disappear. The fragmented legal interest protection system is the limitation and characteristic of the systematic work of criminal dogmatics. The theory of guilt is a regional interpretation of the unit crimes not expressly stipulated in the law rather than a holistic interpretation based on the criminal code and the principle of the rule of law. This kind of interpretation "takes the mechanism of criminal law as a functional element of social reality" instead of a fundamental issue about justification. In the latter, criminal dogmatics is used to control the boundaries of the scope of punishment. The criminal law is fragmented and incomplete and cannot protect all the legal interests in social life but can only combat those infringements of legal interests that should be punished and protect important legal interests. This selective protection of legal interests is precisely the limitation of criminal law from the perspective of crime theory. To punish unit crimes, the criminal law establishes "prohibition norms to safeguard a predetermined legal order". As the last resort and barrier of the legal system, the incompleteness of the criminal law has been generally accepted by people. Moreover, "criminal law" was originally limited to the task of protecting individual legal interests from infringement, which is also called the criminal law serving the rule of law. However, the current development trend of criminal law is increasingly deviating from this "rule of law orientation". The guilt theory about unit crimes not expressly stipulated by the law is not to protect individualized legal interests but to safeguard the socialized and collective legal interests; it is not to serve the rule of law country but cater to the purpose of a welfare state; it is not an interpretation compatible with criminal norms but is produced based on the policy needs of preventing and punishing crimes. Therefore, the guilty theory goes contrary to the trend and requirement of criminal doctrinalization and a distinct embodiment that the criminal law of China strays from the rule of law country orientation. The guilt theory in fact breaks through the formal provisions of the criminal law by substantive interpretation and breaches criminal norms for the consideration of interests; it is out of the consideration of substantive interests that such acts seriously infringe upon the legal interests, and fears that non-prosecution would indulge crimes, thus extensively "introducing the principle of balance of interest into the interpretation and application of civil and criminal laws".[10] However, such interpretation is an interpretation about the current law when there are express provisions in the law, rather than criminalization interpretation when there are no express provisions in the law. If an act should be criminalized due to serious infringement of legal interests, it means that the balance of interests transcends the basis for the application of criminal law norms, which constitutes the dissolution of the criminal law norms, the principle of *nulla poena sine lege* and the principle of rule of law. Legal interest is the core concept and important doctrine of criminal dogmatics, which should be used for the realization of the basic goal of formal rule of law in legal dogmatics, rather than to expand the connotation and extension of legal interests, increase the arbitrariness and operability of criminalization and topple the dogmatics in the name of dogmatics.

5.3.3 Reaffirmation of the formal rule of law and decriminalization interpretation of constituent elements

It needs to be pointed out in particular that the Amendment (9) still adopts the doctrine of legality that "a unit that commits…crime, should be punished…" rather than applying the legislative interpretation about unit crimes. This means that the interpretation did not fundamentally shake the position of doctrine of legality. The precedence of formal rule of law over substantive rule of law is upheld through the provisions about unit crimes in the Amendment (9).

This just gives an opportunity to reflect on the theory of criminal law: the theory of guilt of unit crimes without express provisions in the law may be dubious. According to the theory of guilt, since all unit crimes that are not clearly stipulated in the law can be investigated for criminal responsibility in accordance with legislative interpretations, why does the Amendment (9) still adopt the doctrine of legality? Especially when the legislative interpretation clearly stipulates that the natural person could be investigated for criminal liability for unit crimes not expressly stipulated by the law, there are 11 articles in the Amendment (9) (including paragraph 1 of Article 260, Article 283, Article 285, Article 286, paragraph 1 of Article 286, paragraph 1 and 2 of Article 287, paragraph 1 of Article 307, paragraph 1 of Article 308, Article 313 and paragraph 1 of Article 390) that add stipulations about unit crimes for 12 charges, greatly expanding the scope of unit crimes in the criminal law of China. It can be seen that the Amendment (9) did not ignore the unit crimes not expressly stipulated in the law as the legislative interpretation provides a solution but disregards the legislative interpretation and returns to the doctrine of legality about unit crimes in Article 30 of the criminal law; this seems to imply that judicial and legislative interpretations that deem unit criminal acts not expressly stipulated in the law guilty are actually temporary makeshifts and do not represent the affirmation of the theory of guilt in criminal law theory; perhaps it also means a correction to the legislative interpretation that makes criminal norms retreat, violate the legal dogmatics and compromise the rule of law; if the above conjectures are not accurate, at least it shows that the theory of guilt for unit crimes that are not expressly regulated by law is not safe, and it is neither in line with the original intention of the legislation nor in line with the legislative reality to apply the concept of guilt to all unit crimes not expressly stipulated in the law. Therefore, re-emphasis on the doctrine of legality for unit crimes in the Amendment (9) demonstrates that the guilt theory may lack normative legitimacy and theoretical justification, which should be treated with caution instead of being promoted; meanwhile, this also suggests that how legislative and judicial interpretations about unit crimes in the criminal law of China should be unified and develop still remains to be solved.

How to deal with unit crimes that are not expressly stipulated in the law has always been the focus of criminal law legislation and justice in China, which has undergone development and theoretical controversy from the theory of innocence to the theory of guilt. The theory of guilt ignores the explicit provisions about unit crimes in Article 30 and specific provisions of the criminal law and expands in disguise unit crimes to all crimes through the punishment of the relevant supervisors and directly responsible personnel of the unit, so that all crimes in the criminal code can actually be committed by the unit. This interpretation violates the provisions of Article 30 of the criminal law rather than adapting to it. The scientific interpretation of criminal law should start with criminal regulations but the theory of guilt renders the criminal norms invisible and retreats to an inferior position to interpretations of the interpreters; and obliterates the ruleism and results in the spreading of the utilitarianism of fighting crime. The theory of guilt is a new model of shift of responsibility and strengthens individual responsibility to make up for the shortcomings of the enterprise, which is not conducive to the construction of a modern enterprise system and also blurs the boundaries between natural person crimes and unit crimes. In terms of criminal law theory, Chinese criminal law adopts the viewpoint of "real entity theory" in the continental law system, and recognizes that units can become the subject of crimes, which establishes the normative basis for investigating the unit's criminal liability by the legislative model that "if an act is prescribed by law as a crime committed by a unit, the unit shall bear criminal responsibility" and thus makes it an inevitable conclusion that "for unit crimes not stipulated in the law, the unit shall not bear criminal responsibility". In the process of the rule of law construction in China, we must ensure the supremacy of formal rule of law norms and establish the basic perspective of legal dogmatics. If Chinese criminal law is to practice doctrinalization, it must abide by the normative principle. The researches about legal dogmatics are centered on the normative issues of actual life events, so legal dogmatics should first pay attention to the existing legal system, such as the principle of *nulla poena sine lege* and other existing systems, and then accommodate various values generally recognized by the society. This means that formal justice and formal rule of law are the premises of legal dogmatics; the study of specific issues such as unit crimes should not ignore criminal law norms, abandon formal doctrines such as the principle of *nulla poena sine lege* or blindly yield to utilitarianism.

5.4 Conclusion

Protecting all impaired legal interests is an impossible task for criminal law. The incompleteness of criminal law protection is maintained through the principle of *nulla poena sine lege*, stated through criminal law norms and realized through criminal dogmatics. The criminal law norm itself is not "perfect", nor is it a categorically clear rule. It allows the existence of normative constituent elements or unwritten constituent elements or other constituent elements that require value judgment or reference to other legal norms, which determines that the criminal law norm itself is tolerant to decriminalization interpretation about constituent elements. In the safeguard of the principle of *nulla poena sine lege*, we have always emphasized "no crime without law or no punishment without law", but in reality, many acts that should not become constituent elements are directly or indirectly deemed as constituent elements. To uphold the true principle of *nulla poena sine lege* and prevent it from being used as an excuse to exclude individual constituent element or even criminalization, criminal dogmatics should affirm the decriminalization interpretation of constituent elements to fix the principle of *nulla poena sine lege* from the front and fully implement it through the progressive transmission of the hierarchy theory.

Notes

1 Liu Yanhong: *Views on Substantive Criminal Law (Second Edition)*, Renmin University of China Press, 2019, p. 239.
2 Liu Yanhong: *Views on Substantive Criminal Law*, Renmin University of China Press, 201e, p. 92, 91.
3 See Jiao Baoqian: Concept of Legal Dogmatics and Its Evolution, *Studies in Law and Business*, 2006 (4).
4 See Zhang Xiang: Formal Rule of Law and Legal Dogmatics, *Chinese Journal of Law*, 2012 (6).
5 See Zhang Mingkai: *A Preliminary Discussion on Legal Interests*, China University of Political Science and Law Press, 2000, p. 364.
6 see Zhang Mingkai: *Research on Fraud Crime and Financial Fraud Crime*, Tsinghua University Press, 2007, p. 373–374.
7 See Wang Liangshun: On the Criminal Liability of Unit Members Participating in the Pure Natural Person Crimes, *Study in Law and Business*, 2013(2).
8 See Cai Daotong: Priority Application of Special Articles over Ordinary Articles, *The Jurist*, 2015(5).
9 [Germany] Kinderhauser: German Criminal Law Dogmatics Between Adaptation and Autonomy, translated by Cai Guisheng, *Journal of National Prosecutors College*, 2010 (5).
10 See Wang Lida: A Preliminary Study on the Research Orientation of Legal Hermeneutics: A Methodological Reflection, *The Law Monthly*, 2000 (9).

6 Illegal Decriminalization

From the Perspective of Elimination of Misfeasance

6.1 Preconditions for the establishment of illegality under the three-tier theory

6.1.1 Essence of traffic negligent crime: Establishment of the obligation of consequence avoidance

The traffic negligent crime refers to the criminal act that the person engaged in traffic and transportation fails to exercise reasonable care to avoid the occurrence of criminal facts and damages the legal interests while having foreseen the consequences. Obviously, the duty of care of traffic stands at the core of traffic negligent crime and comprises the obligation of consequence foresight and consequence avoidance. In light of the characteristics of traffic activities and the minimum needs of modern social life, the obligation of consequence avoidance should be regarded as the essence of traffic negligent crime.

Undoubtedly, traffic and transportation activities entail great risks and may give rise to disasters and accidents at any time. The old theory of negligence holds that an act failing to fulfill the obligation of consequence foresight should be convicted of traffic negligent crime. As a result, the doer driving a vehicle on the highway would generally be aware of the danger of their behavior and possible consequences when hazardous results occur, and almost all traffic accidents could be deemed as the traffic negligent crime, which is not different from the consequence liability. For example, *Person A* drove a four-wheel car at a normal speed on a road and saw from a distance a frightened bull dashing around on the road; *Person A* reacted immediately to slow down the car and turn on the left-turn signal to drive into the next lane in order to avoid the bull; however, the frightened bull charged at a fast speed and hit exactly the front of the vehicle intended to turn left, causing the vehicle to hit and kill the pedestrian *Person B*. According to the old theory of negligence, *Person A* could foresee possible consequences of his act and took necessary consequence avoidance measures but still did not prevent causing the death of another person, who should be convicted of traffic negligent crime. Here, the acts that should belong to *force majeure* are also treated as crimes, which consequentially would greatly enlarge the punishment scope of traffic negligent crime and stagnation of activities in the traffic field, thus running

DOI: 10.4324/9781003456773-7

against the development requirements of the times. In order to maintain the basic life of modern society and meet the minimum needs of social operation, the activities in the field of traffic can only be evaluated from the social significance of the behavior and the function of criminal legal interest protection. For this reason, criminal law scholars have created the theory of allowable danger, allowing such dangerous behaviors to exist within a reasonable range, and limiting the scope of punishment for negligent crimes in such fields as transportation and medical industry; the method of delimitation is to take the obligation of consequence avoidance as the essence of negligent crimes in foregoing fields, that is, even if the doer has foreseen that his behavior may cause damage to legal interests and has fulfilled the obligation of consequence avoidance, it shall not constitute negligent crime. Therefore, for similar accidents caused by the frightened bull, *Person B* has made utmost endeavors to forestall consequences but they are still unavoidable. *Person B* shall not be investigated for responsibilities of traffic negligent crime. It can be seen that the new theory of negligence could better delimit the punishment scope of traffic negligent crime and help overcome the defects of the old theory of negligence.

The driving behavior is dangerous, routine and universal in the developing society; the new theory of negligence greatly encourages the normal existence of traffic and transportation behaviors from the perspective of social usefulness and confirms the internal compatibility between social development and dangerous traffic activities; regarding the establishment of negligent crimes for traffic and transportation behaviors, the new theory of negligence undoubtedly has more natural affinity, pertinence and modernity. Therefore, against the backdrop of the widespread use of vehicles in the rapidly developing society in China, the new theory of negligence should be adopted and the obligation of consequence avoidance should be deemed as the essence of traffic negligent crime in light of the characteristics of traffic and transportation activities and the theory of negligent crime.

6.1.2 Normative consequence avoidance possibility: Premise of the theory of protection purpose of duty of care norms

1 Causality, obligation of consequence avoidance and protection purpose of duty of care norms

Taking the obligation of consequence avoidance as the essence of traffic negligence means that the obligation of consequence avoidance could fully and reasonably explain the negligent liability. However, the new theory of negligence regards the objective external duty of care as the benchmark behavior, and "what benchmark behaviors are is still ultimately decided by the obligation stipulated by the administrative ban regulations". In other words, benchmark behaviors in traffic negligent crimes must be judged by the traffic administrative regulations. However, in many cases, the fulfillment of the obligation of consequence avoidance cannot be determined merely based on violation of traffic rules, since for many behaviors that even violate traffic rules, it is still difficult to immediately infer that the doer could avoid consequences; whether there is a causal relationship between the violation and traffic accident should also be evaluated; only when the consequence is incurred by a behavior violating the protection purpose of traffic regulations could the doer by investigated for responsibilities. "To judge whether the doer exercises the duty of care, we should compare whether the behavior of the doer conforms to the requirements of the duty of care, and should not determine whether the doer breaches the duty of care simply from the damage results that have occurred".

For example, when *Person A* was not speeding, *Person B* suddenly crossed the road, and *Person A* immediately braked but still caused the death of *Person B*. Later, it was found that the car driven by *Person A* had exceeded the speed limit in a certain road section half an hour before. In this case, although *Person A* was found speeding half an hour before the accident, it is not sufficient to investigate *Person A*'s responsibilities of traffic negligent crime. The traffic regulations on the speed limit of cars are intended to enable drivers to have enough time to react by braking, avoiding or stopping under emergencies, so as to prevent deaths or injuries of other persons. This causality between purpose and result also only relates to the exact time and spot when and where the accident occurs. *Person A* was unable to foresee the causality between the speeding half an hour ago and the subsequent death of *Person B*, which had no correlation with the normative protection purpose. In the traffic negligent crime, "each traffic rule is in fact a preventive rule whose purpose is to prevent the consequence by stipulating certain measures". Therefore, only when the consequence is the result that the rule attempts to prevent can the subject be condemned for violating the rule. The purpose of the "so-called" rule is also the protective purpose of duty of care norms, which are established for the prevention of traffic hazards; only when the "causality satisfies" the "normative protection purpose" can the doer be investigated for the responsibility for traffic negligent crime.

Accordingly, whether the damage of legal interests in the field of traffic is caused by the violation of the protection purpose of duty of care norms becomes a major standard to judge the establishment of traffic negligent crime. In other words, "in occasions when the doer violates traffic rules, whether this violation of traffic rules leads to the consequence" becomes quite attractive. Does this merely belong to a question of causality or obligation of consequence avoidance? If it belongs to the former, there is no point discussing violations of duty of care norms from the level of the essence of traffic negligent crime, and the discussion could be carried out in accordance with the common practice of discussing the causality theory, namely the conformity of constituent elements. Nevertheless, such discussions are not satisfactory for negligent crimes. The causality is to solve the relation between an act and its results, which must acknowledge the existence of "a negligent act", while for the negligent crime, the existence of negligent act is induced reversely after the occurrence of hazardous consequence. For this reason, the criminal law theory has always held a controversial attitude based on the negative position on whether the negligent crime has the act of perpetrating. Under this circumstance, there are obviously obstacles to expect solving the above problem through the conformity of constituent elements and the theory of causality; the view of solving the problem as a causal one should be negated. If discussions are made at the level of obligation of consequence avoidance, the opinions are also divided. The old theory of negligence holds that whether the causal process conforms to the protection purpose of duty of care norms should be solved as the problem of consequence foreseeing possibility and consequence avoidance possibility, namely view on factual consequence avoidance possibility; while the new theory of negligence believes that the foregoing question should be solved as the problem whether there is obligation of consequence avoidance or increase of risks, namely view on normative consequence avoidance possibility. How should we treat these two different doctrines of the new and old theories of negligence?

2 Premise of protection scope of duty of care norms: doctrine of normative consequence avoidance obligation based on causality foreseeing possibility

In terms of the function of consequence foreseeing possibility, the principle of criminal liability and burden of proof of traffic negligent crime, the doctrine of normative consequence avoidance obligation based on causality foreseeing possibility should be advocated.

First, the function of the consequence foreseeing possibility in helping judge the selection of consequence avoidance measure determines that the doctrine of normative consequence avoidance obligation should be adopted. Along with the alternate development of the old and new theories of negligence, although both theories acknowledge the role of consequence foreseeing possibility in the establishment of negligent crime, the consequence foreseeing possibility is the premise of consequence avoidance obligation in the old theory of negligence and decides on the establishment of negligence; in the new theory of negligence, the consequence avoidance obligation determines the establishment of negligent crime while the consequence foreseeing possibility is merely the premise of consequence avoidance obligation and has the "function of providing standards for the selection of consequence avoidance measures". Meanwhile, the new theory of negligence "emphasizes on the behavior, so, not only the consequence with the constituent elements but also the causal process giving rise to the consequence are deemed as the object of foreseeing possibility". This suggests that whether it is possible to foresee the violation behavior under the situation of violating traffic rules causes the consequence is a matter of consequence foreseeing the possibility of traffic negligent crime; foreseeing this issue could help judge the possibility of consequence avoidance and selecting which measure to prevent the consequence. The foregoing question is also a matter of judging whether the causal process between the violation of traffic regulations and the consequence of damage of legal interests conforms to the protection purpose of duty of care norms, in brief, a matter of judging the correlation of the protection purpose of duty of care norms. Therefore, the application and analysis of the theory of protection purpose of duty of care norms are closely related to the existence of consequence avoidance obligation. In a word, the function of the possibility of foreseeing the consequence in helping select consequence avoidance measures has allowed the possibility of foreseeing the consequence based on the causal process to evolve into an issue of possibility of avoiding consequence in the level of criminal norms; the view that whether the causal process conforms to the protection purpose of duty of care norms boils down to the normative consequence avoidance possibility is considered a matter of course.

Second, the doctrine of normative consequence avoidance obligation circumvents the practice of punishing the doer who does not foresee the causal process, which is in violation of the principle of criminal liability. An act that conforms to the constituent elements of traffic negligent crime must be an act with the violation of consequence foreseeing obligation as the premise and violation of consequence avoidance obligation as the core, so whether there is a causal relationship between dangerous driving and the consequence determines whether the resulting damage of legal interests is unavoidable by the doer or incurred by others. If there is no inherent causal link between the dangerous driving behavior and the consequence, the driver shall not be held criminally liable for his own behavior. For example, *Person A* drove a car after drinking a small amount of alcohol and ran over the cyclist Person B who suddenly turned left. It was found afterward that even if *Person A* did not drink, the collision was still unavoidable. Therefore, even if some behaviors violate traffic rules, it is still difficult to infer immediately that the actor could prevent the consequence. The purpose of alcohol prohibition is to ensure that the actor has normal capability of judgment and control to react normally to accidents, thus preventing the occurrence of traffic accidents. In this case, intake of a small amount of alcohol by *Person A* does not affect the normal handling of the sudden appearance of Person B and the causal process between *Person A*'s violation and *Person B*'s death does not conform to the protection purpose of the alcohol prohibition norm, so *Person A* shall not be investigated for the responsibility of traffic negligent crime. It can be seen that punishing the doer who is impossible to foresee the causal relationship is not only an improper expansion of the punishment scope for traffic negligent crime but also contrary to the principle of accountability of the modern criminal law. The doctrine of normative consequence avoidance possibility that affirms the correlation of the protection scope of the duty of care norms offers reasonable criteria for the establishment of the liability of traffic negligent crime.

Last, from the perspective of practices of traffic negligent crime, the doctrine of normative consequence avoidance obligation could achieve a reasonable distribution of the burden of proof for traffic negligent crime to reach the balance of power between the prosecution and the defense parties.

As the old theory of negligence takes the obligation of foreseeing the consequence as the essence of traffic negligent crime, an act with the harmful consequence of traffic accident could basically be ruled illegal, and the defendant, namely the suspect, who is proven by the public prosecution organ able to foresee the occurrence of the harmful consequence, could be convicted; on the contrary, according to the new theory of negligence, even if the public prosecution organ proves that the defendant is able to foresee the occurrence of harmful consequence, the defendant cannot bear criminal responsibility if he could present evidence to prove that he has made the utmost endeavors to avoid the consequence. The rule of burden of proof in criminal proceedings is "the burden of proof lies with the person asserting a proposition", so the burden of proof in criminal cases generally falls on the prosecution party on behalf of victims. However, under the doctrine of consequence avoidance obligation advocated by the new theory of negligence, the burden of proving the innocence of the defendant is shifted from the prosecution party to the suspect, namely the defendant, which is called the inversion of the burden of proof. Is it feasible to apply the inversion of the burden of proof to the field of traffic negligent crime without explicit legislative provisions? The answer is yes.

On the one hand, like other accidental crimes such as environmental pollution crime and medical negligence crime, the traffic negligent crime demonstrates extremely complicated causal relations and the assumption of the burden of proof by the defendant is more conducive to the identification of the case facts and realization of litigation proof. If the causality of environmental pollution crime is particular for the progressiveness and long-time span between the pollution act and its consequence and difficult to affirm due to the involvement of professional knowledge, the particularity of the causality of traffic negligent crime lies in that the consequence of traffic accident is often caused by many reasons, including the behavior of the driver, behavior of the victim, conditions of the vehicle and other conditions of the road; some of these behaviors violate the traffic administrative regulations, some are legal and some are accidental; the identification of the nature of these acts also implicates the expertise of road traffic. Therefore, it is generally difficult for the victims of traffic negligent crimes to present evidence about the existence of causality. On the other hand, in accordance with the principle of "the closest relation" with the evidence, the party that holds the evidence should present the evidence. Among the various reasons, the defendant, as the driver, is generally most clear about these circumstances and presentation of evidences by the driver could fully explain whether the consequence is caused by his violation of rules. This is because the vehicle driver not only knows road traffic rules and understands the nature of their acts (such as whether driving under the influence, how fast they drive and whether the turn signal has been turned on) but also is fully aware of whether their behaviors of driving motor vehicles violate the rules; however, the victims do not necessarily know, particularly some pedestrians who have never come into contact with vehicles or cannot drive at all do not know whether the behavior of the motor driver violates the rules. After the accident occurs, it is obviously unrealistic to have the "claimant" or the victim that knows little about the driving behavior; that the party holding the evidence, namely the defendant, to present evidence, meets the effectiveness requirement of the rules of evidence. "The distribution of the burden of proof is originally strictly enforced in the pure litigant-centered litigation structure, but cannot be strictly implemented when the power-centered principle has a say. In the old criminal procedural law based on power-centered principle, if the defendant does not claim and prove facts in his favor, the facts may be ignored or remain unknown. In this sense, it can also be said that the defendant also bears certain burden of proof". Therefore, in the traffic negligent crime, if the pedestrian does not know which kind of measures the driver has taken to avoid the consequence and the judiciary is also unable to collect sufficient evidence to prove it afterward, the defendant then could present reasonable proof and make clear those "ignored or unknown" facts to prove that he has taken consequence avoidance measures but is unable to avoid the consequence, who then could not be held criminally liable for the consequence of traffic accidents; this belongs to decriminalization proof and it is obviously more favorable to the defendant to provide evidence by himself. Finally, after the traffic accident occurs, the victim is either dead or injured, or even in coma, who is utterly unable to present evidence about whether the consequence of the accident is caused by the violation of rules by the defendant. Even if in his right mind, the victim suffering physical and mental trauma is expected to bear the burden of proof is obviously adverse to the balance of power between the prosecution and defense parties and to the fair and just settlement of the case.

In summary, in the criminal proceedings of traffic accidents, the burden of proof lies with the defendant to prove whether they have taken measures to avoidance the consequences or fulfilled their obligation to avoid the consequences at the time of the accident. Therefore, adopting a standardized doctrine of obligation for consequence avoidance is beneficial to properly allocate the burden of proof in a reasonable manner.

6.2 Negation of causality and elimination of illegality

The premise for application of the protection purpose of duty of care norms to judge causality is clarified, namely whether the normative consequence avoidance obligation should be promoted, suggesting that the theory of the protection purpose of duty of care norms is applicable at the level of the consequence avoidance obligation, the essence of traffic negligent crime. So, what is the basis of applying the protection purpose of duty of care norms in the traffic negligent crime? What kind of element does the protection purpose of duty of care norms belong to in the traffic negligent crime? Is there any necessity or significance of such application?

6.2.1 Primary positioning of the protection purpose of duty of care norms: Traffic administrative regulations as the behavioral criteria

The core of the protection purpose of duty of care norms includes "duty of care norms" and "protection scope". To have an accurate understanding, we must take into account the basis of the protection purpose of duty of care norms, namely traffic administrative regulations as the behavioral criteria for traffic negligent crime.

The new theory of negligence takes the consequence avoidance obligation as the essence of the negligence. However, whether the consequence avoidance obligation has been fulfilled cannot stay within the category of subjective and internal psychological responsibility; it entails judging from the outside whether the doe has fulfilled the objective duty of care, namely having taken actions to avoid the consequence; this objective behavioral criterion is based on the regulations on traffic administrative bans, that is, “the foundation of the duty of care is the various regulations on administrative bans, typically traffic rules of the road traffic law”. On the one hand, except for a few natural crimes, such as death caused by negligence or serious injury caused by negligence, the vast majority of negligent crimes are administrative offenses, and one of the most common administrative negligent crimes is the traffic negligent crime. For administrative offenses, the criminal legislation generally uses blank provisions, and the economic administrative regulations must be invoked to determine whether the behavior of the doer is illegal. Therefore, concerning the traffic negligent crime, it is normal to judge the behavior violating the objective duty of care based on the traffic administrative regulations. On the other hand, determining the fulfillment of the consequence avoidance obligation based on the compliance with traffic regulations can better facilitate the identification of traffic negligent crime as the administrative crime in judicial practices. “From the perspective of society, the transportation behavior that complies with the traffic regulations is the proper legal behavior”, while the traffic regulations are “the result of comprehensively anticipating the possible dangers based on experience and thinking; the existence of traffic regulations proves: in this field, there may be the risk of accidents if these regulations are violated”. For example, Article 133 of the Criminal Law of China stipulates that whoever violates regulations governing traffic and transportation and causes the death or heavy losses of property shall be convicted of the crime of traffic accident. Here, whether the driver has fulfilled the obligation of foreseeing the consequence shall be analyzed according to the situation at the time of driving; before a conclusion is drawn, whether the driver had performed the obligation of consequence avoidance needs to be evaluated based on violation of traffic rules. Therefore, the setting of the “behavioral criteria” for traffic negligent crime based on whether the traffic rules are complied with can avoid discursive conviction of the negligent behavior by the judiciary and also make the judgment of traffic negligence easier and rule-based.

Whether the traffic regulations are complied with is one standard to judge whether the doer has fulfilled the consequence avoidance obligation of the traffic negligent crime, so traffic regulations are the duty of care created for traffic and transportation personnel. Therefore, the so-called duty of care norms in the protection scope of the duty of care norms refer to, on the one hand, criminal norms and their duty of care and on the other hand, traffic regulations, the subordinate norms of criminal norms on administrative crimes. These traffic regulations have no precedence over the criminal law and are only meaningful under the criminal law from the task of criminal norms in defining criminal wrongfulness, which exists to satisfy the purpose of avoiding damage of legal interests as required by the criminal law. Therefore, like "duty of care norms", the "protection purpose" here refers to both the legal interest protection purpose of the criminal law and the normative purpose of traffic regulations.

6.2.2 *Systematic positioning of the protection purpose of duty of care norms: Objective illegality element or subjective responsibility element*

Which kind of element does the connection between the protection purpose of duty of care norms and the consequence belong to in the traffic negligent crime? This is the essential question to be addressed when the protection purpose of duty of care norms is used to judge the establishment of the traffic negligent crime. It should be first noted that analysis of the establishment of the traffic negligent crime with the protection purpose of duty of care norms needs not be carried out under the objective imputation theory. According to some scholars, requiring the consequences of damage to legal interests caused by the traffic and transportation actor to be the result of violation of the protection purpose of duty of care norms means that "if the result caused by the actor's breach of the duty of care falls outside the protection scope of the violated norms, there is no connection with illegality". Such duty of care norms and corresponding special requirements on illegality connection "amount to applying the objective imputation theory to negligent crimes". For example, Roxin, Puppe and other scholars advocate that the behavior of negligent offenders must be connected with the occurrence of consequence in terms of the protection scope of duty of care norms, and "the causality between the consequence and the inadmissible risk created by the perpetrator is inadequate for objective constituent elements; this consequence should be covered by the protective purpose of provisions on risk avoidance".[1] Only when the actor's breach of obligation actually leads to the consequence can the consequence be attributed to the actor, that is, the harmful result is caused by the act violating the protection purpose of the norms. For example, when *Person A* illegally overtook another vehicle, the overtaken party was frightened and had myocardial infarction, who as a result died. Roxin believes that legal provisions on prohibition of overtaking are aimed to prevent traffic accidents such as collisions caused by dangerous overtaking but do not cover the occurrence of myocardial infarction. Therefore, the death of the overtaken party from sudden myocardial infarction could not be imputed to the overtaking party. Here, as for whether the protection purpose of duty of care norms is violated, "the boundary of imputation" should be delineated "based on objective foreseeability and avoidability on the constituent element consequence and controllability of human behavior over the occurrence of causality". Roxin's application of the protection purpose of duty of care norms in the negligent crime is in fact closely related to the actor's subjective foreseeing ability and the possibility of avoiding the consequence. In the overtaking case, the overtaking person may be able to foresee that his overtaking behavior may cause traffic accidents, but it is impossible for him to foresee the sudden myocardial infarction of the overtaken person, so the death of the overtaken person from sudden disease obviously lies beyond the possibility of foreseeing by the overtaking person who thus is unable to fulfill the obligation of consequence avoidance. Therefore, the so-called theory of the protection purpose of duty of care norms is actually to judge the breach of the protection purpose of norms by virtue of the obligation of foreseeing the consequence and the obligation of avoiding the consequence; further, it determines the imputability with elements that belong to illegality. Thus, when the consequence caused by the behavior falls within the protection scope of norms and the behavior violating the obligation of consequence avoidance leads to the consequence, the consequence can be imputed to the said behavior in law. It is the task of the objective attribution theory to review the specific circumstances under which the obligation of consequence avoidance exists. For the behavior with the obligation of consequence avoidance, the consequence can be attributed to the actor; otherwise, the imputation is impossible. All in all, in negligent crimes, the protection purpose of duty of care norms tends to express the following thinking, "The observance of duty of care norms may or even should avoid the occurrence of the consequence". What the objective imputation theory needs to solve is to ascertain whether the possibility of consequence foreseeing and the possibility of consequence avoidance is violated; this question is just the content of the traffic negligent crime with the possibility of foreseeing the causality as the premise and the obligation of consequence avoidance as the essence. As described above, the protection purpose of duty of care norms is the theory to determine causality in the doctrine of normative consequence avoidance possibility. In this case, there is no need to apply the theory of the protection purpose of duty of care norms by introducing the objective imputation theory to the negligent crime.

Secondly, the protection purpose of duty of care norms independent of the objective imputation theory should belong to the illegality element in the traffic negligent crime. According to the new negligence theory, even if the driver foresees that his behavior may cause harm to the society, the establishment of the traffic negligent crime should also reckon into whether the driver's driving behavior is within the scope of social equivalence. If the behavior does not run away from social equivalence, the driver shall not be held criminally liable even if the death of another person is incurred. In other words, unlike the old theory of negligence that highlights consequences, the new theory of negligence emphasizes on the behavior and the process of the behavior damaging legal interests, namely whether the process leading to the consequence conforms to the requirement of the legal order. The driver's driving behavior would constitute negligent crime only when it belongs to inattention not allowed by the society. In this way, the establishment of negligent crime not only requires harmful consequences but also whether the actor has effectively fulfilled the obligation of consequence avoidance and taken corresponding measures in the process of the occurrence of the consequence. In short, the establishment of negligent crime is not just a matter of Erfolgsunwert or consequence without value but also a matter of Handlungsunwert or behavior without value. What is the inattention not allowed by the society? It implicates whether certain measures have been taken to avoid the consequence; whether traffic regulations are observed while driving; whether the causal process between the actor's violation of traffic regulations and the resulting harmful consequence is illegal, which is the key to judging the establishment of the traffic negligent crime. This causal process does not fall under the scope of subjective and internal responsibility but the scope of objective behavior, which judges whether the actor takes actions to avoid the consequence from the outside and is consistent with the view of the behavior without value that illegality represents negative evaluation about the specific behavior of the actor. Therefore, it focuses on whether the development of the causal process between the behavior and the consequence conforms to the scope of social equivalence and embodies the question of illegality or legality. Consequentially, the duty of care is not an abstract question that is isolated from the concrete attitude or consequence but becomes an issue regarding the evaluation about whether a certain attitude with causal relation to the consequence constitutes inattention. In accordance with the new theory of negligence, the causal relation that the violation of the protection purpose of duty of care norms leads to the consequence demonstrates that the behavior is illegal, which could arouse the emotion of punishment; if the causal process between the behavior and the consequence does not breach the protection purpose of duty of care norms, it is a legal behavior within the scope of social equivalence.

To sum up, the protection purpose of duty of care norms advocated by the objective imputation theory tackles essentially the question of the possibility of consequence avoidance, which lies at the core of the traffic negligent crime, so the use of the theory of the protection purpose of duty of care norms needs not to be conditioned on the objective imputation theory; as a theory judging the existence of causality between the behavior violating traffic regulations and the harmful consequence, the protection purpose of duty of care norms answers whether the development of causal process in the traffic negligent crime conforms to the legal order, which is not an element of responsibility but an element of illegality in the negligence crime.

6.2.3 Necessity and significance of applying the protection purpose of duty of care norms to analyze the establishment of traffic negligent crime

From the perspective of actual effect, the protection purpose of duty of care norms can work out questions that cannot be resolved by previous doctrines and reasonably define the scope of traffic negligent crime through purposeful interpretation.

First, the protection purpose of duty of care norms can work out questions that cannot be resolved by previous doctrines. Regardless of whether the prediction of the causal process belongs to the problem of consequence avoidance obligation, the main theory in China and Japan today is adequate cause theory only in terms of the technical level of the judgment of causation. However, due to its vague and uncertain content, it is difficult for the adequate cause theory to distinguish whether there is a causal relationship between the violation of traffic regulations and the damage of legal interests; based on the essence of the traffic negligent crime, namely the obligation of consequence avoidance, analyzing the establishment of causal relation in the normative consequence avoidance possibility with the theory of the protection purpose of duty of care norms becomes an effective means to determine the liability of the traffic negligent crime.

The adequate cause theory is built on the theory of conditions. Under this premise, it holds that the causation exists only when the conduct is an adequate cause of the consequence in accordance with the experience of ordinary people in society. "The adequate causation has two characteristics: first, excluding the inadequacy situation in the theory of conditions, that is, based on the conditional relation, confining from the law the causation within the scope of general possible occasions in terms of the daily life experience; second, judging the adequacy based on the social life experience of ordinary people at the time of the conduct".[2] For this reason, to judge whether there is adequate causation, we must first "eliminate the inadequacy situation in the conditional theory". This is actually to determine the factual scope of causation, observe and find out which facts and consequences are of causal relationships; in this stage, the reasons are screened. To ascertain whether "there is adequacy" between the determined conditions and consequences obviously requires not logical reasoning at the level of pure natural science probability nor neutral formal considerations but entails common sense judgment of adequacy grounded on the objective facts caused by the actor and in combination with thinking about criminal norms like the actor's possibility of foreseeing and possibility of avoiding the consequence as well as criminal policies and legal purpose, so as to ultimately determine whether and how the consequence could be attributed to the actor. However, although there are different assertions in the adequate cause theory for judgment of adequacy, such as the subjective doctrine, objective doctrine and compromise doctrine, their differences are only limited to whether there is a situation generally difficult to recognize at the time of conduct.[3] If the consequence of conduct is general rather than abnormal in daily life and with high probability, and is not different to recognize by the ordinary people at the time of the conduct, there is adequacy. For example, *Person A* drove in the reverse direction on a one-way street and did not speed, while *Person B* suddenly crossed the road; seeing this, *Person A* slammed on the brake but knocked down and killed *Person B*. Should *Person A* be held responsible? According to the adequate cause theory, it seems that *Person B*'s death caused by *Person A*'s driving on the wrong side is not an extremely special or extremely unlikely abnormal situation, so *Person B*'s death may be attributed to *Person A*. This means that the adequate cause theory is likely to lower the threshold for the causation of traffic negligent crime and expand the punishment scope of traffic negligent crime. Maybe opponents reach a conclusion negating *Person A*'s liability, but this just exposes the fatal flaw of the adequate cause theory, that is, adequacy is not a legal concept with clear and normative connotation after all; it is the different views on adequacy that sow the seed of controversy over the adequate cause theory. Due to its inherent problem, the adequate cause theory is doomed to encounter problems that are difficult to be reasonably defined for their abstractness and uncertainty upon addressing the traffic negligent crime or even general criminal causal relations. If the protection purpose of duty of care is employed, it is held that although the actor's breach of traffic regulations on prohibition of driving in wrong directions leads to the harmful consequence of *Person B*'s death, this consequence is not the one that rules on prohibition of driving in wrong directions have intended to prevent. Legal provisions on prohibition of driving in wrong directions on one-way streets are aimed to prevent collisions of vehicles rather than preventing traffic accidents caused by the pedestrian crossing the road. This interpretation may circumvent the dispute about whether there is causation between *Person A*'s violation and *Person B*'s death when the adequacy is utilized; this is because the protection purpose of duty of care norms is a clear and normative legal concept and it is evidently easier and more convenient to analyze whether the development of the causal process is legal.

Apart from the inherent problem of the adequate cause theory, the application of the theory of the protection purpose of duty of care norms to the traffic negligent crime also has special significance. Traffic and transportation involve a wide range of activities and the violations of different subjects often overlap, posing difficulties for the judgment of adequacy.

Second, the theory of the protection purpose of duty of care norms belongs to purposeful interpretation of the traffic negligent crime, which could effectively limit the punishment scope of the traffic negligent crime.

The theory of the protection purpose of duty of care norms has long been used to confine the scope of damages in the field of civil law. Although the civil law determines the liability for damages and the criminal law determines the liability for criminal punishment, the establishment of civil and criminal liability is both based on the causation between the conduct and the consequence. Therefore, with reference to the relevant theory in the civil law, considering that the result of damage to legal interests is required to correspond to the protection purpose of duty of care norms, the theory of the protection purpose of duty of care norms can be regarded as the result of the purposive interpretation of the criminal law traffic negligence crime. What's more, whether the actor should be held responsible for the damage of legal interests due to fault belongs to judgment of illegality and naturally should be based on the protection purpose of duty of care norms.

Considering the different purposes of each specific traffic rule, the purposive interpretation of traffic negligence crime can reasonably limit the scope of traffic negligent crime. Traffic regulations are intricate and different traffic administrative regulations are different not only in contents but also in purposes. These traffic laws and regulations with different purposes are also the basis for judging whether the obligation of avoiding the result has been fulfilled. In order to avoid reaching the expanded conclusion that violation of the traffic regulations constitutes the breach of consequence avoidance consequence so as to investigate the responsibility of the perpetrator, the use of the theory of protection scope of duty of care norms is undoubtedly of great practical significance: according to the specific situation of different traffic accident offenders, the theory of protection scope of duty of care norms is generally employed to reasonably limit the causation of traffic negligent crime and shrink its scope, thus keeping the traffic negligence responsibility from being reduced to consequence responsibility.

6.3 Judgment criterion and judicial application of decriminalization of illegality

In accordance with the theory of the protection of duty of care norms, only when the consequence of damage to legal interests is caused by breach of the protection scope of duty of care norms can the actor be identified as obligatory to avoid the conduct, namely having the obligation of avoiding the consequence. Nevertheless, the intricate traffic rules have diverse normative purposes; some are certainly aimed at preventing and avoiding accidents and death and injury, such as the regulations on speeding and overtaking; some clearly cater to administrative purposes, such as a driver shall carry the motor license and driver license while driving, so they should not be treated as the same. Besides, as provisions on protection of safety, the majority provisions of care are intended to (at the same) protect the safety of other traffic participants, such as provisions about speeding and overtaking, but there are provisions that only serve to protect the safety of the driver, such as the driver shall wear a safety belt.[4] Obviously, the traffic negligent crime should be analyzed in combination with the purpose of legal interests' protection of criminal norms and the different purposes of the subordinate traffic administrative rules. In this way, the violation of duty of care norms cannot be generalized but should be considered in combination with the specific situation of the case and the purpose of norms violated; whether the norms really have the purpose of protection should be tested from the specific case, because only through the specific case can we determine whether the compliance of norms can properly prevent the consequence. To this end, the following will focus on specifically analyzing the violation of the protection purpose of duty of care norms and possibility of avoiding the consequence in light of different categories of traffic rules of diverse purposes and traffic cases in judicial practices.

6.3.1 Judgment on violation of duty care norms aimed at ensuring traffic safety

The purpose of most traffic regulations is to prevent and reduce traffic accidents and ensure traffic safety, including no speeding, no driving under the influence or after taking state-controlled psychotropic and narcotic drugs, no fatigue driving and observing traffic lights and traffic signs. Nevertheless, as traffic safety rules, some of them are mainly for the purpose of ensuring the safety of others, such as the prohibition of speeding, while others are for the purpose of ensuring the safety of drivers themselves, such as wearing safety belts and helmets. The judgment conclusions of traffic accident cases will be different when traffic safety rules targeted at different objects are applied.

1 Judgment of violation of duty of care norms aimed at protecting the safety of others

If the violation of traffic rules with the aim of protecting the safety of others leads to the death or injury of others, does its causal process necessarily meet the protection purpose of duty of care norms? We should not jump at generalizing.

If some violations of the traffic rules with the aim of protecting the safety of others result in the death of other people and the causal process does not satisfy the requirement of the protection scope of duty of care norms, the traffic negligent crime cannot be established. The above-mentioned speeding case of *Person A* is an example. If some violations of the traffic rules aimed at protecting the safety of others result in the death of other people and the causal process may satisfy the requirement of the protection scope of duty of care norms, the establishment of traffic negligence can be determined. For example, *Person D* drove a minivan from places A to B; when he reached a national highway with large traffic flow, *Person D* over-sped and failed to observe clearly the changes of the front road and pedestrians; as a result, his right rear view mirror collided with the shoulder of *Person E* walking along the road who fell and was run over and killed by the Santana car driven normally by *Person C*. It was identified that *Person E* died of multiple composite injuries caused by car crash. In this case, *Person D*'s speeding should be subject to the requirements of the protection purpose of norms on the prohibition of speeding, so his conduct constituted the traffic negligent crime while *Person E* and *Person C* were innocent.

First, *Person E* walking along the roadside had no responsibility. Unlike the fully closed expressway, the national highway belongs to open first-class highway and pedestrians are allowed to walk on it but should walk along the kerb. *Person E* walking along the side of the national expressway does not hinder the movement of vehicles in any way who therefore shall not be held responsible for the consequence. Second, *Person C* should not bear responsibilities, either. *Person C* drove normally on the national highway; although *Person C* may realize that there are pedestrians on the national highway, in accordance with the traffic regulations, pedestrians on the national highway are only allowed to walk along the kerb and not cross arbitrarily; moreover, *Person C* was unable to foresee the falling of *Person E*. *Person E* fell at the instant of collision with the speeding vehicle of *Person D* and at that moment, *Person C* drove at a normal speed from the normal distance from *Person D* to the site, who obviously was unable to avoid. If *Person C* saw from the distance that *Person E* was knocked down but did not take measures, thus running over and killing *Person E*, then *Person C* should be investigated for responsibilities. In other words, since it was impossible to foresee the consequence that *Person E* would be run over and killed, *Person C* should not be required to avoid the consequence of *Person E*'s death. For *Person C*, that *Person E* was run over and killed by the vehicle was unexpected. Third, that *Person D* knocked down *Person E* and caused *Person E* to be killed by the following vehicle was a behavior in violation of the protection purpose of norms against speeding; there was a causal relationship between this behavior and the death of *Person E*, so the death of *Person E* should be attributed to *Person D*. *Person E* was hit at the shoulder by *Person D* and was not injured, but it was this collision that caused *Person E* to fall and then be run over by the following vehicle. *Person D* collided with the shoulder of *Person E* due to a lack of attention to pedestrians at the roadside and failure to keep an appropriate distance from *Person E*; if *Person D* drove at a normal speed, he would not necessarily knock down *Person E* even when it did not keep a proper distance from *Person E*; besides, the higher traction from speeding than a vehicle running at a normal speed made *Person E* fall. The sudden knockdown of a pedestrian on the national highway is an extremely dangerous situation and such accidents often occur in an instant so that the rear vehicle is impossible to foresee. *Person D* who should have foreseen all these failed to take necessary measures for the safety of *Person E* due to speeding, ultimately resulting in the death of *Person E*. The protection purpose of provisions against speeding is to urge the driver to keep sober and focused so as to observe comprehensively the safety of pedestrians or other vehicles and detect in time and take necessary measures to diffuse traffic dangers. The death of *Person E* in this case is incurred due to *Person D*'s violation of the protection purpose of the prohibition of speeding, so *Person D* was convicted of the traffic negligent crime accordingly.

2 Judgment of violation of duty of care norms aimed at protecting the safety of oneself

Although some traffic laws and regulations are also rules to ensure safety, these safety rules are not intended to ensure the safety of other vehicles or pedestrians and other traffic participants, but to ensure the safety of the drivers. For the violation of such traffic safety norms, the doer should not be investigated for criminal responsibility even when the harmful consequence of traffic accidents occurs; in other words, the causal process in these cases does not fall under the protection purpose of duty of care norms, so the consequence cannot be attributed to the doer. Wearing seat belts and helmets are typical duty of care norms to ensure the safety of drivers.

For example, *Person A* drove from west to east with *Person C*, while *Person B* drove from north to south; all these three people did not wear helmets and the two vehicles collided at the intersection without traffic signs and markings, resulting in mild injuries of *Person A* and *Person B* and death of *Person C*. Should *Persons A* and *B* undertake criminal liabilities for the death of *Person C*? Upon investigation, *Persons A* and *B* and *Person C* all violated the provisions that "motorcycle drivers and passengers should wear helmets as required"; *Person B* also violated the provision that "if there is no traffic sign or line marking, the driver should stop and watch before entering the intersection, and let the vehicle coming from the right side pass first", but in accordance with the theory of protection purpose of duty of care norms, *Person A* in this case should not be held liable for the death of *Person C* and *Person B* should bear the responsibility of traffic negligence for the death *Person C*. First, although *Person A* did not wear a helmet, the purpose of wearing a helmet was to ensure the safety of the motorcycle driver so as to protect the life and health of the driver from damage in the event of a collision instead of ensuring the physical safety of the passenger *Person C*. In other words, the result of *Person C*'s death was not caused by *Person A*'s failure to wear the helmet, and there was no causal process consistent with the protection purpose of duty of care norms on wearing helmets, so *Person A* should not bear criminal responsibility for *Person C*'s death. Second, for the same reason as above, *Person B*'s failure to wear the helmet was also not related to the death of *Person C* in the sense of the protection purpose of duty of care norms, but according to legal provisions, when *Person B* drives his motorcycle from north to south at an intersection without traffic signs or line markings, he should stop and watch before entering the intersection and let the vehicles coming from his right side, namely the motorcycle driven by *Person A* from west to east, pass first, but *Person B* failed to do so, thus leading to the collision with *Person A* and the death of *Person C*. The provision that "if there is no traffic sign or line marking, the driver should stop and watch before entering the intersection, and let the vehicle coming from the right side pass first" is just to guarantee that vehicles at the intersection could pass orderly to prevent collisions or other accidents. The death of *Person C* was caused by *Person B*'s violation of the protection purpose of the duty of care norms that the driver should stop at the intersection and let the vehicle coming from the right side pass first, so *Person B* should be held responsible for the death of *Person C*. It can be seen that even if a traffic accident has occurred, the doer should not be investigated for the responsibility for traffic negligent crime based on his violation of the duty of care norms aimed at protecting the safety of oneself.

6.3.2 Judgment of violation of duty of care norms aimed at traffic administration

Many provisions in traffic laws and regulations only serve the purposes of administration and have no significance or role in protecting the safety of drivers, passengers or other pedestrians and vehicles. For example, unregistered motor vehicles are prohibited from driving on the road; vehicles without license plate are prohibited from driving on the road; blocking or defacing the license plate of the motor vehicles is prohibited; the driver should carry the driver license and motor license. These traffic laws and regulations are only for the convenience of the traffic administrative department in the management of vehicles and drivers, and effectively dealing with traffic accidents. For these traffic laws and regulations that are for the purpose of maintaining traffic administrative order rather than ensuring traffic safety and preventing road hazards, violations by the doer should not constitute the traffic negligent crime.

Person A drove normally on a city highway. *Person B* illegally crossed the road on the non-pavement section; *Person A* hit on the brake urgently but as *Person B* had already reached the front of *Person A*'s vehicle, and *Person A* was unable to avoid it and hit and kill *Person B*. It was later found that *Person A* did not carry a driver license. In this case, although *Person A* violated the duty of care norms on carrying the driver license, *Person A* could not be determined in violation of the obligation of foreseeing the consequence nor was required to undertake the obligation of avoiding the consequence. Norms on carrying the driver license are merely aimed to fulfill the requirement of inspection and management by the traffic police on the way rather than preventing running over and killing others. The effective factors for analyzing whether *Person A* is responsible for *Person B*'s death are: whether *Person A* can foresee *Person B* crossing the road and whether *Person A* has taken the avoidance measures required by the traffic regulations. Traffic regulations stipulate that a motor vehicle shall slow down when passing a crosswalk or shall stop to give way when a pedestrian is passing the crosswalk; when a motor vehicle is passing a road without traffic signal and a pedestrian is crossing the road, it shall give way. *Person B* crossing the road did break the regulations but this does not mean that *Person A* could turn a blind eye to it without taking any avoidance measures. However, in this case, *Person A*, who was driving normally, tried to stop and avoid *Person B* after he saw *Person B* crossing the road but was unable to give way as *Person B* was too fast, thus resulting in the death of *Person B*. Therefore, *Person A* should not be responsible for the death of *Person B* based on the negligent crime. It can be seen that without violation of the protection purpose of duty of care norms that protect traffic safety, *Person A*'s disregard of the protection purpose of duty of care norms to ensure the traffic administration cannot be regarded as the reason for the establishment of the traffic negligent crime.

If it is difficult to distinguish diametrically whether the regulations aimed at traffic and transportation safety are to protect the safety of others or the safety of the driver, it is easy and usually clear to distinguish between the norms targeted at traffic administration and norms to ensure road traffic safety. The road traffic administrative regulations have more static characteristics, such as carrying a driver's license or prohibiting the random alteration of vehicles, which have no impact on or relationship with the driving of vehicles on the road and the safety of themselves and others. Distinguishing between traffic safety norms and administrative management norms is of great significance for determining the traffic offense of the doer and whether the causation in the traffic accident with casualties meets the protection purpose of duty of care norms; if the latter is violated, the establishment of causation can usually be ruled out through the protection purpose of duty of care norms.

6.3.3 Judgment of violation of multiple protection purposes of duty of care norms at the same time

The situation of the traffic accident offender with multiple causes and one consequence is more complicated. For example, the driver has violated the traffic regulations to ensure the safety of others as well as those to ensure his own safety or contravened concurrently more than two traffic regulations to ensure the safety of others or violated norms to ensure traffic safety and traffic administrative norms. In addition, in the traffic accident with multiple causes and one consequence, it is necessary to ascertain the causal process between the violations and the consequence to meet the protection purpose of duty of care norms.

One day, as requested by Mr. Li, Mr. Fu drove an unlicensed lorry carrying 20 tons of ore (overloaded), which occupied the driveway on the other side and collided with another lorry coming from the opposite direction and fell off the road; Mr. Fu and the other two passengers in the lorry died on the spot. According to the investigation by the traffic police department, Mr. Fu was mainly responsible for the accident. In this case, should both Mr. Li and Mr. Fu be investigated for responsibilities? Some scholars believed that Mr. Li, knowing that his vehicle was unlicensed, still employed others to drive and instructed them to transport overloaded ores, who had two acts of instigating others to drive illegally. According to the relevant judicial interpretation of the Supreme People's Court, if the owner of a motor vehicle instigates or forces others to drive illegally and cause a major traffic accident, he shall be convicted of the crime of traffic accident and punished accordingly. Therefore, the behaviors of Mr. Li constituted the traffic negligent crime. Opponents held that the behaviors of Mr. Li did not constitute a crime since "the accident in this case was caused by driving in the driveway on the other side, which was due to the improper handling of Mr. Fu during the driving and had no connection with Mr. Li's instigation of overloading".[5] The author believes that, inculpation is obviously a positive answer to the adequacy between Li's behavior and the result under the guidance of the adequate cause theory, which is also a wrong conclusion; although the view of innocence is correct, the traditional causal relation is inevitably used as the keynote, which therefore not only exposes the shortcoming of insufficient reasoning but also fails to pinpoint the essence of the problem: why is the accident caused by driving in the driveway on the other side rather than by overloading? Based on the theory of the protection purpose of duty of care norms, Mr. Li in this case should not be held responsible but Mr. Fu should.

First, the unlicensed vehicle running on the road was in violation of the norms for the purpose of traffic administration, which had no connection with the occurrence of the traffic accident and could be disregarded. As for Mr. Li's instigation of Mr. Fu to transport overloaded cargo, the causal process between this and the death of Mr. Fu did not meet the protection purpose of duty of care norms against overloading. In accordance with the Regulations on Administration of Over-Limit Transportation Vehicles on Highway, when the vehicle is overloaded, the stability will be undermined and the centrifugal force will increase while turning, so the vehicle at a high speed is very easy to overturn; when the vehicle is overloaded, the braking effect will be reduced and meanwhile the acceleration will increase when the vehicle goes downhill, which will cause the center of gravity of the vehicle to move forward and the vehicle to lose control, thus resulting in accidents. Although the lorry driven by Fu was overloaded, the road section where the accident occurred was straight and smooth, without turning or downhills; the vehicle fell off the road not because the brake did not work or there was turning, and the fact of overloading had no connection with the accident. In other words, there was no causal process between overloading and accident results, which met the protection purpose of the duty of care norm on prohibition of overloading, so Mr. Li should not bear criminal responsibility for the deaths of Mr. Fu and several other passengers. Second, the causal process between Mr. Fu's occupation of the driveway on the other side and the resulting deaths of himself and the passengers accorded with the protection purpose of the duty of care norm on prohibition of driving in the driveway on the other side. The traffic regulations stipulate explicitly that the norms prohibiting motor vehicles from overtaking the vehicle ahead or occupying the driveway on the other side are aimed at guaranteeing the traffic order so as to prevent hindering the normal running and ensure the passage priority of vehicles in the driveway on the other side and meanwhile keeping vehicles in opposite directors from collisions. It was due to the occupation of the driveway on the other side that Fu's lorry collided with another lorry running in the opposite direction and led to deaths and injuries; even if the vehicle driven by Mr. Fu was loaded with a normal quantity of cargo, it would fell off the road due to collision with another lorry while running in the driveway on the other side. Therefore, the causal process between Fu's occupation of the driveway on the other side and the resulting deaths of himself and the passengers conforms to the protection purpose of the duty of care norm against running in the driveway on the other side, so Mr. Fu should be responsible for the deaths of other people.

In a word, the determination of the traffic accident offense with multiple causes and one consequence is the same as that with one cause and one consequence; however, the multiple causes must be examined one by one, so as to clarify what kind of behavior results in a causal process that conforms to the protection purpose of duty of care norms, thus reasonably establishing the traffic negligent crime.

6.4 Conclusion

A behavior that formally conforms to the constituent elements is not necessarily given a negative evaluation in the criminal law. The purpose of decriminalization of illegality is to negate the criminal illegality of the act but does not exclude the civil or administrative illegality of the act, which are not contradictory. This is because different legal norms have different normative purposes, which also makes them self-consistent in the corresponding normative fields. Although a certain act violates the prepositioning law, it cannot be treated as crime directly and whether the act results in the damage of legal interests or dangers of damaging legal interests and whether there is a causal relation with the consequence of legal interests damage should be analyzed to obtain a complete judgment about the illegality in the three-tier theory.

The essence of traffic negligent crime is the result avoidance obligation, but only when there is the possibility of result avoidance can the actor be held liable for avoiding the consequence; if the consequence is not caused by the behavior that violates the protection purpose of duty of care norms, it means that the actor does not have the possibility of avoiding the consequence. Therefore, the judgment of the essence of traffic negligent crime is preconditioned on the possibility of consequence avoidance, while the judgment of consequence avoidance possibility is based on the possibility of foreseeing the consequence. The theory of protection purpose of duty of care norms can concretize the judgment about the possibility of foreseeing the consequence as the premise of consequence avoidance obligation and then explains the illegal behavior of the traffic negligent crime, which renders the measurement of the illegality of the traffic negligent crime more objective and aligns with the core preposition of the modern crime theory that "illegality is objective" and "responsibility is subjective". The imputation of the damage to legal interests that establishes the responsibility for the traffic negligent crime must conform to the protection purpose of duty of care norms and exclude circumstances that the harmful consequence is not caused by the violation of the protection purpose of norms despite of the seemingly causation, thus effectively limiting the scope of the traffic negligent crime. The theory of protection purpose of duty of care norms, which is more of the concept of criminal law, also makes the identification of traffic negligence more operational and standard.

The discussion of negligent crime in China's criminal law theory has not been based on the essence of negligent crime. In the field of traffic negligent crime, whether the essence of traffic negligent crime is the obligation of foreseeing the consequence or the obligation of avoiding the consequence is not clear; this leads to the analysis of the establishment of traffic negligent crime without considering its essence, and the letter of identification of traffic accident liability is often used to replace the determination of the traffic negligent crime in the criminal law, namely taking the letter of liability identification as the direct basis for the establishment of traffic negligent crime, which greatly broadens its scope. Unfortunately, in China's judicial practice, the court often determines the establishment of the traffic negligence crime directly according to the letter of identification of traffic accident liability. Such practice that takes the identification letter of administrative liability as the direct basis for conviction and punishment in the criminal law broadens the scope of traffic negligent crime, which is undoubtedly wrong. This phenomenon is naturally the result of a series of reasons, such as lack of sound awareness of rule of law in China and blurry boundary between administrative responsibility and criminal responsibility. Another important reason is the failure of the criminal theory to interpret above similar cases in combination with the essence of traffic negligent crime and how it should be understood and applied, but only the causation as the objective constituent element is analyzed based on the adequate cause theory or the accidental and positive causation theory that are not fully convincing in the explanation of the causation of traffic negligent crime. If the criminal theory of China could investigate the causation of traffic accident crime from the essence of traffic negligent crime and highlights the protection purpose of various duty of care norms in traffic rules and the special "correlation" between the violation of traffic rules and the consequence,[6] namely determining the causation in the traffic negligent crime by the theory of protection purpose of duty of care norms and whether the consequence avoidance obligation and traffic negligent crime could be established, the criminal theory and practice in China could present a reasonable explanation about the establishment of traffic negligent crime from the legal norms and effectively shrink the scope of traffic negligent crime, thus eliminating the myth of taking the letter of administrative responsibility of traffic accident as the basis for the establishment of traffic negligent crime.

Notes

1 [German] Claus Roxin: *Die Lehre von der objektiven Zurechnung*, translated by Xu Yuxiu. *Chengchi Law Review*, 1994(50).
2 Zhang Mingkai: *Outline of Foreign Criminal Law (second edition)*, Tsinghua University Press, 2007 edition, p. 123.
3 See Ma Kechang editor-in-chief: *General Introduction to Foreign Criminal Law (Civil Law System)*, Renmin University of China Press, 2009 edition, p. 117.
4 See Lin Yuxiong: *General Principles of the New Criminal Law*, published by the author in 2006, p. 483.
5 See Li Fuyan: Should the Owner Be Convicted for Accidents Due to Overload—the Key Is to Ascertain Whether There Is a Causal Relationship between the Overload and the Harmful Consequence, *Procuratorial Daily*, March 4, 2009, p. 3.
6 Lin Yuxiong: *General Principles of the New Criminal Law*, published by the author in 2006, p. 483.

7 Decriminalization of Culpability

Analysis Based on the Relativity of Illegality

7.1 Principle of illegality relativity: Relationship between the legal effects of criminal law and civil law

According to the principle of illegality relativity, criminal law and civil law are relatively independent and need not strictly follow each other. In order to explore the mutual influence between the effect of criminal law and the effect of civil law, appropriate cases are those criminal and civil overlapping ones.

In March 1997, Deng and Chen divorced by agreement and agreed that the house jointly possessed by them located in place A belonged to Chen and completed the ownership transfer registration procedure in March 2001. In September 2005, Deng stole the property ownership certificate of Chen and falsified the identity card of Chen along with Zhang to transfer the house to his own name (property ownership certificate No. 30077296). Later, Zhang mortgaged the house ownership in the name of Deng and obtained a mortgage loan of RMB 100,000 from the Bank of China Nanchang District Sub-branch of Wuxi, which was repaid by Zhang in October 2008. In November 2008, under the instigation of Zhang, Deng transferred the above house to Zhang's wife in the form of false transaction (property ownership certificate No. 1000108617). Then, Zhang mortgaged the house ownership in the name of Liu and secured a loan of RMB 170,000 from the Industrial and Commercial Bank of China Wuxi Branch ("ICBC Wuxi Branch"), for which one Wuxi investment guarantor served as the guarantor and assumed the joint and several liabilities. Zhang's whereabouts were unknown after repaying RMB 15,000 for the above loan.

Later, Chen detected the above-mentioned behavior of Deng and Zhang and appealed to the Chong'an District People's Court of Wuxi to start the administrative proceedings. In November 2009, the court decided to revoke the X.F.Q.Z.No. 30077296 property ownership certificate approved and registered by Wuxi Municipal Housing Administrative Bureau in September 2005. In April 2010, ICBC Wuxi Branch filed a civil lawsuit to the Nanchang District People's Court of Wuxi on the ground that Liu failed to repay the loan as agreed and requested to exercise the house mortgage right and recover the loan in advance and demanded the above Wuxi investment guarantee company to undertake joint and several liabilities. In March 2011, the Nanchang District People's Court of Wuxi held in

DOI: 10.4324/9781003456773-8

the first instance that the mortgage loan contract signed between the ICBC Wuxi Branch and Liu was valid and Liu constituted a breach of contract, so it ruled to sustain the above claims of ICBC Wuxi Branch. In June 2012, the third person Chen, unsatisfied with the judgment of first instance, filed a lawsuit against the Beitang District People's Procuratorate of Wuxi. Chen claimed that Deng and Zhang stole the property ownership certificate without her knowledge and applied for mortgage loans to the Bank of China Nanchang Sub-branch of Wuxi and ICBC Wuxi Branch through false transactions of the property involved; the above acts constituted serious violations of laws and the bank also did acquire the property in good faith and could not exercise the right of preferred payment on the mortgaged property.

Subsequently, the Beitang District People's Procuratorate of Wuxi filed a public prosecution with the Beitang District People's Court of Wuxi against Zhang's suspicion of loan fraud crime. In April 2013, the Beitang District People's Procuratorate of Wuxi decided that Zhang transferred the property involved to his wife Liu for the purpose of illegal possession and obtained fraudulently a bank loan of RMB 170,000, who was suspected of the crime of loan fraud; Zhang was sentenced to imprisonment for five years and six months and a fine of RMB 60,000 in accordance with the law. In May 2013, the Beitang District People's Procuratorate of Wuxi prepared a protest report regarding the civil judgment issued by the Nanchang District People's Court of Wuxi; the protest report held that the criminal judgment of the Beitang District People's Court of Wuxi as the new evidence sufficed to overturn the civil judgment of the Anchang District People's Court of Wuxi and that the property ownership transfer registration and mortgage loans should be determined invalid, requesting the Wuxi Municipal People's Procuratorate to lodge a protest. Then Wuxi Municipal People's Procuratorate lodged a protest with the Wuxi Municipal Intermediate People's Court. After that, Wuxi Municipal Intermediate People's Court remanded the case to the Nanchang District People's Court of Wuxi for retrial, which maintained the original judgment as the facts found in the retrial were consistent with those in the first instance. Chen was unsatisfied and filed an appeal with the Wuxi Municipal Intermediate People's Court, which sustained the original judgment after the second instance.

The controversial issues in this case include: first, does the exercise of the mortgage right by the ICBC Wuxi Branch over the property involved constitute acquisition in good faith? Second, is the loan contract signed by Wuxi ICBC and Liu legal and valid? Third, would the effect of the civil judgment be affected by the subsequent civil judgment?

7.1.1 Nature of acquisition of the mortgage right by the third party (bank) in the real estate loan fraud crime

In criminal and civil overlapping cases, if the behavior of the doer is identified as a crime, such as the behavior of Zhang in this case was identified as the crime of loan fraud, the house that Zhang used to obtain fraudulently the loan has been mortgaged to the bank, so could the bank acquire the collateral in good faith? This question matters to the validity of the mortgage. Based on the facts of this case, one of the core issues is whether the bank could acquire the mortgage right of the house involved in good faith.

In accordance with the Article 106 of the Real Right Law, to constitute the *bona fide* acquisition of the general real right, there are four elements: (1) the conduct of the doer is unauthorized disposal; (2) the transferee is in good faith when accepting the property; (3) corresponding consideration; (4) the transferred property should be registered (immovables) or delivered (movables) in accordance with laws. However, due to its particularity compared with the general real right, the real right for security is a subordinate one in accordance with Article 172 of the Real Right Law and Article 5 of the Real Right for Security Law, so the validity of the security contract (clause) depends on the validity of the master contract (namely the master creditor's right or debt). Therefore, the *bona fide* acquisition of the real right for security has a fifth element, namely (5) validity of the master contract.

Since the real estate is of high value and involves significant interests, its transfer is subject to registration that has the function of the announcement and public evidence; once the party in interest makes announcements in line with the method prescribed upon change of the real right, it is bestowed full effect by the law. Even if the announcement is defective, the *bona fide* transferee, based on the reliance on the announcement, is not responsible for the return and could still obtain the real right. This system has intended to protect the safety of trading activities and the *bona fide* third party. The following section presents discussions in combination with the constituent elements:

1 No right of disposal. When there is a legal and effective mortgage right, Liu has the possibility to dispose of it. However, Deng falsified materials and fraudulently transferred the property to himself, which should be invalid, and his sale of the property to Liu belonged to unauthorized disposal and Liu did not pay consideration, so it is evident that Liu's conduct did not constitute acquisition in good faith and Liu had no right of disposal.
2 Consideration. In this case, there should be no dispute about bank lending as the consideration for obtaining the mortgage right.
3 Real estate registration. The property involved in this case was registered for mortgage after both parties signed the mortgage contract.
4 Good faith. In this case, the bank has inspected the property ownership certificate and handled mortgage registration with the housing administrative bureau. Based on the credibility of this registration, the bank should be considered in good faith.
5 Effect of the master contract. Whether the mortgage contract is effective depends on two conditions: a. whether the mortgage contract has the elements for a contract to take effect; b. the mortgage contract is a subordinate one, whose effectiveness is decided by that of the master contract (loan contract). In this

case, the mortgage contract had the general elements to take effect, which satisfied the first condition. Therefore, the validity of the mortgage should be determined by the effectiveness of the loan contract.

7.1.2 Whether the establishment of the real estate loan fraud crime affects the validity of the loan contract

First of all, as mentioned above, whether the bank acquired the real right for security on the house involved is boiled down to the validity of the loan contract in this case. According to the provisions of the civil law in China, there are five main conditions of contract invalidity: (1) the subject is not qualified, and the doer does not have the corresponding capacity; (2) the expression of intention is untrue, and one Person enters into a contract by means of fraud or coercion, which damages the national interests; (3) malicious collusion to damage the interests of the state, the collective or a third party; (4) covering up illegal purpose in legal form; (5) other circumstances of damaging the social and public interests or violating mandatory provisions of laws and administrative regulations. According to the above legal provisions, to determine whether the loan contract is valid, it is necessary to examine whether the loan contract has the required elements of a valid contract and whether it belongs to the prescribed circumstance of invalidity.

Whether the subjects of the loan contract were qualified should be clarified, namely whether the contractual parties had the corresponding civil capacity. In this case, whether Zhang could replace Liu to become a party to the contract deserves careful study. A contract is an agreement between the parties to establish, change or terminate a civil relationship. As one of the reasons for the occurrence of debt, the most important feature of the contractual relationship compared with other civil legal relationships (such as real right relations) lies in its relativity, that is, the contractual relationship can only occur between specific subjects; only a party to the contract can make a request or bring a lawsuit against the other Person Concerned based on the contract, so the contracting parties are only those that sign the contract and bear rights and obligations to each other. In this case, Zhang enjoyed the contract interests and assumed the obligations to replace the position of Liu as the contracting party, but this should not cover up the fact that he was essentially a third party. Therefore, the parties to the loan contract in this case were Liu and ICBC Wuxi Branch and had full civil capacity when signing the contract, so the contracting parties were obviously qualified.

Analysis should be made to find out whether this case belonged to the circumstance that one person committed a fraud to damage the national interests. In this case, Liu concealed the fact that the loan was actually disposed of and repaid by Zhang, causing the bank to get into misconception and enter into the loan contract; if the bank knew, the bank would not issue the loan in dispute to avoid risks, so it could be determined that Liu committed a fraud. However, the lending by the bank was merely an ordinary commercial behavior and did not involve the national interests, so despite being concluded by means of deceit, this loan contract did not jeopardize the national interests and should be valid, but this contract could be altered or rescinded in accordance with the Paragraph 2 of Article 54 of the Contract Law.

Whether there was any malicious collusion to damage the interests of the state, the collective or a third party. "Malicious collusion" emphasizes the existence of "malicious intent" on both sides. As mentioned above, one party to the loan contract in this case, ICBC Wuxi Branch, had performed the duty of due diligence on the mortgage loan materials and did not have malicious intent, let alone malicious collusion.

Whether the social public interests were damaged and mandatory provisions of laws and administrative regulations were violated. The loan contract in this case was a contract whereby the borrower borrowed money from the lender and repaid the loan and interest prior to the expiry date. The parties concerned voluntarily reached the contract through negotiation on an equal footing, which conformed to the form requirement of the bank loan contract and did not damage the public interest or violate mandatory provisions of laws and administrative regulations.

It can be noted that whether the bank acquired in good faith the real right for security over the house involved was ultimately decided by whether Liu in the loan contract "was concealing the illegal purpose in a legal form". In this case, in disregard of the subjective motive of Liu, from the series of civil acts that Liu mortgaged the house under her name to secure a loan from the bank and both parties signed a written mortgage loan contract, there were general elements for the establishment of a contract and conformity with the formal elements of the contract should refer to the "legal form" here. Whether there was an "illegal purpose" needs to be further explored.

Liu, a party to the loan contract, applied for a loan from the bank not for herself but for her husband Zhang; Zhang's whereabouts were unknown after getting the loan and repaid RMB 150,000, suggesting that Zhang intended to embezzle the fund or obtain the fund by deception. Obviously, the conduct of Zhang should be subject to the negative evaluation by law. Moreover, due to the marital relationship between Liu and Zhang, objective evidence could also prove that Liu, as the wife of Zhang, participated in the whole process of loan: (1) execution of the purchasing contract in the house transaction and handling of property ownership transfer registration with the housing administrative bureau; (2) execution of the loan contract with the bank; (3) mortgage of the house to the bank and handling the registration; Liu had fault during the whole process.

1 The transaction of the house was fictitious without real payment of the house price and was aimed at creating the collateral for securing the mortgage loan from the bank. In accordance with the legal procedure of house transaction, Liu needed to sign personally the house transaction contract and handled the ownership transfer registration with the housing administrative bureau. With full

civil capacity, Liu should fulfill the duty of due diligence for her own behaviors and bear corresponding responsibilities.

2 As for the loan contract, Liu, as a borrower, applied for a loan from the bank, not for her own use but for her husband Zhang. If her husband had applied for the loan by himself, he might have not been granted the loan; Liu was only a tool for Zhang to secure the bank loan, but in light of the relativity of the contract, the bank was only required to conduct risk evaluations about the counter-party Liu and the mortgaged house before deciding to issue the loan. Despite that Liu was equivalent to the tool used by Zhang, she had the intention to exploit policy loopholes when engaging in this act and should be fully aware of the whereabouts of a large amount of money and the consequences, so she should be responsible for her own acts.
3 In the process of mortgaging the house to the bank and going through the registration process, knowing that the property did not belong to her or her husband Zhang, Liu still mortgaged the property in dispute to the bank, who had a malicious intention with a view to meeting the lending requirements of the bank and obtain the loan. Liu concealed their loan intention and still used the house as collateral even though she knew there was a major flaw in the ownership of the house; Liu violated her pre-contract obligations and had the intention to possess the fund.

As mentioned above, Liu obtained the bank loan by way of mortgage of an illegal property ownership, while the amount loaned was all disposed of by her husband Zhang, with Zhang bearing the repayment obligation. Zhang's subsequent behavior showed his intention to acquire the loan by deception, and Liu also had indirect "illegality" of purposes and evaded the law and exploited policy loopholes to get the money from the bank without considering the repayment. In addition, the criminal judgment of loan fraud crime could also act as eloquent evidence about Zhang's "illegal purpose", which then corroborated that his wife Liu had indirect "illegality" of purposes or at least played a supporting role in helping Zhang fraudulently obtain the loan. As the "illegal purpose" in the civil law is different from the strict subjective imputation standard in the criminal law, once the purpose of the behavior is inferred from its appearance, the criminal judgment about conviction of "loan fraud crime" would inevitably play a supporting role in the establishment of the illegal purpose of this case. This should then be discussed in the case of whether Zhang had committed the "loan fraud crime". Zhang helped Liu obtain the house ownership through illegal means and went through the real estate registration, which has the effect of announcement and public evidence, so could it be identified as the "false property ownership certificate" in the loan fraud crime? The answer is yes since this certificate is fictitious in content although real in form. The criminal law and the civil law have different standards for the authenticity of the property ownership certificate: the civil law judges more from the form, where a civil act is effective if it has the general elements stipulated and conforms to the statutory form; the criminal law judges more from the substance, which focuses on protecting the legal interests. Therefore, some acts that appear to conform to the requirements of civil conduct may be considered invalid or false in criminal law. Of course, this does not mean that a legal act in civil law would be determined illegal in criminal law but that the above act, despite registration and announcement, should not be considered legal from the civil law, since it is merely legal in form but illegal in substance. Therefore, Zhang ought to be convicted of loan fraud crime. The question lies in whether the criminal judgment about convicting Zhang of loan fraud crime ("purpose of illegal possession" that Zhang had subjectively) could affect the prior civil judgment. In other words, would the "purpose of illegal possession" of Zhang cause the loan contract between Liu and ICBC to comply with the circumstance of "concealing the illegal purpose by legal form" so as to identify the contract as invalid?

7.1.3 Determination of the influence of criminal judgment on civil judgment in the real estate loan fraud crime

In judicial practice, any judgment needs to trace back to its legal basis. Similarly, if the effect of criminal judgment is considered to have precedence over that of civil judgment and could affect the criminal judgment, there should also be a corresponding legal basis. In the criminal and civil overlapping case, the determination of the validity of the contract may be affected by the conclusion of the criminal judgment, that is, if new evidence is found in the trial of the criminal case and suffices to overturn the original civil judgment and ruling, this satisfies the conditions for the person concerned to apply for retrial in Article 200 of the Civil Procedure Law and the person concerned could initiate the trial supervision procedure. However, this influence has no necessary connection with the effect of the criminal judgment.

As for this case, "concealing the illegal purpose by the legal form" does not emphasize the existence of the illegal purpose among the contract signatories but intends to safeguard the seriousness of the law to keep people with ulterior motives from exploiting legal loopholes and illegally circumventing the legal regulation. However, the inference that the parties in this case have "illegal purposes" was not based on the criminal judgment of Zhang but on existing evidence about the subjective intention of Liu. Although there was no direct evidence proving that Liu knew her husband Zhang's intention to take possession of the loan, Liu applied for a loan from the bank in the name of house purchase; later, Liu did not occupy or use the house nor repay the loan, which could demonstrate that all acts of Liu were only aimed to obtain the loan for other purposes and had the intention of evading the law. Therefore, Liu should be responsible for her indiscretion and improper motive in this case.

Based on the above analysis, the criminal judgment would not affect the civil judgment. The existence of "concealing the illegal purpose by the legal form" in the loan contract was determined based on Liu's own fault and motivation of evading the law, so the loan contract was invalid and so were the subordinate mortgage contract and the guarantee contract. The analysis and handling of criminal and civil overlapping cases are different from those of single criminal or civil cases, especially when the determination of the effectiveness of the above contract directly relates to the handling results of criminal and civil cases, there are greater controversies. Such cases should not be determined as valid or invalid without discretion but should be analyzed based on the content of the contract and whether the principle of reciprocity is violated at the time of execution. At the same time, for the determination of civil cases and criminal cases, it is necessary to distinguish between criminal and civil legal principles and apply them accurately to prevent the error of "impairing the civil principles by the criminal ones" or "criminalizing by the civil principles".

7.2 Decriminalization significance of the responsibility element in the criminal law different from that in the civil law

The criminal judgment and the civil judgment would not necessarily affect each other and the responsibility element also has different decriminalization significances in the criminal law from the civil law. Throughout the criminal legislation and precedents of various countries worldwide, the understanding of illegality has increasingly become a critical factor in determining the culpability and its degree.

Case: To attract clients, the operator of pub A made coupons of the same size as the hundred Yuan note and took them to the police station for inspection but was not criticized for these. Therefore, the pub operator produced formal coupons at ease and distributed them. However, he was identified with the "act of making items confused with the currency" and was investigated for criminal responsibility. In this case, could the operator be determined to lack awareness of illegality and be given mitigation or exemption of responsibility accordingly?

In the field of civil law, the actor's awareness of the constituent elements of civil liability is only limited to factual elements and the awareness of illegality affects the establishment of civil liability. Taking tort liability as an example, the subjective awareness (fault or non-fault) of the actor does not affect the assumption of responsibility, and there is no so-called illegal awareness; for fault liability, what affects the establishment of the fault is always factual elements, under either the "subjective standard doctrine", "objective standard doctrine" or "comprehensive standard doctrine", but the positions may vary; the actor's attitude to the criminal norms, that is whether having the awareness of liability, is not considered.

In the field of criminal law, the actor's understanding of relevant criminal elements is a major constituent element for the judgment of culpability. Regarding the question whether the "criminal element" here only comprises the pure factual knowledge or covered the attitude to legal norms, there exists the doctrine of unnecessary awareness of illegality and the doctrine of necessary awareness of illegality. Considering that the judgment of illegality awareness may affect the existence and severity of criminal responsibility, thus exerting a substantive impact on sentencing, it is of great practical significance to clarify the systematic status of illegality awareness theoretically.

7.3 Illegality awareness as a new cause of decriminalization under the theory of normative responsibility

As mentioned earlier, the construction of civil responsibility tones down the fault elements; the awareness of fault is only limited to factual one and the awareness of illegality does not affect the establishment of fault. In contrast, due to the severity and particularity of criminal responsibility, whether the awareness of illegality affects the judgment of culpability and to what extent affects the criminal responsibility would exert material impact on the distribution of criminal responsibility of the actor in practice. Therefore, the following section will elaborate and analyze the divergences of major doctrines of illegality awareness in terms of criminal law.

7.3.1 Foothold of the doctrine of unnecessary illegality awareness: Theory of psychological responsibility

The systematic position of illegality awareness is a question of how the illegality awareness is distributed among the elements of responsibility. For a long time in the German and Japanese criminal law academia, the doctrine of unnecessary illegality awareness occupies a dominant position and the intentional offender is not required to have the recognition of the illegality of the act. Regarding the distribution of elements, the awareness of illegality is not the constituent element of criminal responsibility. The doctrine of unnecessary illegality awareness that excludes the awareness of illegality from the construction of criminal responsibility is generally recognized in the current criminal law theory.

The modern illegality awareness is not built based on the theory of psychological responsibility. According to the theory of psychological responsibility, responsibility is not the evaluation of the behavior, but the evaluation of the actor; only when the actor's motivation conflicts with the "social psychological coercion" effect of the law, can the actor be condemned. Therefore, "the development of the concept of culpability has to depend on the essence of the concept of responsibility for the inner person", which is the requirement of legal norms for specific individuals. The theory of psychological responsibility is deeply influenced by the way of thinking in natural science and takes the culpability as the factual evaluation of subjective components of crime, namely psychological fact, rather than value evaluation. In this way, the concept of culpability is the second category of crime behind the concept of illegality, and the objective illegality and subjective responsibility are clearly distinguished. On this basis, the psychological responsibility discriminates between intentional and negligent responsibility, which constitute the whole content of the elements of culpability along with the ability of imputation. Therefore, the knowledge of intention is also limited to factual knowledge, and the knowledge of illegality is naturally excluded from the elements of culpability.

Undeniably, illegality awareness is unnecessary to be relatively rational and convincing. It is well known that citizens' knowledge of the law is an important prerequisite for their law-abiding and the state's judicial power to intervene in their illegal acts; otherwise, it is difficult to guarantee the freedom of movements of citizens and the criminal law system centered on human rights protection will also face challenges. However, on the one hand, law is a historical category and there may be completely opposite provisions for the same behavior at different times. For example, many crimes related to the ethics of sex in the feudal era have obviously no basis for punishment today; on the other hand, for the majority of crimes, people have a general understanding of their illegality and there is no need to judge the awareness of illegality after their behavior. Therefore, for the sake of maintaining legal authoritarianism and judicial economy, the law presumes that the perpetrator knows the law before committing a criminal act, which then forms the concept of "no exemption from responsibility without knowledge of the law" influential in modern law. Along this way of thinking, it is not difficult to draw a conclusion: awareness of illegality is a fact that precedes the constitution of crime, which therefore needs not to be included in the crime theory; in other words, the judgment of any level in the three-tier system is all based on the actor's knowledge of illegality and so is the judgment of culpability.

However, in essence, the theory of psychological responsibility has obvious weaknesses. First, judgment of culpability is fact-based. Whether there is a measurable fact for intent is questionable; however, whether the *means rea* could be established to confirm the doer's culpability is a value evaluation and should be judged by certain standards. For example, there is often no dispute about the intent of malicious behavior. However, whether the behavior constitutes the intent in the sense of intentional injury crime and confirms the behavioral culpability has divided opinions. The value evaluation exists independently beyond factual judgment and is an open element. The theory of psychological responsibility excludes the element of value evaluation and would cause a closed culpability system that lacks the space for development. Second, the connection between the subjective element and the objective element is ignored. Although culpability is mainly a subjective phenomenon, it must be based on the subjective fact. In other words, intent and negligence are not completely dependent elements and their judgments should take a comprehensive consideration of the actor's loyalty to legal norms. As a result, the theory of psychological responsibility remains an immature scheme of culpability.

7.3.2 Attribution of the doctrine of necessity of illegality: Normative theory of responsibility

To overcome the shortcomings of the theory of psychological responsibility, the normative theory of responsibility came into being. The normative theory of responsibility takes "Neo-Kantianism" as its philosophical foundation and holds that the world is divided into the real material world and the unreal value (conceptual) world, which are independent of each other; it denies that the object can be understood from itself in terms of epistemology and emphasizes the initiative of the subject in understanding the object. The Neo-Kantianism advocates the methodological dualism in which objective reality is separated from the value world, so the concept of criminal responsibility transcends the factual level in the field of responsibility to give rise to the concept of culpability and realizes the conversion of the criminal responsibility class from the real world to the value world. In accordance with the normative theory of responsibility, three conditions must be satisfied to condemn the illegal behavior and together constitute the necessary and sufficient conditions of culpability: first, the actor must have the capacity to assume the criminal responsibility, namely with a normal mental state and of the legal age for responsibility; second, the actor's behavior and consequence must be of psychological connection, namely intent and negligence; third, there is no objective situation that hinders the free choice of behavior. Even if the actor carries out the anomie in a dilemma of choice, the criminal law should not punish him, thus leading to the theory of expectation possibility.

The doctrine of the necessity of illegality awareness holds that the illegality awareness is a normative evaluation element of criminal responsibility; only in the occasion of illegality awareness could the actor be held accountable. However, although the doctrine of the necessity of illegality awareness has earned the consent of the majority of people in the community of criminal law, the internal debates rise and fall and none of the doctrines is highly persuasive. Preliminarily, the introduction of the value evaluation into the normative theory of responsibility is a methodological change, which breaks the limitation of the traditional fact-based concept of criminal responsibility and has distinct improvements compared with the prior system. Nevertheless, although the normative theory of responsibility integrates the illegality awareness into the system of criminal responsibility, no further demonstration could explain how the illegality awareness is distributed among the elements of criminal responsibility. Then, it is necessary to return to the general principle of criminal law and re-examine the illegality awareness to tackle the question that the normative theory of responsibility is unable to define the systematic position of the illegality awareness.

7.4 Path of decriminalization for substantive illegality awareness under the principle of criminal-civil relativity

7.4.1 Relativity of illegality awareness elements from the perspective of criminal and civil overlapping

As described above, in the field of civil law, the illegality awareness is not a constituent element of fault and does not affect the establishment of civil responsibility; in the field of criminal law, the illegality awareness would at least affect the severity of responsibility. Therefore, another question needs to be answered: what is the cause of the difference in systematic position of illegality awareness? This is determined by the different normative purposes and nature of civil responsibility and criminal responsibility.

The primary purpose of civil responsibility is to make up for damage, that is, only after the established damage occurs will the existence and severity of civil responsibility matter; in other words, the civil responsibility lies in determination of the existence and severity of objective damage, while the subjective fault of the actor is only the auxiliary element for determination of responsibility, which, despite necessary, just need to meet the standard of fault in the sense of daily life. Moreover, out of the consideration of some special circumstances, the civil legislation stipulates the non-fault responsibility; even if the actor has no subjective fault, the actor should assume the responsibility, which almost completely eliminates the influence of subjective factors on civil responsibility.

In contrast, the criminal responsibility has triple purposes. First, from the perspective of the infringed legal interests (including individual, state and social legal interests), the protection of legal interests is the primary purpose, which is consistent with the overall purpose of the criminal law. In order to fully protect legal interests, we do not need to wait until the legal interests are damaged to investigate the criminal responsibility of the perpetrator; there is the possibility of investigating the criminal responsibility of the perpetrator with the criminal law.

7.4.2 Form and substance of awareness of illegality

Illegality concerns both the form and substance. "Formal illegality means that the actor violates legal provisions and the prohibition or order of the law". Accordingly, when an act conforms to the constituent elements of a crime and there is no cause for elimination of misfeasance, it shall be deemed illegal in form. "Substantive illegality refers to (antisocial behavior) that endangers the society. Illegal acts are damages to major interests of individuals or groups protected by law, and sometimes damage or harm to a legal interest. The infringement of life interests, namely legal interests, protected by legal norms is contradictory to the purpose of legal orders that regulate the common society". According to the provisions of the criminal law of China, what the criminal law prohibits is the behavior that has the infringement of legal interests or the danger of infringement of legal interests (behavior that is harmful to society). Therefore, substantive illegality is pertinent to the social harmfulness of the behavior.

Usually, in order to ensure the effectiveness of criminal law norms, it is only necessary to recognize the substantive illegality, that is, only to recognize the social harmfulness of the behavior. However, in exceptional cases, for the purpose of decriminalization, the perpetrator is required to recognize the formal illegality of the behavior. The reasons are as follows: first, the perpetrator is required to realize that formal illegality is adverse to regulating criminal behaviors. Substantive illegality, namely social harmfulness, belongs to the basic content of good and evil, and people are usually easy to recognize and make free choices at the time of behavior; while formal illegality requires selecting those punishable from substantive illegal behaviors and is a higher level concept. If the awareness of formal illegality is required for the establishment of an intentional crime, the power to judge culpability will inevitably be transferred to the hands of the criminal, which is undoubtedly the indulgence of crime. Moreover, from the perspective of the relationship between substantive illegality and formal illegality, in a society where the rule of law is relatively sound, the basic judgment of good and evil, right and wrong (substantive illegality) is available to normal citizens, but what kind of behavior deserves criminal punishment (formal illegality) can only be judged by the state. Second, total negation of the necessity of awareness of formal illegality will in some cases block the proper decriminalization path. For some crimes, the substantive illegality is ambiguous. In other words, no matter how advanced the legislative technology is, it is impossible to require citizens to establish a unified value of good and evil. At this time, if the actor violates the law based on reasonable trust, there is no need to punish him. The behavior of the operator in the case at the beginning of this section has the characteristics of such reasonable trust to a certain extent.

Because of this, in general, the establishment of an intentional crime only requires the awareness of the substantive illegality (social harmfulness) of the act; in exceptional cases, for the sake of decriminalization, the awareness of formal illegality should also be included in the judgment of culpability. The following will examine the distribution of illegality awareness elements in the circumstance of intent and negligence, respectively.

7.4.3 Awareness of illegality as an intent element

Awareness of illegality is an element of intent. According to the provisions of Article 14 of the criminal code of China, the establishment of an intentional crime must first recognize the substantive illegality (social harm) of the act, which seems to mean that only the knowledge of the facts of constituent elements is the content of intent knowledge, but if the perpetrator conducts an illegal act based on reasonable reliance and there are sufficient and reasonable reasons to believe that the perpetrator does not have the motivation to confront the law, the perpetrator cannot be imposed too severe intentional liabilities. In order to resolve this logical contradiction, we must rely on the following understanding: usually, as long as the actor has substantive illegality, it is presumed that the actor has the knowledge of illegality; however, when the actor commits illegal acts based on reasonable reliance, it negates the presumption of illegality awareness set by the criminal law norms, thereby preventing intentional responsibility. That is to say, awareness of illegality is a presumed intentional element. When the actor recognizes the social harmfulness of the act, as long as the criminal law clearly stipulates that the act is a crime, it can be presumed that the actor has an awareness of illegality.

Generally speaking, only when the following two conditions are met can we determine that the perpetrator has no awareness of illegality, thereby preventing intentional liability: first, it is difficult to judge the substantive illegality, which is often seen in non-traditional natural crimes and needs to be judged in light of specific circumstances. Second, based on reasonable trust, these two elements are indispensable, namely even if the perpetrator has a substantive awareness of illegality but carries out illegal acts based on laws, court judgments or opinions of public agencies with reasonable and reliable reasons, it cannot prevent intentional liability.

7.4.4 Possibility of awareness of illegality as an element of negligence

The possibility of awareness of illegality is an element of negligence. Just like the relationship between intention and negligence, the awareness of illegality and the possibility of awareness of illegality are concepts of different degrees of the same problem. Negligence involves the possibility of foreseeing the result of the constituent elements and then violating the obligation to avoid the result. But as its premise, the perpetrator must form an attitude of disregard for legal norms. Therefore, from the conclusion – as emphasized by most scholars – the perpetrator is exempted from responsibility when there is no possibility of illegality awareness. However, it is not because the possibility of illegality awareness is an element of responsibility, but because it is an element of negligence that prevents liability. If the possibility of awareness of illegality is positioned as the element of responsibility, then it is impossible to explain why intentional liability is exempted in the absence of awareness of illegality, because the premise of awareness of illegality is that the perpetrator has the possibility of awareness of illegality. The essential meaning of negligent crime is to investigate the motive of the perpetrator to disregard the prohibitive norms stipulated in the criminal law. Therefore, negligence liability can only be established when the perpetrator has the possibility of forming an illegal motive. Intentional crimes require the knowledge of normative elements, and correspondingly, the possibility of the existence of normative elements in negligent crimes must be affirmed. Therefore, the awareness of constitutive element facts and its possibility belong to the factual aspect of awareness, and the awareness of illegality and its possibility belong to the normative aspect of awareness, which unifies the factual judgment and value evaluation.

After the above review, the final conclusion can be drawn: the awareness of illegality and the possibility of awareness of illegality progressively belong to the elements of intention and negligence. For an illegal act that meets the constituent elements, if the actor lacks the possibility of knowing the illegality while satisfying other elements of guilt, the establishment of the crime is excluded; if the actor has the possibility of knowing the illegality but does not recognize the illegality of the behavior, it constitutes a crime of negligence; if the perpetrator has the awareness of illegality, an intentional crime is established.

7.5 Conclusion

According to the principle of relativity of illegality, the effects of criminal law and civil law are relatively independent. The complexity of criminal-civil cases that can best reflect this problem lies in the complexity of their legal relationships. For the resolution of such cases, it is necessary to grasp the core logic of the case, find the corresponding legal relationship and identify the corresponding legal basis.

The intricate legal relationships should be clarified, and finally, the conclusion of the case solution is drawn. If the doer makes the main contract invalid because of "covering up the illegal purpose in a legal form", the invalidation of the main contract cannot be based on the impact of the criminal judgment, and the criminal judgment does not have the effect higher than that of the civil judgment.

The systematic status of the awareness of illegality is also relative among criminal and civil laws. In the field of civil law, since facts are the core of liability, the requirements for the actor's fault are relatively relaxed, and the awareness of illegality is not a constituent element of fault. In the field of criminal law, the awareness of illegality is the normative element of judging guilt. Therefore, it is necessary to re-examine its systemic status based on the general principles of criminal law. In terms of the distribution of elements, it is advocated to focus on the protection of human rights, and to regard the awareness of illegality as an intentional element to ensure the freedom of action of citizens; based on the old theory of negligence, the possibility of illegal cognition is taken as the constituent element of negligence, so as to clarify the starting point of guilt. Therefore, in the absence of illegal awareness, the intentional responsibility is eliminated, and the negligent crime is established; in the absence of the possibility of illegal awareness, the negligent responsibility is eliminated to deny the establishment of a crime.

8 Decriminalization of Procedural Legitimacy

An Analysis Based on the Perspective of Criminal Integration

8.1 Criminal evidence rules based on criminal integration: For the purpose of decriminalization

Since Amendment (8) made drunk driving a criminal offense, the minimalist provision of "whoever drives a motor vehicle under influence on the road shall be sentenced to criminal detention and fined" has triggered discussions about how and whether to establish a decriminalization system for drunk driving. At present, criminal law scholars mainly focus on "stubbornly being within the discipline of criminal law, repeatedly discussing whether the proviso of Article 13 of the criminal law can be applied to this crime. However, regardless of the conclusion, it is impossible to tackle the contradiction between the legislative type of drunk driving crime similar to the foreign police offense crime and the proviso of Article 13 of the criminal law of China as a condition similar to that of foreign decriminalization of felonies".[1] It can be said that the criminalization of drunk driving and pick pocketing is to some extent the product of the "strict but not draconian" legislative model of foreign criminal laws, which is fundamentally different from crimes under the traditional "draconian but not strict" legislative model of the criminal law of China. Disregarding the changes in the criminal legislation model, they still continue to analyze the problem with the traditional thinking of whether Article 13 can be applied to these new crimes, which constitutes intentional neglect of decriminalization issues under the new legislative model and a vulgar interpretation of new issues such as how to decriminalize after conviction of the police offense crime in foreign countries. For this reason, how to break from the traditional established thinking and open up a decriminalization channel for drunk driving is a major problem facing criminal law theorists and practitioners.

Since the determination of "drunk driving" as the substantive element of the crime of dangerous driving under influence depends on the appraisal opinion of the criminal procedure law on the evidence of alcohol content, this gives rise to a common problem of this crime in the procedural law and the substantive law, that is, how to strictly control the evidence and thus strictly control the crime. How to improve the probative effect of identification evidence of blood alcohol content, so as to resolve the risk of violating the defendant's human rights that may

DOI: 10.4324/9781003456773-9

be brought about by only a single piece of evidence, thus finally satisfying the requirement on the appropriateness of criminal punishment based on the principle of *nulla poena sine lege* through the guarantee of procedural law; how to question the probative force of blood alcohol content identification evidence in combination with the rule that isolated evidence cannot determine a case in criminal proceedings; how to solve the problem of conviction evidence when there is no blood alcohol test result but only breath alcohol test result, or only circumstantial evidence without any alcohol test result; all these are theoretical and practical problems that need to be solved urgently in the process of the establishment of the crime of drunk driving. Under the current situation, it is difficult to solve the decriminalization of drunk driving behavior from within the criminal substantive law, since this kind of behavior involves both the procedural and substantive law issues, it is advisable to change the perspective, and based on the thinking of criminal integration, to establish evidence rules in criminal proceedings for the criminalization of drunk driving behaviors, so as to strictly guard the threshold for incrimination, and exculpate drunk driving behaviors that do not meet the standard of evidence.

8.1.1 Theoretical and practical problems of drunken dangerous driving crime: How to establish effective rules of evidence

According to relevant legal documents, whether a driver's blood alcohol content reaches 80 mg/100 ml is the only criterion for judging whether an intoxicated driver constitutes a crime of dangerous driving, whose importance is evident. Therefore, we must attach great importance to and standardize the collection of "evidence" in accordance with the law. Countries that have criminalized drunken driving for many years such as America and Canada "explored and found that in the past few decades, many innocent people have been wrongly convicted based on scientific evidence". As a new crime that has been implemented not long ago, there have been no wrongful convictions of drunk driving crimes in China; however, from the perspective of preventing unjust, false and wrongful convictions, it is obviously necessary to promptly discuss the issue of evidence for the conviction of drunk driving cases.

Based on the analysis of judicial practice, there are three prominent evidentiary issues in drunk driving cases, namely, whether a breath alcohol test result can be used to convict a person without a blood alcohol test, whether a blood alcohol test result can be used to convict a person without a breath alcohol test result and whether a conviction can be based solely on circumstantial evidence in the absence of either breath or blood alcohol test results.

8.1.1.1 Evidence-related issue 1: Whether a breath alcohol test result can be used to convict a person without a blood alcohol test

If a driver flees by car or otherwise to evade or refuse to take a blood sample for a blood alcohol test after a breath alcohol test, can the breath alcohol test results alone be used for conviction?

At present, relevant laws and regulations of China stipulate three procedures for drunk driving cases: first, breath alcohol test, blood alcohol test and then applying for re-identification. However, in practice, it is impossible to fully implement the two-stage process from breath to blood alcohol test for evidence collection in drunk driving cases. Judicial practice shows that "some drunk drivers use various tricks to evade punishment, and the most typical one is to leave the scene after causing an accident, wait until the alcohol has completely volatilized before surrendering, when the judiciary is unable to determine the blood alcohol concentration at the time of driving".

For example, Case 1. At 11:00 p.m. one day, when the breath alcohol test result was 113 mg/100 ml, Xiao drove away from the scene while taking advantage of the police taking notes.

The question reflected in this case is, when the result of the breath alcohol test meets the establishment standard for drunk driving, and a blood alcohol test on the driver cannot be conducted, can the decision be made directly based on the result of the breath alcohol test? Are breath test results evidence in a criminal case, and if so, which statutory form of evidence does it belong to? What is the evidentiary relationship between breath and blood alcohol test results? What is the respective status of the two in the evidentiary system of drunk driving cases? Also, if there is a large discrepancy between a driver's breath and blood alcohol test results, which should prevail?

For example, Case 2. At about 9:20 a.m. one day, *Person A* ran a red light and was stopped by the traffic police, who was discovered driving under the influence of alcohol. The traffic police then conducted a breath alcohol test on *Person A*, and the result was 95 mg/100 ml. Subsequently, *Person A* was taken by the traffic police to a medical institution for a blood test and arrived there one and a half hours later. The subsequent blood alcohol test result was 76.5 mg/100 ml. At this time, should the results of the breath or blood alcohol test prevail?

8.1.1.2 Evidence-related issue 2: Whether a blood alcohol test result can be used to convict a person without a breath alcohol test result

Drunk driving cases are currently only based on the blood alcohol content of the driver for conviction, which is a typical crime inculpated based on a single piece of evidence. If there is no breath but only a blood alcohol test result, can a driver be convicted?

Case 3. *Person B* was riding a motorcycle home from work after drinking and hit a pile of stones on the side of the road. The traffic police conducted an alcohol test on him and found that the ethanol content in his blood was as high as 236.26 mg/100 ml.

In this case, there was only a blood alcohol test result, no breath alcohol test and other circumstantial evidence. Can *Person B* be convicted of dangerous driving under influence? If *Person B* applies for re-examination on the grounds that the blood alcohol content test result is inaccurate, how should the case be handled?

Article 32 of the Procedural Regulations clearly stipulates that if the criminal suspect has doubts about the accuracy of the blood test appraisal opinion, "he may submit a written request for re-examination appraisal within three days from the date of delivery of the Notice of Appraisal Conclusion by the case-handling department". However, compared with other judicial appraisals such as re-identification of mental patients, the blood alcohol content is affected by alcohol volatilization and absorption and digestion by the human body, and the accuracy of the re-identification within three days is even more doubtful. Therefore, the pivotal position of the blood alcohol content value in the drunk driving case determines that this evidence should be treated more cautiously.

8.1.1.3 Evidence-related issue 3: Whether the conviction can be based on circumstantial evidence when there is neither breath nor blood alcohol test results

In some cases, neither the breath alcohol test result nor the party's blood alcohol test result is available, and only relevant circumstantial evidence proves that the party may have been driving under the influence of alcohol, which might constitute the crime of dangerous driving under the influence of alcohol. At this time, can the driver be convicted based on these circumstantial evidences?

Case 4. Mr. Yuan drove his wife Mrs. Hu and friend Yao to a banquet in a neighboring town and drove in the reverse direction while drinking and speeding, resulting in the death of two people on the motorcycle on the spot. Yuan asked his wife Hu to take the blame and asked Yao to give false testimony. Later, Hu went to the public security organ to "surrender", claiming that she was driving the vehicle that caused the accident. After being exposed, the public security organ took Yuan's blood for a test, but at this time Yuan's blood alcohol content was far below the drunk driving standard. The judiciary finally determined that Yuan was "drunken" driving based on the circumstantial evidence obtained from Yao who was accompanying him, friends who were drinking with him and hotel waiters and, finally, found him guilty of traffic accidents. In this case, Yuan was found to have drunk driving circumstances "mainly presumed from circumstantial evidence", but whether this approach is appropriate is really debatable.

The above three evidentiary problems in drunk driving cases all reflect that in practice, since drunk driving cases mainly rely on identification evidence of blood alcohol content, when the evidence is either inaccurate or inconsistent with the breath test results or is not available, it is difficult to determine the circumstances of drunk driving or drunk driving crime, and how to deal with the case when the relevant evidence cannot be confirmed.

8.1.2 Establishment of criminal evidence rules for drunk dangerous driving: Focusing on the probative power of evidence

According to the relevant provisions and principles of the criminal procedure law, the following evidence rules can be established for evidence collection and identification in drunk driving cases, that is, the results of a breath alcohol test alone cannot be used as conclusive evidence, and the results of a blood alcohol test alone can be used as evidence for conviction after verification; in the absence of breath and blood alcohol test results, the circumstantial evidence could not lead to the conviction.

8.1.2.1 Evidence rule no. 1: The results of a breath alcohol test alone cannot be used as conclusive evidence

Article 6 of the Drunk Driving Interpretation stipulates: "The blood alcohol content inspection and appraisal opinion is the basis for determining whether the criminal suspect is drunk. If the criminal suspect has reached the drunk standard stipulated in Article 1 of this Opinion after the breath alcohol content test but escapes before the blood sample is drawn, the results of the breath alcohol test can be used as the basis for determining their intoxication". The explanation clearly establishes that the breath alcohol test results can be used as evidence for conviction; however, this provision is obviously inappropriate.

The litigation proof model of China is corroborative, which requires at least two or more pieces of evidence to determine the facts of the case, which could support each other (with the same direction) and eliminate self-contradictions and mutual contradictions, thus forming a stable and reliable evidence framework. Whether the evidence is reliable can only be confirmed through the mutual corroboration of the evidence. The results of the breath alcohol test alone, no matter whether other evidences can corroborate each other, cannot support the establishment of the crime of drunk dangerous driving.

1 The subject of the breath alcohol test does not have the qualifications of a legal appraiser. The breath alcohol test belongs to forensic identification and should be carried out by specialized forensic identification personnel. However, in judicial practice, the breath alcohol test of drivers is carried out by the traffic police. The traffic police, as case investigators, are obviously different from the legally qualified appraisers and do not have professional appraisal skills and knowledge and cannot guarantee the accuracy of appraisal opinions. "The appraisal opinion may also be wrong due to the qualifications, appraisal level and professional ethics of the appraiser". "The scientificity, authenticity and authority of the appraisal opinion do not depend on the appraisal opinion itself to a large extent, but depend on the professional qualifications, appraisal process and judgment capacity of the appraiser".[2] At the same time, the police undertake the breath alcohol testing, which also violates the provisions of Article 28 of the new Criminal Procedure Law that investigators shall not serve as appraisers at the same time. The breath alcohol test itself violates the relevant provisions of the Criminal Procedure Law and the Identification Management Regulations in the identification procedure. Therefore, no matter what the result of the breath alcohol test is, it should not be used as an expert opinion and cannot be used alone as evidence for a drunk driving case.

2 The accuracy of breath alcohol test results is still questionable. Breath alcohol test results are often only of probable accuracy. Moreover, drunk driving has just been criminalized, and there is no legislation to provide detailed regulations on the standards of breath alcohol testing equipment and how to ensure its accuracy. The accuracy of the equipment has been questioned, and the reliability of police breath tests cannot be guaranteed. In addition, many substances such as mouthwashes, breath sprays and cough syrups also contain alcohol, which can also lead to alcohol in the oral cavity after ingestion. However, all the procedural regulations on drunk driving identification in China do not require the police to ask the driver before conducting the preliminary breath test whether they have drunk alcohol or ingested other substances that may affect the accuracy of the breath alcohol test within 15–20 minutes before the test. At the same time, because the police do not have professional qualifications for breath alcohol testing, it is difficult to ensure timely and effective disinfection of the identification equipment. In practice, there are also concerns about how to ensure that the testing equipment does not become the source or medium of disease transmission.

   During the breath alcohol test, other factors can also often lead to inaccurate test results. Some types of preliminary breath test devices react to specific substances rather than alcohol, such as ether, chloroform, acetone, acetaldehyde and even cigarettes.[3] In the judicial practice of China, there was a case that "after eating 'egg yolk pie', a person can be found out for drunk driving".[4] Based on the breath alcohol test, if you eat one egg yolk pie, the alcohol value is 26 mg/100 ml, then, if you eat less than four egg yolk pies, the alcohol value can meet the standard for establishing a drunk driving crime; a person who has eaten liqueur chocolates or kissed another person having drunk alcohol could be found "driving under the influence" via the breath alcohol test.[5] All of the above show that breath alcohol test results are difficult to become conclusive evidence in drunk driving cases. Because of this, in the judicial practice of foreign drunk driving cases, the preliminary breath test results generally cannot be used and adopted as final evidence in criminal proceedings.

3 The results of the breath alcohol test should be used as the basis for filing and investigation and should not be used as evidence for finalizing the case. The "National Standards" stipulates that "a person with the blood alcohol content greater than or equal to 80mg/100ml" should be convicted of drunk driving; the relevant regulations of the Ministry of Public Security point out: "After the person concerned is seized, in order to avoid legal investigation, if the person drinks alcohol before the breath alcohol test or blood sample and the blood alcohol content reaches the drunk driving standard after testing, the case should be filed for investigation. If the party meets the drunk driving standard after the breath alcohol test and escapes before the blood sample is drawn the case will be filed for investigation based on the breath alcohol content". This shows that, on the one hand, the "alcohol content

in the blood", not the alcohol content in the breath, should be used as the evidence for the concluding evidence of a drunk driving case; on the other hand, although the breath alcohol test results cannot be used as the basis for determining the establishment of a drunk driving crime, they can be used as a basis for filing a drunk driving case and its extended meaning can provide probabilistic guidance for the police to predict whether the driver may be in an intoxicated state.

However, in practice, some judicial personnel or judicial departments turn a blind eye to the above provisions. Instead, they believe that "if the suspect evades the standard test, the conclusion of the on-site breath test can be used as conclusive evidence". "As long as there is sufficient evidence, even if the alcohol content is not tested, it can also be handled as drunk driving". According to this, if the driver's blood alcohol content cannot be checked, as long as there is a breath alcohol test result, the crime of drunken dangerous driving can be established. However, as mentioned earlier, the subject of the breath alcohol test does not meet the qualification requirements for the identification subject, which leads to the problems with the legality of the results as evidence; the test results are also affected by many factors and are not accurate, and their objectivity is even more questionable; in the absence of corroboration with the results of the blood alcohol test, only the testimony of witnesses and circumstantial evidence do not have the probative effect required for conviction evidence. Using breath alcohol test results as conclusive evidence not only violates the provisions of the "Guiding Opinions" that breath alcohol test results be used as the "basis" for "filing a case for investigation" but is also contrary to the basic principles of the evidence law. Only the breath alcohol test result is not enough at all; directly accepting the breath alcohol test results as the final evidence is an inappropriate way that expands the conviction and violates human rights and must be guarded against. Although the results of the breath alcohol test of Xiao in Case 1 and *Person A* in Case 2 have reached the conviction standard for drunk driving, according to the above analysis, due to the lack of the most important blood alcohol test results, these two people cannot be convicted.

In short, the subject of the breath alcohol test is not qualified as a judicial authenticator, the accuracy of the test equipment is also questionable, and the accuracy, reliability and authority of the test results cannot be guaranteed; the breath alcohol test results mainly work to enable the police to predict whether a person is driving while intoxicated, and can be used as the basis for filing a case for investigation, but cannot be directly used as conclusive evidence in criminal proceedings; the relationship between it and the blood alcohol content test results is that between preliminary proof materials and final conclusive evidence. In practice, we should minimize the practice of convicting based solely on the results of the breath alcohol test and try to collect and determine the conviction and sentencing based on the results of the blood alcohol test, so as to strictly control the conviction of drunk driving.

8.1.2.2 Evidence rule no. 2: The result of a blood alcohol test alone can be used as evidence for conviction after verification

1 The uniqueness of drunk driving cases determines that a conviction can be based only on identification evidence of blood alcohol content, which does not violate the principle of being unacceptable as uncorroborated evidence.

In a drunk driving case, as long as the driver's blood alcohol content reaches 80 mg/100 ml, it could prove the establishment of the crime of drunk driving without any other evidence; no matter how sufficient the other evidence is, there is no blood alcohol content test result to prove the crime of drunk driving. Therefore, for drunk driving cases, no other evidence can prove the driver's guilt, but the evidence of blood alcohol content; in other words, the crime of drunk dangerous driving belongs to the crime that only attaches importance to "one piece of evidence of guilt", which is its particularity.

However, for the crime of drunk dangerous driving, the blood alcohol content is the direct and original evidence of the case, and its probative force is higher than any other evidence in the drunk driving case, which could fully establish the crime. The conviction based solely on evidence of blood alcohol content does not violate the principle of being unacceptable as uncorroborated evidence; conviction only based on breath alcohol tests or other relevant circumstantial evidence falls within the scope of the afore principle. Under the premise of objectiveness and authenticity, the direct evidence of a case can contain the information of the main facts of the case alone, which can not only prove that the crime has occurred but also prove that the crime was committed by the criminal suspect, instead of only proving a part or fragment of the constituent elements of a crime like the circumstantial evidence. Therefore, the direct evidence of the case can prove that the main facts of the case are established. It can be said that in the crime of drunk dangerous driving, the blood alcohol content is the direct evidence that can prove the main facts of the case. The principle of being unacceptable as uncorroborated evidence is mainly "aimed to protect the rights of the defendant and prevent mis-recognition of the facts of the case; for some evidence that is obviously weak in probative force, other evidence is required before it can be used as a rule for concluding a case". The probative force of the content appraisal opinion is not "obviously weak" but also can directly prove the main facts of the case. Among all the evidence in the drunk driving case, its probative force is the strongest.

In particular, the principle of being unacceptable as uncorroborated evidence has special warning significance for cases of conviction based on confession alone, rather than for cases of drunk driving, which are mainly based on the conclusions of biological tests. In China, "confession is the king of evidence"; the phenomenon of convicting only by confession was and is still a relatively common phenomenon in criminal judicial practice. Therefore, the principle of being unacceptable as uncorroborated evidence is of special significance for preventing convictions based on oral confessions alone. Article 64 of the Criminal Procedure

Law stipulates: "The judgment of all cases must emphasize evidence, pay attention to investigation and research, and not readily rely on oral confessions. If there is only the defendant's confession and no other evidence, the defendant cannot be found guilty and sentenced to punishment; without the defendant's confession, if the evidence is sufficient and reliable, the defendant can be found guilty and sentenced". Accordingly, if there is only the defendant's confession without other relevant evidence to corroborate it, the probative force of the confession as evidence itself is still in doubt. If there are only oral confessions, the facts are unpredictable and cannot be disapproved; a conviction based on this violates the principle that isolated evidence does not stand. In the recent Zhang Gaoping case that has attracted much attention, "the only direct evidence" "comes from the confession of the 'prison leader' Yuan Lianfang", while the most important DNA identification evidence is excluded.[6] The judiciary determined Zhang Gaoping as the criminal in the rape and murder case of the young girl Wang Dong based on this confession evidence only. But in a drunk driving case, regardless of whether there is a confession, the driver will not be convicted; the driver's blood alcohol level must be verified to ascertain whether having reached the standard for drunk driving before conviction. Obviously, the principle that isolated evidence does not stand is particularly pertinent for cases of conviction based on oral confession alone. For drunk driving cases convicted based on biological test conclusions, when the conviction is based on the driver's blood alcohol content, it is due to the requirements for the establishment of the crime and does not violate the principle that isolated evidence does not stand.

In addition, only blood alcohol test results without the breath alcohol test results may not necessarily be isolated evidence in the true sense. It is the consensus of the criminal procedure law academia and judicial practice circles in China that being unacceptable as uncorroborated evidence or isolated evidence cannot conclude the case. "There is only one piece of incriminating evidence in the case. Since this evidence is 'uncorroborated' and cannot be confirmed by any other evidence, it is difficult to determine whether it is true or false. Of course, the judge cannot make a decision based on this uncorroborated evidence".[7] Obviously, the so-called uncorroborated evidence, in criminal proceedings, means that the incriminating evidence is uncorroborated. The concept of uncorroborated evidence is relative, as there is no absolute uncorroborated evidence, and the drunk driving case is no exception. According to judicial practice, the "evidence of a drunk driving case should include the following main aspects: (1) the process of seizure; (2) the testimony of witnesses; (3) the confession of the criminal suspect and the simultaneous audio and video recording at the scene; (4) the breath alcohol content test report and blood alcohol content identification conclusion. (5) blood extraction transcripts; (6) identification materials of the criminal suspect". It can be seen that the results of the blood alcohol content test are evidence of guilt and the main evidence that can directly prove the facts of the case to be proved; only this evidence is relative to cases without breath alcohol test results; in addition, even if there are no breath alcohol test results, there are witness statements, confessions of criminal suspects or other evidence to prove that they are driving under influence.

In short, the conviction based on the results of the blood alcohol content test just reflects the uniqueness of the drunk driving case and does not violate the basic principle of evidence law that being unacceptable as uncorroborated evidence. As long as it is verified to be true and the identification evidence of blood alcohol content is objective and accurate as well as of legal source, and the obtaining procedure does not violate the legal provisions, it can be used as evidence for conviction.

2 The identification evidence of blood alcohol content must be verified before it can be used as conviction evidence in drunk driving cases.

Paragraph 2 of Article 48 of the Criminal Procedure Law stipulates that "evidence must be verified before it can be used as the basis for conviction". Article 53 of the Criminal Procedure Law stipulates that "the evidence is reliable and sufficient, and shall meet the following conditions: (1) facts of conviction and sentencing should be proved by evidence; (2) The evidence on which the case is based has been verified through legal procedures; (3) Based on the evidence of the entire case, reasonable doubts have been ruled out for the facts identified". This requires the conviction evidence in the crime of dangerous driving, that is to say, blood alcohol identification must be objective, relevant and legal and, at the same time, reach a degree of certainty and adequacy. If the objectivity of blood alcohol identification evidence is in doubt, it can only be used as evidence for conviction after reasonable doubts have been excluded.

Blood alcohol content testing evidence's objectivity is also a question about whether the evidence is accurate. The evidence must reflect the objective truth of the case, with clear facts and sufficient evidence. In other words, if there is no doubt about the objectivity of the blood alcohol content testing evidence, then it is necessarily accurate. However, the level of objectivity (accuracy) required for evidence of driving under the influence is a controversial topic in evidence law theory and practice. Based on relevant provisions and legal analysis in criminal procedure law, the objectivity of blood alcohol content testing evidence only needs to meet the standard of excluding reasonable doubt.

First, from a criminal law theory perspective, if the objectivity of evidence is required to reflect the truth of the case, then the evidence must fully prove the facts of the case and restore its true nature. This requirement means that the evidence in criminal cases should meet the highest standard of objective truth. This is beneficial for the investigation and prosecution of cases but ignores the practical operability of the evidence standard in court. Second, from the analysis of criminal procedure practice in China, the lack of a neutral adjudicator in pre-trial procedures means that "demanding that the police and prosecutors reveal the facts of the case objectively and truthfully is somewhat unrealistic". If the standard of "clear facts and sufficient evidence" reflects an "absolute certainty" and "objective certainty", then requiring this highest level of proof before the trial is logically contradictory. If the investigation and prosecution procedures require absolute correctness, then why do we still need the trial process? Therefore, emphasizing absolute certainty and truthfulness is not in line with judicial reality or the inherent legal principles of litigation procedures. Regarding the objectivity of blood alcohol content evidence in driving under the influence cases, the standard of excluding reasonable doubt should be applied. Third, the legislation in China's criminal procedure law also establishes the standard of excluding reasonable doubt as proof of the case's facts. Although paragraph 2 of Article 48 of the law seems to establish "excluding reasonable doubt" as a lower level provision of "clear and sufficient evidence", the requirement for "excluding reasonable doubt" is based on the "comprehensive evidence of the whole case". Therefore, evidence that can exclude reasonable doubt based on comprehensive evidence of the whole case is considered clear and sufficient evidence. Therefore, blood alcohol content testing evidence that meets the standard of excluding reasonable doubt can be used to identify the driver's offense of dangerous driving under the influence, even if there is no other evidence to corroborate it. As a result, in judicial practice, cases with only blood alcohol content testing results and no breath alcohol testing results are processed as dangerous driving under the influence cases.

Case 5. One day in 2011, Mr. Zhu was reversing his car in a parking lot in Ezhou, Hubei and collided with another parked car, causing damage to both vehicles and a dispute to arise. When the police smelled alcohol on Mr. Zhu, they asked him to take a breathalyzer test, but he refused to cooperate. The police took Mr. Zhu to a hospital in the city for a blood test, which showed that his blood alcohol content was 158 mg/100 ml. Although only Mr. Zhu's blood alcohol test result was available in this case, the evidence of blood alcohol content was obtained under normal conditions, and the refusal to take the breathalyzer test was due to Mr. Zhu's refusal. This evidence could prove the main facts of the case. Although there was no breathalyzer test result or other circumstantial evidence presented in the case, Mr. Zhu was still convicted of drunk driving and sentenced accordingly.

In fact, the standard of excluding reasonable doubt is not only the objectivity standard of criminal evidence, but also the standard of the legality of evidence. This is because, in criminal proceedings, the usual standard for proving guilt is to exclude reasonable doubt. The legality of evidence requires that the evidence be obtained in accordance with legal procedures, and evidence obtained in violation of legal procedures is not legal. If the legality of the blood alcohol content determination opinion is questionable, it must also be excluded from reasonable doubt before it can be used as evidence for conviction. "The crime facts must be based on 'evidence', and the evidence must be based on 'legal investigation' before it can be used as a basis for the court's judgment. This indicates that the core issue of modern criminal procedural law is the pursuit of the rule of law procedure". For the crime of drunk driving, in addition to complying with the provisions of the Criminal Procedure Law on evidence collection etc., the aforementioned "Procedural Regulations" must also be followed. Chapter Three of this regulation provides detailed provisions on the investigation procedures for drunk driving cases, including regulations on breathalyzer tests, blood alcohol content testing conditions and procedures, and oral summons, interrogation and restraint of drunk drivers. However, many detailed issues regarding evidence collection in drunk driving cases cannot be found in the Criminal Procedure Law. For drunk driving cases, the acquisition of blood alcohol content identification evidence mainly involves a fundamental issue: Can the police use forced measures to collect evidence when the suspect refuses to cooperate with the police test? Among them, the most common coercive measures are as follows: forced interception and forced testing. Whether the evidence obtained by using these two coercive measures is legal has become a question that must be answered. Obviously, this involves how to exclude reasonable doubt to ensure the legality of blood alcohol content identification evidence, which is a more detailed issue.

8.1.2.3 Evidence rule no. 3: Conviction cannot be based solely on circumstantial evidence when there is no breath or blood alcohol test result

Since the introduction of the criminal offense of drunk driving, although the incidence of drunk driving has decreased significantly, "drivers evading alcohol tests and shifting blame behavior also frequently occur". This means that in practice, some drivers may indeed have driven under the influence of alcohol and may even have been drunk driving, but due to various reasons such as driver escape or shifting blame, there is no alcohol test opinion to prove it. That is, there is no breath alcohol test result, nor is there a blood alcohol content test result, but there may be some other relevant evidence, such as witness testimony from passengers, restaurant owner's testimony, video evidence etc. These circumstantial evidences may be able to prove that the driver drove after drinking alcohol. At this time, can the drunk driving offense be established based solely on this circumstantial evidence? Currently, there seems to be a trend toward criminalizing such behavior, that is, even if there is no alcohol test result, as long as other circumstantial evidence can prove it, both the offense of drunk driving and the offense of dangerous driving while intoxicated may be established. The aforementioned Case 4 is an example of this.

In Case 6, on a certain evening, after a Santana car was involved in a traffic accident, several men and women obstructed the police from enforcing the law, and the driver of the car took the opportunity to abandon the car and escape. After investigation, it was confirmed that the perpetrator was the person in charge of the Nanshimeng Taxation Branch of the National Taxation Bureau in Xingtai County, and he had driven a government vehicle under the influence of alcohol. Some people believe that "if a driver abandons the car and escapes when checked by the traffic police, and there is other testimony or evidence that the driver had been drinking, it should be considered as drunk driving". Therefore, it is argued that the offense of dangerous driving while intoxicated is established in this case. Similarly, in the aforementioned Case 4, where Yuan and Hu shifted blame, the local judicial authorities believed that "if there is other relevant evidence proving that the perpetrator had been drinking, the perpetrator can be deemed to have driven a motor vehicle under the influence of alcohol", so Yuan was deemed to have the "driving after drinking" offense. In these two cases, although it seems that the drivers were driving under the influence of alcohol, conviction based solely on circumstantial evidence without any alcohol test results not only violates the constituent element requirements of the substantive criminal law for the offense of dangerous driving while intoxicated but also violates the basic principles of the criminal procedural law regarding the presumption of innocence.

From the perspective of criminal substantive law, convicting solely based on circumstantial evidence without any alcohol test results violates the principle of legality. Article 22 of the "Amendment (8)" sets out the constitutive elements of the crime of dangerous driving caused by drunk driving as "driving a motor vehicle under the influence of alcohol". Without alcohol test results, it is impossible to determine the blood alcohol content of the driver. If the conviction is based solely on circumstantial evidence, it is equivalent to rendering the standard for establishing drunk driving meaningless and indirectly amending the provisions of the criminal law on "drunk driving", violating the principle of legality. In dealing with crimes of drunk driving, which are not set out in specific circumstances and can only be established by "driving under the influence", it is better to strictly require evidence and strictly control the threshold for prosecution. All cases where there is doubt about the facts should not be prosecuted as crimes, which is more acceptable to both theoretical and practical workers.

From the perspective of criminal procedural law, convicting solely based on circumstantial evidence without any alcohol test results violates the presumption of innocence principle. According to the presumption of innocence principle, "the presumption of innocence is an important principle in the criminal justice system of modern rule of law countries. Although 'exclusion of reasonable doubt' does not directly express the presumption of innocence, it implies this idea: only when all reasonable doubt has been eliminated should the defendant be found guilty".[8] This means that in cases where there is doubt about the fact of drunk driving, if reasonable doubt cannot be eliminated, the driver cannot be found guilty. Even if other evidence is detailed, if there is still controversy over whether the driver actually committed drunk driving, "if the question of whether the crime has been committed is a matter of controversy, then the fact should be proved to the extent of excluding reasonable doubt". If the degree of excluding reasonable doubt cannot be reached, the presumption of innocence principle should be applied. Paragraph 4 of Article 171 of the Criminal Procedure Law stipulates that "for cases of secondary supplementary investigation, if the people's procuratorate still believes that the evidence is insufficient and does not meet the conditions for prosecution, a decision not to prosecute shall be made". Article 49 stipulates that "the people's procuratorate shall bear the burden of proving the guilt of the accused in a public prosecution case". Therefore, in the case of drunk driving, if there is no alcohol test result during the investigation and prosecution stage, the public prosecution agency should request that the public security agency supplements the investigation. If the evidence issue of alcohol test results cannot be resolved after the supplementary investigation, drunk driving should not be prosecuted. If the blood alcohol content evidence of the driver cannot be obtained, it means that the burden of proving that the suspect is guilty cannot be fulfilled by the prosecution, and the judge's reasonable doubt about the facts charged cannot be eliminated. At this time, if the driver is convicted based solely on other circumstantial evidence, it is in fact a presumption of guilt. Even if the case enters the trial stage, "as long as the court cannot form a conviction of guilt based on solid evidence after a lawful investigation, the defendant is presumed innocent and the court should render a verdict of not guilty".[9] In other words, in the case of "drunk driving" where there is a lack of direct evidence to prove the crime, such as the results of an alcohol test, the court can only determine the driver's innocence based on the presumption of innocence principle.

Case 7. The suspect Kong who drove under the influence of alcohol collided with an electric bicycle, causing minor injuries to two people; Kong fled the scene and was arrested four days later. However, at this point, it was no longer possible to supplement the alcohol content test.

Although there are a large number of witness testimonies from relevant personnel in this case, it should not be assumed that Kong has committed the crime of drunk driving type dangerous driving based solely on this evidence. After China incorporated the value of "respecting and safeguarding human rights" into Article 2 of the Criminal Procedure Law, it is necessary to gradually "eliminate the influence of the mandatory punishment system, strictly collect and review evidence in accordance with the requirements of the legal due process, and achieve relative substantive truth as the goal of proof". Therefore, it must be clear that substantive truth is not only relative, but "the discovery of substantive truth is not the only purpose of criminal procedure law, and it is not equivalent to 'guilty must be punished' or 'relentlessly pursue and prosecute the defendant at any cost.' Criminal proceedings are governed by other criminal procedural purposes, among which the rule of law principle and its many derived principles are the most important. The discovery of substantive truth can only be done within the limits of the rule of law, and the presumption of innocence is a core principle".[10] In the absence of any alcohol test results, it means that the facts of the case have not been effectively revealed; convicting the suspect solely based on relevant circumstantial evidence cannot rule out reasonable doubts about whether the suspect has committed drunk driving.

In fact, in cases where the facts of "drunk driving" are questionable due to the lack of any alcohol test results, not convicting the suspect based on the presumption of innocence principle may seem unfavorable to protecting road traffic safety and combating drunk driving crimes. However, starting from the fundamental idea of human rights protection in the rule of law, this approach has more advantages than disadvantages. In the field of criminal justice, the evolution from arbitrary justice to procedural justice is considered a major change in legal history. The presumption of innocence principle provides a basis for various human rights protection systems for criminal suspects and defendants in criminal proceedings. The realization of state punishment power must be based on a legitimate legal process. In the absence of alcohol test results for the suspect, convicting them solely based on relevant circumstantial evidence will not only lead to an unlimited expansion of drunk driving crimes but also relax the conviction standard of "clear criminal facts and sufficient evidence" in the Criminal Procedure Law. This will ultimately lead to the expansion of criminal liability and the broadening of the scope of drunk driving crime punishment, which is detrimental to the protection of citizens' human rights.

8.1.3 Summary

To deepen the understanding of drunk driving crimes that rely on alcohol content identification evidence to solve the problem of substantive convictions, a criminal-integrated research method is adopted. This not only stems from the characteristics of drunk driving cases themselves but also can absorb the criminal procedure law evidence theory to establish strict rules of evidence for conviction, thereby truly realizing the spirit of human rights protection in criminal law. The inclusion of "respecting and protecting human rights" in the Criminal Procedure Law not only sets a clear boundary for "punishing crimes" but also provides a safety belt for public power in criminal proceedings. It is of great significance for understanding the mission of the Criminal Law's first article in China, which requires that the exercise of state's penal power, punishment for crimes and protection of national and people's interests cannot be at the cost of sacrificing citizens' human rights protection. The establishment of evidence rules for drunk driving cases is precisely to achieve the requirement of the principle of legality of crimes and punishments in the substantive aspect, that is, the appropriateness of criminal punishment regulations, to fully realize the guarantee function of the principle of legality of crimes and punishments in criminal law and the task of respecting and protecting human rights in criminal procedure law. The establishment of the above evidence rules for drunk driving cases can provide operational experience rules for judicial practice and establish a mechanism for excluding drunk driving behavior. Rather than just staying at the level of substantive law, analyzing the applicability of the crime concept in drunk driving cases from the perspective of criminal law logic theory, or more abstractly discussing the "leniency and severity" of criminal policy, it is better to combine the uniqueness of drunk driving crimes and establish a specific system of evidence rules for drunk driving cases from the level of criminal procedure law to strictly regulate the process of conviction. By attempting to establish evidence rules for drunk driving cases, we can reflect on the provisions of the "Interpretation of Drunk Driving" which only convicts based on breath alcohol content testing results, and be cautious about the inappropriate practice of theory and practice only relying on breath alcohol testing results or even circumstantial evidence to expand the scope of conviction, and advocate the presumption of innocence principle in the Criminal Procedure Law for drunk driving cases without blood alcohol content testing results to implement human rights protection for drunk driving suspects or criminal defendants in practice.

8.2 How to exclude objectivity and legality of evidence to achieve conviction of a crime

8.2.1 Reflections from cases

Case 1: Kong Moyuan and Zhang Mohong and three others, after drinking alcohol, hit a mother and daughter with a car (minor injuries). After getting out of the car, they not only failed to help the victims but also beat the husband of the injured woman and fled the scene. The next day, Kong Mozhi confessed to the crime, claiming that he was driving under the influence of alcohol and that Kong Moyuan was covering for him.

Case 2: The defendant, Li, drove a two-wheeled motorcycle without a license after drinking alcohol and took his wife, Du, home. At around 7:30 pm, he collided with another two-wheeled motorcycle and, after the parties, failed to reach a settlement, the victim reported it to the police. In order to create an illusion of drinking after the accident, Li drank a bottle of beer around 8 pm and was later caught by the traffic police. At 9:20 pm on the same day, his blood alcohol content was found to be 165.4 mg/100 ml.

According to relevant regulations, the opinion of blood alcohol content is the most important evidence for convicting drunk driving cases. Regardless of whether the results of the blood alcohol content test can be corroborated by the results of the breath alcohol content test or other circumstantial evidence, or even if only the blood alcohol content test results are available as evidence, as long as the evidence meets the proof standard required by the Criminal Procedure Law, it can be used as evidence of conviction. In the Criminal Procedure Law, the proof standard refers to the degree of proof required to prove the facts to be proved by the evidence used, as stipulated by the Criminal Procedure Law. According to the principles of the Criminal Procedure Law, evidence must have objectivity, relevance and legality in order to meet the requirements of the proof standard.

8.2.2 Judgment standard for objectivity of blood alcohol content evidence in drunk driving crimes: Excluding reasonable doubt

To determine the objectivity of the evidence of blood alcohol content test, it is necessary to clarify the standard to be achieved by excluding reasonable doubt. "The standard of excluding doubts. Generally, evidence cannot be judged as true or false, that is, evidence cannot be completely confirmed as true or false. The truth or falsity of evidence is expressed by the 'degree' between truth and falsehood, that is, the credibility of the evidence. The doubts of evidence should be reasonably excluded, rather than absolutely excluded, that is, the degree of truth of evidence is greater than the degree of falsehood of evidence". Therefore, as long as the degree of truth of the evidence of blood alcohol content test is higher than the degree of falsehood, it can be considered objectively true. The objectivity of the evidence of blood alcohol content test depends on a series of conditions, "mainly based on some basic principles that should be followed in its formation process. These principles have universal significance for the identification of evidence and belong to axiom principles". Therefore, as long as the blood alcohol content test results are obtained in accordance with the above principles and there is no doubt that cannot be reasonably excluded, the objectivity of the evidence can be proved.

The drunk driving case must be determined based on the opinion of the blood alcohol content test, which belongs to a fact that can only be judged based on specialized knowledge and experience, in line with the necessity principle. According to relevant regulations, the blood alcohol content test must be conducted by "inspection and appraisal institutions of public security organs at or above the county level or other qualified inspection and appraisal institutions recognized by public security organs". The qualified appraisal personnel in these appraisal institutions are generally not familiar with the drunk driving parties, ensuring their neutrality in the appraisal process. These appraisal personnel can also apply reliable scientific knowledge to accurately reflect the object of appraisal, so there are generally no problems in terms of the principles of objectivity, neutrality and scientific reliability.

As for the principle of authenticity of the source, there may be more problems because the accuracy of the blood alcohol content test in the drunk driving case depends on factors such as obstacles set up by the driver or their physical condition. Specific analysis should be conducted based on the specific situation. As mentioned earlier, if the driver runs away and cannot undergo a blood alcohol content test, it has been discussed and will not be repeated.

If the driver asks someone to take the blame for them, it should be handled with caution due to differences in blood alcohol content between different subjects in the blame-shifting case. If the relevant video footage on the road shows that the driver was temporarily replaced before being caught by the police and the blood alcohol content of the previous driver had reached the standard for filing a case, the driver can be convicted of the crime of drunk driving. However, if there is no clear evidence that the driver was switched before being caught by the police, even if the blood alcohol content of the "switched" driver has reached the standard for prosecution, this type of case cannot be criminally convicted. If the blame-shifting case is clear, such as if *Person A* has indeed taken the blame for *Person B*, but *Person A*'s blood alcohol content test result did not reach 80 mg/100 ml, and *Person B* has fled, it cannot be criminally convicted. In summary, the characteristic of the crime of drunk driving is that it must involve driving after drinking. Only when the evidence proves that the drinking subject and the driving subject are the same person and their blood alcohol content test results have reached the standard for conviction can they be criminally convicted.

If the driver is drinking water or alcohol on the spot when checked by the traffic police, two different situations should be dealt with separately: in the first situation, if the driver is drinking water or other drinks to dilute the alcohol in their body, there may be issues with the probative force of the blood test results, regardless of whether the result reaches the standard for filing a case or not. Even if the result shows that the blood alcohol content of the driver has reached the standard for filing a case after dilution, they can be convicted of the crime. However, if it does not reach the standard, it cannot be concluded that the crime would have been established if there was no dilution. In other words, the classification of such cases should be based on the actual results of the blood alcohol content test, and not on unfavorable inferences for the suspect.

In the second circumstance, as in Case 2, whether the crime can be directly punished depends on the strength of the evidence. For new crimes such as drunk driving, there are currently no clear regulations in legislation or judicial interpretation for such issues. In judicial practice, "for those who have drunk alcohol before breath testing or blood testing, and obstructed law enforcement work before blood testing, all are investigated based on the actual alcohol content tested". However, using actual alcohol content as a standard for investigation does not necessarily mean that it can be used as evidence for conviction. During the investigation process, there is obviously a problem of further verifying whether the evidence of "actual tested alcohol content" is "indeed sufficient". According to a voluntary test of "drunk driving standards" organized by a large domestic newspaper media, the human body does not reach the drunk driving standard within 10 minutes after drinking, and no one even reached the standard of 20 mg/100 ml for the conviction of drunk driving. However, the alcohol content in the body after 1 hour of abstinence from drinking was the highest among the volunteers, which then showed a decreasing trend. It can be seen that drinking on the spot to confuse the test does not mean that it cannot be used to identify the true or false alcohol content in the body. The threshold for blood alcohol content is not simply "blood + alcohol" because it takes a certain amount of time for alcohol to dissolve into the bloodstream after drinking. If the blood alcohol content test is immediately conducted on the driver after drinking, the accuracy of the identification opinion is generally not affected by the fact that the driver just drank alcohol. The result displayed is basically the blood alcohol content of the driver before drinking in front of the police. If the identification opinion shows that the case has reached the standard for investigation, the case can generally be convicted and sentenced accordingly. However, if, like Li in Case 2, the measurement was taken after an hour, it is highly likely that the test showed the alcohol content in his blood after drinking and fleeing. At this time, the evidentiary force of the identification opinion is obviously weaker than the opinion formed by immediate identification after drinking. If there is not enough identification technology to indicate that the opinion is verifying the blood alcohol content before that, the driver cannot be convicted of drunk driving. It can be seen that the evidentiary force of blood alcohol content identification after the driver drinks alcohol in front of the police is inversely proportional to the time interval between drinking and blood alcohol content identification. The closer the time interval, the stronger the proof; the longer the time interval, the weaker the proof. From the perspective of evidence science, whether the evidence obtained between drinking and blood testing can be accurately used as evidence for conviction, and how to deal with the blood alcohol content identification evidence obtained during the intermediate interval, which is neither too short nor too long, require further refinement in theory and practice around the issue of "focusing on fixed driver blood alcohol content and further standardizing evidence collection". In summary, the objectivity of the evidence of blood alcohol content testing can be established as long as it meets the standard of excluding reasonable doubt. When the objectivity is in doubt, it may be appropriate to apply the presumption of innocence principle in criminal procedure law and not prosecute the driver as a criminal.

8.2.3 Legality assessment of evidence in forced stoppage and evidence collection: An Analysis based on the non-natural rights view of driving rights

Case 3: Mr. Wang drank about 250 ml of liquor while having dinner with friends and later drove his friend home. On the way, he had a traffic accident with a pedestrian, Mr. Zhang. After the police arrived at the scene, Mr. Wang refused to cooperate, so the police forcibly drew his blood. The test showed that his blood alcohol concentration was over 80 mg/100 ml. Mr. Wang believed that the police's forced blood draw violated his personal rights and filed an administrative compensation lawsuit to the court.

Since "alcohol emboldens people", there are often cases where suspects refuse to cooperate with police testing during the collection of blood alcohol concentration test evidence. In such cases, is the evidence collected by police using coercive measures legal?

Firstly, according to Article 8 of the "Procedural Regulations", "If a traffic police officer on duty on a road discovers that a motor vehicle driver is suspected of drunk driving, he or she shall conduct a breath alcohol test". Article 9 provides that if a party is suspected of drunk driving a motor vehicle, blood samples should be taken to test the alcohol content in the body. Therefore, forced stoppage based on the reasonable suspicion is in compliance with China's legal regulations. Certainly, when investigating and handling other crimes under criminal law, the crime and the victim have often already appeared, and subsequently, the suspect is locked down based on objective behavior or the victim's report before arrest and other investigation work is carried out. However, drunk driving is identified before a traffic accident occurs and before it is determined to be drunk driving. There is no so-called criminal behavior or direct victim, nor is there clear evidence, so the legitimacy of forced stoppage and punishment for drunk driving needs to be questioned. Moreover, police's forced stoppage may violate the right of passage of those who are not drunk driving. It seems to affect "the autonomy of citizens". Therefore, further analysis is necessary. Article 83 of the "Road Traffic Law" stipulates that "traffic police investigate and handle road traffic safety violations" as their power, and Article 115 stipulates that traffic police who "illegally stop and inspect normally running vehicles" should be given "administrative sanctions". These provisions indicate that the police's forced stoppage of vehicles is not a power that can be exercised arbitrarily, but must comply with legal regulations. For investigating drunk driving, forced stoppage must be based on the "discovery of suspected drunk driving by motor vehicle drivers". Therefore, as long as the forced stoppage is based on reasonable suspicion, it is legitimate in procedure.

On the one hand, from a legal perspective, forced stopping seems to involve a game between power and rights, infringing on the driving rights of drivers. However, in reality, forced stopping is for the better protection of the rights of road users. Through forced stopping based on reasonable suspicion, hidden dangers or actual hazards of unsafe driving can be eliminated, ensuring the normal exercise of driving rights of other drivers on the road. Article 1 of China's Road Traffic Law explicitly states that "this Law is enacted for the purpose of maintaining road traffic order, preventing and reducing traffic accidents, protecting personal safety, protecting the property safety and other lawful rights and interests of citizens, legal persons and other organizations". This clearly indicates that when the police exercise their power to forcibly stop and investigate illegal vehicles, they are doing so for the better protection of the driving rights of drivers. "When drunk driving poses a serious threat to public safety, the behavior is no longer purely a private act. As an administrative law enforcement department, they can exercise appropriate investigation powers over the driving vehicle and driver from the perspective of serving the public interest".

On the other hand, although driving behavior is a right, it is not a natural right but a privilege granted by administrative law. Driving rights are clearly different from natural rights such as the right to life, health and equal freedom, which are innate and should be enjoyed by everyone. Driving rights are a developmental conferred right, that is, a right that is granted by the state to those who meet the requirements of the motor vehicle management regulations and pass the examination for a driving license, and provide corresponding road conditions, thus developing the interests of citizens themselves. In legal theory, compared with natural rights such as the right to life and health that everyone is born with, rights such as driving rights that are granted to certain individuals or groups by law are often referred to as special rights. It is precisely because "the principle that driving is a privilege rather than a natural right has been recognized by the courts of common law countries for almost 100 years".[11] More specifically, driving rights are a qualified privilege, that is, a restrictive special right that requires certain qualifications. Since "driving a vehicle on a public highway is not a natural right but a special privilege, it is subject to reasonable regulation for the public benefit",[12] and since driving rights are a conferred right that individuals are allowed to engage in certain activities and obtain benefits after administrative permission, and "the essence of administrative permission is the intervention or restriction of administrative power on private rights", it certainly needs to be subject to reasonable regulation for the public benefit. Therefore, the police's forced stop based on reasonable suspicion is completely legal, and the blood alcohol content test evidence obtained after taking such a forced measure is admissible.

In practice, the main sources of reasonable suspicion for police to forcibly stop vehicles are as follows: the police's own discoveries and reports from others. The first is their own discoveries, such as abnormal driving on the road. The second is reports from others. Drunk driving reports can be divided into two types: real-name reporting and anonymous reporting. For real-name reporting where the identity of the reporter is known and the reported facts are also clear, if the driver refuses to stop during the investigation, the police have the right to stop the vehicle. At this time, the real-name reporter's report can be considered a "reasonable suspicion" for the forced stop. Anonymous reporting determines that the truthfulness of the reported content is lower than that of real-name reporting, so it is difficult to uniformly consider forced stop based on this report as "reasonable suspicion", otherwise, there is a risk of violating human rights. Therefore, before stopping the vehicle based on this information, the police need to "observe the driver's abnormal driving behavior by themselves", and the forced stop of the vehicle at this time can be considered a reasonable suspicion and therefore legal. In summary, whether the police forcibly stop the vehicle based on their own observation of abnormal driving behavior or based on a report from others, the observed or reported facts must reach a level of reasonable suspicion of drunk driving behavior, otherwise the forced stop is illegal and the evidence obtained cannot be used as evidence of conviction.

Secondly, there is the issue of the legality of the blood alcohol content test results obtained through mandatory testing of drivers. This issue, like mandatory traffic stops, involves the legality of the means of obtaining evidence, and therefore, the analysis of the reasons for police mandatory traffic stops also applies to mandatory testing as well. It should be noted that like mandatory traffic stops, mandatory testing must also be based on the police's reasonable suspicion. Only when the police reasonably suspect that the driver's behavior may be related to drunk driving can they force the driver to undergo a blood alcohol content test. Generally speaking, drivers who refuse to cooperate with testing, such as by tightly closing their car doors or fleeing the scene, often do so because they may have been drinking and driving. Therefore, when faced with abnormal behaviors such as sleeping in the car or refusing to cooperate with testing behind tightly closed doors or windows, the police can reasonably believe that the driver is likely to be driving under the influence of alcohol. The use of forced testing methods, such as breaking windows, can be considered as being based on reasonable suspicion, and the blood alcohol content test results obtained can naturally be considered legal.

Although the legality of mandatory testing can be confirmed under procedural law, there is still great room for improvement in China's system design for dealing with whether mandatory testing methods can be used to investigate drunk driving cases. In the future, when facing the special charge of drunk driving, which relies on identification evidence as the essential element for determining the existence of the crime, and whether or not the crime has been committed, and facing the uniqueness of obtaining evidence, the legality of forced testing and other mandatory means of obtaining evidence should be directly conferred to the police through system design. This will ensure that police evidence collection work proceeds smoothly, while also reasonably assigning citizens the obligation to cooperate with evidence collection in order to better protect their rights.

If a driver applies for a re-examination based on the grounds of forced interception or forced testing in violation of procedural laws, how should it be handled? At this time, "unless there is evidence to prove" "there is an obvious or determined violation of relevant procedures in the sampling procedure", otherwise, "the identification application submitted by the party will not be evaluated one by one like the second instance of the second instance case. It should be based on the judgment of judicial personnel, especially the court, to determine whether there is indeed or may exist a need for identification to be carried out". There is often a certain time interval between re-examination and initial examination, and alcohol in the human body has volatility. Therefore, the accuracy of the initial examination opinion is undoubtedly higher than that of the re-examination opinion. "The limited resources of evidence are the basic laws and starting points of evidence law".[13] To effectively combat drunk driving, we should highly value the hard-won blood alcohol content test identification evidence. Unless the party has clear evidence to prove that there is an obvious violation of procedural laws in the sampling test procedure, a re-examination should generally not be supported. This is also the reason why not all reasons for re-examination applications are supported in judicial practice.

For example, after drinking with friends, *Person A* drove home and happened to pass by a section of road where police were conducting vehicle inspections. *Person A* refused to undergo a breathalyzer test, so the police decided to take a blood sample. *Person A* resisted and assaulted the police officers. The two officers forcibly took *Person A* to the hospital for a blood test, which showed that their blood alcohol level was 87 mg/100 ml. *Person A* refused to admit to drunk driving. In this case, the blood alcohol content test obtained by the police through forced means is objective and legal evidence, which is direct evidence to prove the facts of the case and has relevance to convicting the crime of dangerous driving while intoxicated. Even without *Person A*'s confession or other testimony, or breath alcohol test results, the evidence can still be used to establish the crime. As for *Person A*'s request for re-evaluation, because they only vaguely believe that the evaluation opinion is inaccurate but lack clear reasons, it should not be supported. Of course, if Person A has reasonable grounds to question the previous blood alcohol content test evaluation and meets the conditions for re-evaluation, they can apply for it. How to ensure that the blood sample is consistent with the blood condition during drunk driving? Article 32 of the "Procedural Regulations" only provides an abstract provision on the right to re-evaluate but does not address specific issues related to re-evaluation, such as the number of re-evaluation applications, the deadline for filing, the authority and reasons for filing, and the instruments and institutions used for retesting. In particular, the core issue of preserving and fixing blood evidence samples used in re-evaluation has not been addressed, and neither have other administrative regulations. Regarding this, the author believes that how to preserve blood samples to ensure the accuracy of re-evaluation is not so much a criminal law issue as a medical scientific and technological problem. "Blood sample evidence is a typical 'scientific testing-type' evidence", and "without the support of science and technology, blood samples cannot play their proper evidential role".[14] In short, if a "suspect objects to the evaluation conclusion and applies for re-evaluation, how to ensure that the blood sample does not evaporate, and how to preserve the evidence need to be solved technically".[15] This is also a problem that needs to be further explored in drunk driving cases in the future.

Conclusively, the driving behavior of drivers is a right granted by administrative licensing law, rather than a natural right. It is the duty of drivers to cooperate with the police in their efforts to detect drunk driving for the sake of road traffic safety. In the event that a driver refuses to cooperate, the police have the right to take measures such as forcibly stopping and testing the driver, which are legitimate evidence collection actions carried out by the police in accordance with the Road Traffic Law and procedural regulations. Evidence obtained in this way is neither illegal evidence obtained by means such as violence or threats, as stipulated in Article 54 of the Criminal Procedure Law, nor is it "defective evidence obtained through non-standard evidence collection methods".[16] Therefore, the blood alcohol content obtained through these two methods does not need to be excluded or corrected and can be directly used as evidence for conviction.

8.2.4 Summary

From the perspective of evidence standards, the results of a single breath alcohol content test should not be used as evidence of conviction. Article 6 of the "Drunken Driving Explanation" provides that the results of breath alcohol content tests can be used as evidence of conviction only in cases where the driver avoids blood alcohol content testing. This does not mean that the results of breath alcohol content tests have universal status and value as evidence of conviction in drunken driving cases. From China's current situation, because the subject of breath alcohol content testing does not have a legal qualification as a judicial expert, the accuracy of the testing instruments is also questionable. The accuracy, reliability and authority of the test results cannot be guaranteed. Therefore, the results of breath alcohol content tests can only be used as evidence for the investigation of drunk driving cases rather than as evidence of conviction.[17] In general, only when the results of breath alcohol content tests can be verified with blood alcohol content test results to a certain degree should they be used as evidence of conviction. Therefore, on the one hand, it is necessary to oppose the inappropriate view that "the results of breath alcohol content tests are also applicable to fleeing criminal suspects within a certain range, and the court can use these results to hold them criminally responsible". On the other hand, for single blood alcohol content tests, they should meet the objective and legal requirements to exclude reasonable doubts before they can be used as evidence of conviction. Based on the concept that the right to drive is a special legal permission rather than a natural right, if a driver refuses to cooperate with the testing of blood alcohol content, the police can use necessary coercive measures such as stopping and testing to obtain evidence based on reasonable suspicion, and the legality of such evidence is not in doubt. In cases where there are no results from breath alcohol content tests or blood alcohol content tests, and only circumstantial evidence such as victim statements and witness testimony is available, it cannot be proved that the drunk driving offense has been committed. In such cases, the principle of presumption of innocence should be applied, and the driver should not be prosecuted for a crime.

8.3 Exculpatory role of the defendant's confrontation right in criminal cases

In criminal trials, scientific and specific judicial appraisal evidence plays an increasingly important role in the detection of criminal cases. The modern rule of law is primarily manifested through the justice of the litigation process, and the legitimacy of the judicial appraisal evidence procedure and the reliability of the appraisal evidence directly affect the accuracy of the appraisal conclusions and thereby impact whether procedural justice can be achieved. Judicial appraisal evidence is often generated by instruments composed of hardware and software, such as breathalyzer machines that measure alcohol concentration through exhaled gases, and devices used to create DNA gene maps.[18] According to current law, a suspect can be convicted based on a single piece of evidence alone. Once a suspect is convicted of a serious crime, such as murder or robbery, they may be sentenced to the ultimate punishment of life imprisonment or even the death penalty. Over the past few decades, many studies have revealed an important phenomenon: innocent people have been wrongfully convicted based on a single piece of appraisal evidence. Therefore, it is necessary to pay attention to and research how to avoid the negative impact of the inaccuracy or unreliability of judicial appraisal equipment on the proof effectiveness of appraisal conclusions and how to effectively utilize a single piece of judicial appraisal evidence to support a conviction. China's crime of drunk driving currently only relies on the blood alcohol concentration value of the driver to determine whether or not the crime has been committed, which is a typical conviction based on a single piece of evidence. To ensure the accuracy of the conviction for drunk driving crimes, it is necessary to try to ensure the accuracy of the judicial appraisal conclusion of blood alcohol concentration value. Therefore, this article attempts to construct the defendant's confrontation right with the appraiser in drunk driving crimes, to counter the possibility of wrongful conviction by state authorities and ensure the equality of the positions of the prosecution and defense, ultimately achieving the human rights protection function of criminal law.

8.3.1 Lack of confrontation right: The distorted use of forensic evidence in drunk driving cases in China

Confrontation right refers to the right of the defendant and witness to challenge the unfavorable testimony against themselves face-to-face. It is a judicial system that has long existed in England, America and Europe. Its purpose is to prevent the abuse of state power, achieve judicial fairness through procedural justice and ultimately ensure the human rights of the accused. However, with the emergence of new types of crimes such as drunk driving, forensic evidence is widely used as evidence of conviction in criminal cases. Whether criminal defendants can enjoy the confrontation right in the same way as in cases not convicted based on forensic evidence has become a problem of concern for both criminal procedural law and substantive law. However, in China's current legislation and judicial situation, due to the serious lack of confrontation rights, the inaccuracy and unscientific nature of forensic evidence and the distorted use of forensic evidence in drunk driving cases, China must rethink the rules for the use of forensic evidence in such cases.

Since the inclusion of drunk driving in the regulation of the crime of dangerous driving in the "Amendment (8)", a large number of drunk driving cases have entered the criminal judicial process. The Criminal Law clearly establishes "drunk driving of a motor vehicle" as a constituent element of the offense, but the substantive issue of whether the defendant belongs to "drunk driving" ultimately depends on the procedural determination. "The result of blood alcohol content examination has almost become the only and 'sufficient' basis for judging whether a driver is driving under the influence of alcohol". In judicial practice, the forensic report of blood samples has therefore become unshakable core evidence. The author randomly collected 50 judgments of cases accused of dangerous driving due to

Table 8.1 Frequency of Use of Prosecution Evidence

Type of Evidence	*Frequency of Use by Prosecution*
Forensic report on blood sample	50 times
Witness testimony	36 times
Defendant confession	24 times
Breathalyzer test result	12 times
Victim statement	8 times

drunk driving, which came from Henan Province (30 judgments), Chongqing City (11 judgments), Shaanxi Province (3 judgments), Hunan Province (3 judgments), Hubei Province (1 judgment), Fujian Province (1 judgment) and Guangxi Autonomous Region (1 judgment).

A statistical analysis of the 50 judgments mentioned above revealed that in cases of drunk driving, the most commonly used evidence by the prosecution includes forensic reports on blood samples, witness testimony, defendant confessions, breathalyzer test results and victim statements. The frequency of the use of these types of evidence in these 50 judgments is shown in Table 8.1.

In addition, it was found that all of the 50 judgments mentioned the statement "the defendant did not object to the facts charged (acknowledged the facts) and the evidence submitted by the prosecutor during the court hearing". In other words, in all 50 cases of drunk driving, the defendant and their defense counsel did not only plead guilty but only pleaded for leniency in sentencing. The specific frequency of defense reasons is shown in Table 8.2.

From the above table, it can be seen that the defense arguments made by the defendants and their lawyers are all related to sentencing, and there was no defense for innocence. Therefore, in the randomly selected cases of drunk driving, the defendants were all found guilty. However, the defense on sentencing by the defendants and their lawyers had a good legal effect. In these 50 cases, although the court made guilty verdicts, six different sentencing judgments were made: lenient punishment, lenient punishment with probation, probation, exemption from criminal punishment, no clear expression of leniency or probation (generally expressed as a comprehensive judgment based on the defendant's criminal nature,

Table 8.2 Defense Situations of Defendants and Their Defense Lawyers

Defense Reasons	*Frequency of Use by Defendants and Their Defense Lawyers*
Voluntarily confess guilt and have a good attitude toward confession	44 times
Proactively pay fines and show remorseful behavior	15 times
Actively compensate for the losses of victims	15 times
First-time offender	5 times
The criminal circumstances are relatively light	Twice
The criminal circumstances are minor	Twice

Table 8.3 Court Judgments

Sentencing Decision	*Frequency of Use by Courts*
Lenient punishment	35 times
Lenient punishment with probation	7 times
Probation	Twice
Exemption from criminal punishment	Twice
No explicit indication of leniency or probationary circumstances	3 times
Explicit indication of no leniency or probationary circumstances	Once

circumstances and confession attitude after being arrested) and a clear indication of no leniency or probation. This is shown in Table 8.3.

In summary, in cases of drunk driving, once the prosecution presents the forensic identification report of the defendant's blood sample, the defendant will inevitably be convicted of dangerous driving, with no room for any defense of innocence. It is generally believed that "the current model of integrated conviction and sentencing in litigation" has made the issue of conviction the main procedural and central issue in criminal proceedings, "while the defendant and defense counsel have insufficient participation in the court's sentencing decision-making process and limited influence". However, in cases of drunk driving, the so-called defense has evolved into a "dominant" sentencing defense. As is well known, the right to defense occupies an extremely important position in criminal proceedings, and in a sense, "the history of the evolution of criminal proceedings can also be said to be the history of the development of the right to defense".[19] "The right to defense is an important component of human rights in criminal proceedings, and the protection of the right to defense of the accused is the core and key of the human rights protection system in criminal proceedings". Article 35 of China's Criminal Procedure Law stipulates that "the responsibility of defense counsel is to present materials and opinions proving the innocence, lightness, or mitigation of the criminal suspect or defendant, or to exempt them from criminal responsibility based on facts and laws, and to safeguard the legitimate rights and interests of the criminal suspect or defendant". Any defense in a criminal proceeding necessarily includes defense of innocence and defense of sentencing, and defense of innocence, compared with defense of sentencing, is particularly important because it directly concerns whether the accused's behavior constitutes a crime and whether the right to life and personal liberty will be deprived in the case at hand. Regardless of the probability of success in defending innocence, as long as there is a possibility of successful defense, the defendant can be considered to enjoy complete defense rights. The two defenses of innocence and sentencing are indispensable, and without either defense, the right to defense becomes incomplete, especially the defense of innocence.

It is not difficult to see from the foregoing that some scholars believe that in some cases, defense lawyers do not raise any objections or arguments against the criminal facts and charges because the typical defense of innocence has lost its space due to the defendant's voluntary confession, and the main duty of the lawyer has turned to sentencing defense.[20] The reason for the loss of the defense of innocence is that the forensic identification report of blood samples, as the only basis for determining whether the defendant is guilty or not, is excessively trusted and relied upon by legislators, prosecutors and judges, resulting in the distorted status of the forensic identification report in the entire litigation process. It should be emphasized that although relevant laws and regulations stipulate that forensic experts should testify in court and be questioned, in 50 cases, the number of times that forensic experts appeared in court was zero. Similarly, although relevant laws and judicial interpretations provide for the defendant and their defense counsel to have the right to apply for re-identification, in these 50 cases where the forensic identification evidence of blood samples is so important for conviction, the number of times the defendant and their defense counsel applied for re-identification was actually zero. The reason is that forensic experts have no mandatory obligation to accept cross-examination, which makes it difficult for defendants and their defense lawyers to question the process of producing forensic identification reports of blood samples, including whether the equipment for producing forensic identification evidence is qualified, whether the forensic identification procedure meets the standards, and whether the forensic identification evidence is valid and accurate. Therefore, the application for re-identification is relatively difficult and ineffective. It can be said that defendants and their defense lawyers can only passively accept the "arbitrary disposal" of forensic identification reports without the forensic expert appearing in court for cross-examination.

8.3.2 Introduction of the right to cross-examination: Using application system and remote two-way video technology to implement cross-examination of drunk driving experts

8.3.2.1 Introduction of the right to cross-examination in China's criminal procedural law

As mentioned earlier, in drunk driving cases in China, the court excessively relies on forensic evidence. However, in the case of the accuracy of forensic evidence being questioned, China's legislative, judicial and academic institutions should not turn a deaf ear but should establish the right to cross-examination to construct an adversarial criminal proceeding. This can prevent the defendant from being harmed by anonymous accusers. From the perspective of discovering the truth, the significance of the right to cross-examination lies in ensuring that witnesses provide sworn testimony, preventing witnesses from committing perjury, compelling witnesses to accept cross-examination, providing the jury with an opportunity to observe the witness' words and actions etc. This is the largest legal engine invented to discover the truth. In addition, ensuring the right to cross-examination also helps "prevent the abuse of government power" and "enhance public trust in the case judgment, the judgment-making process, and the law".

Although the right to confront witnesses plays an extremely important role in ensuring the fairness of litigation and protecting the legitimate rights and interests of criminal defendants, witness attendance rates in criminal proceedings in China are extremely low. According to data from the Supreme People's Court's comprehensive statistics, "the witness attendance rate in first-instance criminal cases nationwide is no more than 10%, and in second-instance criminal cases, it is no more than 5%". Statistics from the Ningxia Higher People's Court show that "from 2002 to 2007, the witness attendance rates in first-instance criminal cases were 11.24%, 3.15%, 6.7%, 5.68%, 5.07%, and 5.57%, respectively. In criminal trials, witness attendance rates have shown a downward trend year by year, with an average annual witness attendance rate of only 5%. But even with such a low rate, it is still higher than the national average". In a rule of law country where using legal means to compel witness attendance and giving criminal defendants the right to confront witnesses is already widespread, Chinese law neither specifies the circumstances under which witnesses must appear nor grants criminal defendants the right to confront witnesses who are unfavorable to them in court. Whether witnesses appear and whether defendants have the opportunity to confront witnesses is entirely at the discretion of judges and prosecutors in charge of charging crimes.[21] All of these indicate that the right of criminal defendants to cross-examine witnesses is "illusory" in China.

Criminal trials without the right to confront witnesses can lead to many adverse consequences, such as increasing the likelihood of wrongful convictions due to the defendant's inability to confront witnesses when they do not appear in court; being unfavorable to the accuracy of convicting and sentencing criminal defendants; and causing serious damage to procedural fairness, leading to court judgments being based solely on substantive truth rather than procedural fairness.[22]

Therefore, many scholars in China have suggested that the system of confrontation rights should be established in the procedural law of our country. Some scholars believe that the system of confrontation rights can be established and improved by "establishing the system of confrontation rights through legislative interpretation or judicial interpretation and setting up corresponding guarantee mechanisms". Specifically, this includes "setting up a pre-trial evidence disclosure system, which requires both the prosecution and defense to submit a list of relevant evidence, witness names, and the content of their intended testimony to the court before the trial, so that both sides can cross-examine each other's evidence and decide whether to request that the other party's witness appear in court. Establishing a mechanism for compulsory subpoenaing of witnesses and a punishment mechanism for witnesses who refuse to testify. Establishing an invalidation system for trials that violate the right of confrontation, i.e., trials that violate the right of confrontation should be declared invalid".[23] Other scholars believe that in China's criminal procedural concept and culture, it is necessary to first establish the concept of "confrontation rights" and "give the right of confrontation a certain attribute". On the basis of "establishing the concept and system of confrontation rights",[24] this will promote and guarantee the appearance of witnesses. Some scholars also believe that it is necessary to first establish a "multilevel system of confrontation rights for criminal defendants" and to make the exercise of confrontation rights by defendants in criminal cases with disputed basic facts as the trigger condition. Secondly, "establish a criminal procedural diversion mechanism" to ensure the confrontation rights of defendants in major and difficult cases.[25]

The above-mentioned scholars intend to realize the right of confrontation in China's criminal proceedings through the construction of concepts and specific institutional measures. However, these proposals have limitations, which are reflected in their only solving the problem of witnesses (mainly unfavorable witnesses) accepting confrontation, without addressing whether other key entities in evidence, especially judicial appraisers, need to be cross-examined, and whether confrontation rights necessarily require appearance in court for cross-examination.

8.3.2.2 The inclusion of expert appraisers in the category of cross-examined parties and the analysis of their acceptance of cross-examination in court

The above measures for setting and strictly enforcing the right of cross-examination are reasonable and feasible for ordinary witnesses. However, it is difficult to implement for judicial expert appraisers. Firstly, according to the Criminal Procedure Law of China, judicial expert appraisers do not belong to the category of witnesses. If the only constraint of the right of cross-examination is understood as witnesses, then the defendant in cases involving judicial expert evidence, especially in cases of drunk driving, cannot apply for expert appraisers to accept cross-examination. Therefore, it is necessary to explore whether judicial expert appraisers need to accept cross-examination. Secondly, if expert appraisers are included in the objects constrained by the right of cross-examination, that is, if all expert appraisers must accept cross-examination, then whether it is feasible for expert appraisers to appear in court and accept cross-examination in cases of high incidence of drunk driving and overly dependent on expert evidence becomes a question.

As mentioned earlier, although China currently has relevant laws and regulations that provide for the system of expert appraisers testifying in court, the chances of expert appraisers appearing in court in judicial practice are extremely low. According to incomplete statistics, "in criminal trials before 2000, the average appearance rate of expert appraisers was less than 5%". According to relevant departments, "in 2003, a total of 2,153 cases involving judicial appraisal were heard in the high and intermediate courts of Jilin Province, and only 17 cases had expert appraisers appearing in court for cross-examination, with an appearance rate of only 0.8%". "In 2008, taking Suzhou City, Jiangsu Province as an example, among the cases heard in the two levels of courts in Suzhou City, the judicial appraisal department entrusted 6,009 appraisals, and the 'three major categories' of forensic, physical evidence, and audiovisual data appraisals were 2,831, accounting for 47%. Among them, there were 5,480 cases in which the parties applied for appraisal, and 529 cases in which the court appraised according to its own jurisdiction. Among them, 86 cases required notification of appraisers to appear in court, and only 33 actually appeared in court. It can be said that the vast majority of expert appraisers do not appear in court".

In judicial practice, forensic evidence has the reputation of being the "king of evidence" and plays a crucial role in criminal proceedings. Generally speaking, forensic experts are required to appear in court to participate in cross-examination, and their legal, scientific and reliability issues related to their forensic conclusions are subject to questioning by the accused, prosecutors and judges. This not only fulfills the legal obligation of the forensic experts but also meets the needs and necessary requirements of achieving procedural justice in criminal trials and ensuring the fairness of trial outcomes. Specifically, "from a scientific perspective, the materials and information relied upon in forensic activities are limited, and the time available to make judgments is also restricted. It is impossible to reach absolutely objective conclusions like scientific research".[26] The inherent defects in forensic activities themselves may make it difficult for judges or parties to discover errors in the contents of documents. "In China, the inability to correct forensic errors due to the failure of forensic experts to appear in court to testify has become one of the main causes of wrongful convictions".[27] Only by requiring forensic experts to appear in court for cross-examination can the defects and errors that may exist in the forensic process be discovered. Moreover, "from a legal perspective, requiring forensic experts to appear in court for cross-examination is not only a legal obligation that forensic experts should fulfill but also a necessity for parties to exercise their right to equal litigation and for judges to review forensic opinions".[28] Due to the inherent defects in forensic evidence itself and the requirement of procedural justice, the right to cross-examine should include forensic experts, rather than only being a right of the adverse party.

In general cases, the demand for forensic appraisal reports is low and reliance on forensic evidence is not unique, so requiring forensic experts to appear in court for cross-examination will not overly pressure the prosecutor's office, forensic experts and appraisal units. However, in cases such as drunk driving, where there is a large volume of cases, according to information provided by the Traffic Management Bureau of the Ministry of Public Security, during the seven months of the implementation of the "Amendment (8)" and the revised "Road Traffic Safety Law", public security organs nationwide investigated 33,183 cases of drunk driving, and 19,836 cases have been investigated and transferred to people's procuratorates for examination and prosecution. Based on this conservative estimate, more than 34,000 cases of drunk driving are expected to be prosecuted within a year. As mentioned earlier, the dependence on forensic evidence in drunk driving cases is disproportionately high, coupled with the constraints on the number of forensic experts and work requirements, making it difficult for forensic experts to appear in court for cross-examination. If forensic experts were blindly required to appear in court for cross-examination for every drunk driving case, the prosecuting authority and forensic appraisal institutions would face great financial and time pressures.

In China, requiring forensic experts to appear in court for cross-examination will also create similar financial and time pressures. Especially in "some remote areas, when the court commissions authoritative appraisal institutions in provincial capital cities or even large cities such as Beijing and Shanghai to conduct appraisals, the likelihood of experts appearing in court is low due to the long and expensive travel. Moreover, the lack of unified legal provisions on the reasonable cost of experts appearing in court seriously affects their enthusiasm to do so".

Therefore, it is difficult to require all forensic experts to appear in court for cross-examination in cases of drunk driving due to many obstacles that cannot be objectively regulated by legislation.

8.3.2.3 Feasible path for the defendant in drunk driving cases to cross-examine the expert witness

Since forensic experts need to be cross-examined by the defendant, and in cases of drunk driving, the status of forensic evidence is crucial. Failure to cross-examine the expert witness may lead to a wrong judgment. However, it is not possible to require the expert witness to appear in court for cross-examination in every case of drunk driving.

1 Application system for the defendant to request the appearance of the expert witness in court for cross-examination

Not all defendants and their lawyers question the accuracy of forensic reports. Therefore, many defendants may give up their right to require the expert witness to appear in court after receiving the notification from the prosecuting authority that forensic evidence will be used against them. This not only does not violate the defendant's right to cross-examination but also does not waste judicial resources. In China, many drunk driving cases indeed occur after the driver has consumed a large amount of alcohol, such as driving a vehicle after drinking a whole bottle of 500-ml Chinese liquor with an alcohol content of over 50% and then being arrested by the police for drunk driving, finally being confirmed by forensic examination. If the defendant is allowed to request the appearance of the expert witness in court for cross-examination without any restrictions, it will undoubtedly waste judicial resources. Therefore, when the defendant submits an application to the court, they must state their reasonable doubt about the facts determined by the forensic report. Reasonable doubts include providing relevant testimony or physical evidence to prove that they have not consumed any alcohol or the amount of alcohol consumed is insufficient to exceed the legal limit of blood alcohol concentration etc. Only then can the defendant apply for the expert witness to appear in court for cross-examination. In addition, the defendant must bear the necessary expenses for the expert witness to appear in court for cross-examination. This can alleviate the financial pressure of requesting the expert witness to appear in court for cross-examination. If the defendant indeed consumed a large amount of alcohol and drove, and has no objection to their drunk driving behavior, and needed to bear the expert witness' transportation, food, lodging and compensation for loss of work, they will make a rational choice and not apply for the expert witness to appear in court without any concerns, thus avoiding wasting judicial resources and relieving the many pressures caused by the expert witness appearing in court.

2 Use remote two-way video technology if possible.

Even though an application system can filter out some unnecessary experts who needn't appear in court, due to the large number of drunk driving cases, solely relying on the application system cannot completely alleviate the pressure on experts to appear in court for cross-examination. It is necessary to combine the corresponding technology: remote two-way video technology, to achieve the dual goals of protecting the defendant's right to cross-examination and reducing the pressure on the judicial organs.

Remote two-way video technology reduces the backlog of cases requiring judicial expertise, and the judicial expertise laboratories using this technology have noticed that their ability to provide valuable scientific analysis for the criminal justice system is increasing. These judicial laboratories operate more efficiently, and precious time is not wasted on the road, which means that time can be spent on other important identification work in the laboratory for investigation.

Testifying through two-way video technology is no different from physical appearance in court. This technology does not have an adverse effect on the evidence, and encouraging its implementation is beneficial to both the prosecution and the defendant.

Using remote two-way video technology can satisfy the two key requirements of cross-examination: "face-to-face" and "questioning". Although this face-to-face is not physically close, it is achieved through remote two-way video technology, allowing the defendant, defense counsel, prosecutor and judge to clearly see and hear the words and actions of the judicial experts in the judicial laboratory, creating a sense of closeness. But through a clear visual and audio transmission system, the participants in these courtroom activities can achieve the same questioning effect as the expert's appearance in court.

By using remote bidirectional video technology, the defendants and their defense lawyers can question the expert witnesses about whether they have received the necessary professional training, possessed the professional knowledge required for the appraisal and held the professional qualifications required for engaging in the forensic appraisal business. They can also question the reliability and maturity of the scientific principles and technical methods on which the appraisal conclusion is based. Additionally, they can inquire about whether the appraiser followed the correct experimental steps, whether the reagents were effective, whether the technical equipment was precise and advanced, and a series of other issues related to the accuracy and reliability of the forensic evidence. At the same time, the judge can observe the confrontation process between the defendant and the appraiser and remotely question the appraiser regarding relevant doubts. Ultimately, the judge can make a decision on whether to adopt the forensic appraisal report.

Therefore, China's relevant procedural regulations and judicial interpretations can stipulate that remote bidirectional video technology be used by courts and forensic appraisal institutions in areas where conditions permit. In drunk driving cases, the defendant can choose or request the appraiser to appear in court for confrontation or apply for remote bidirectional video technology for courtroom confrontation. If the appraiser has a reasonable excuse for not appearing in person, then only remote video technology can be used for confrontation.

8.3.3 Summary

Given that in the legislation and judiciary of drunk driving cases in China, the conviction issue overly relies on the forensic evidence of blood alcohol concentration, and the chance of forensic experts appearing in court for cross-examination is almost zero. The defendants and their defense lawyers are unable to question the potentially flawed forensic evidence, thus falling into the dilemma of zero "not guilty" defense, depriving the defendants of their right to a complete defense and ultimately leading to wrongful convictions. The crux of the problem lies in the lack of a cross-examination system in China's Criminal Procedure Law. Taking inspiration from the legislative experience of the United States, establishing a cross-examination system in China and incorporating forensic experts into the regulation of the cross-examination system can solve the problem of cross-examination between the defendants and forensic experts in the absence of enough forensic experts. In drunk driving cases, adopting an application system and remote two-way video technology in the court system and forensic laboratory system in eligible areas not only solves the cross-examination problem between the defendant and forensic expert in the shortage of forensic experts but also solves the problem of witness testimony infringement of the defendant's cross-examination right in other situations. In drunk driving cases, since the forensic report plays an important role in the conviction and sentencing of the defendant, adopting the application system and remote two-way video technology can prompt the defendants and their defense lawyers to question forensic experts during the trial, facilitating the timely discovery and questioning of flaws and issues in the forensic process, and subsequently engaging in not guilty or sentencing defense, which can guarantee the legal rights of the defendant in form and substance and enable justice to be truly realized in a visible manner.

8.4 Conclusion

The determination of the criminal entity element in combination with the characteristics of the forensic identification results should go beyond the Criminal Code and take into account the relevant theories of criminal procedural law on the standards of criminal evidence proof. Based on how to judge the probative force of evidence, relevant rules of evidence should be established to strictly control the conviction standard. The nature of the drunk driving offense, as a type of offense similar to foreign traffic violations, determines that the offense should not be established based on Article 13 of the Criminal Code. Depending on the strength of the evidence in drunk driving cases, the following rules of evidence can be established: the results of a single breathalyzer test can only be used as the basis for initiating a drunk driving investigation and cannot be used as evidence in a conviction; the results of a blood alcohol test can be used as evidence in a conviction and do not violate the principle of single evidence being insufficient in criminal proceedings, but its objectivity and legality must be established by excluding reasonable doubts; and in the absence of either breathalyzer or blood alcohol test results, the crime of drunk driving cannot be determined based on circumstantial evidence alone. By attempting to establish rules of evidence in drunk driving cases, the reliance on the breathalyzer test results alone in judicial interpretations of drunk driving offenses is critically reviewed. The theoretical and practical dangers of relying solely on breathalyzer test results or other circumstantial evidence in convictions are highlighted, and the need to strictly adhere to the evidentiary standards for drunk driving offenses is emphasized in order to fully realize the human rights protection function of criminal law.

Regarding blood alcohol test results, on the one hand, the probative force of such evidence can only be established after reasonable doubts have been excluded. If the principles of necessity, neutrality and expertise in obtaining the identification evidence are followed in the formation of the blood alcohol test result, and there are no doubts that cannot be excluded, its objectivity can be proven. Based on the concept that driving is a special right granted by law rather than a natural right, if a driver refuses to cooperate with a blood alcohol test, the police can use necessary coercive measures such as forced interception and testing based on reasonable suspicion. The legality of evidence obtained through such measures is not in doubt. When the objectivity and legality of blood alcohol test results are in doubt, according to the presumption of innocence principle in the Criminal Procedure Law, the driver should not be prosecuted for a crime. On the other hand, the United States maintains a cautious and skeptical attitude toward forensic identification evidence for drunk driving cases. The legal theory community is concerned about the lack of system safety standards for forensic identification equipment, and the National Academy of Sciences has questioned the accuracy of forensic identification evidence. Therefore, the Federal Supreme Court has given defendants the right to confront forensic experts during legal proceedings. In China, the drunk driving offense determination process should introduce the right to confrontation in a timely manner, include the forensic expert in the scope of the right to confrontation and use application systems and remote two-way video technology to ensure the operability of the right to confrontation. This will ensure the accuracy of convictions in drunk driving cases, protect the defendant's right to a substantive and complete defense and ultimately protect the human rights of defendants.

Notes

1 Liu Yanhong: Evaluation and Reflection on the Current Criminal Status, *Legal Research*, 2013(1).
2 Chen Ruihua: *Criminal Evidence Law*, Peking University Press, 2012 edition, p. 115.
3 Leonard Stamm, *The Top 20 Myths of Breath, Blood, and Urine Tests*, 29 Champion 44, 45–46 (2005).
4 Shan Sijing, Wang Pengfei: "Eating Egg Yolk Pie Will You Drive Drunk? Blood test shall prevail!", *East Asia Economic and Trade News*, July 15, 2012, third edition.
5 See Chen Lixin: Drunk Driving, *Legal Daily*, 8th edition on January 13, 2013.

6 See Zhang Biao: Is it Difficult for 'Bao Qingtian', *Southern Weekend*, May 16, 2013, Edition A1.
7 Chen Ruihua: On the Rules of Mutual Confirmation of Evidence, *Law and Business Research*, 2012(1).
8 Wang Fengxiang: On the Standard of Proof for 'Excluding Reasonable Doubt', *Prosecution Daily*, May 3, 2013, 3rd Edition.
9 Lin Yuxiong: *Strict Proof and Criminal Evidence*, Law Press, 2008, p.167.
10 Ibid.
11 People v. Rosenheimer 102 N.E. 530, 532 (N.Y. 1913).
12 Standish v. Dep't. of Revenue, 683 P.2d 1276, 1281 (Kan. 1984).
13 Long Zongzhi: Research on Several Issues of the Norms and Implementation of Two Evidence Regulations, *Chinese Law*, 2010(6).
14 Wang Zhigang: On the Characteristics of Blood Sample Evidence and the Improvement of Judicial Procedures for Collection, *Politics and Law*, 2012(3).
15 You Chunliang, Cheng Hailong: Shenzhen's Handling of Drunk Driving Cases Faces Multiple Legal Challenges Half a Year Later, *Legal Daily* December 6, 2011, 4th edition.
16 Chen Ruihua: *Criminal Evidence*, Peking University Press, 2012 edition, p.88.
17 See Liu Yanhong: Research on Criminal Evidence Rules for Drunk Driving Dangerous Driving Crimes, *Legal Science*, 2014(2).
18 William C. *Thompson et al, Evaluating Forensic DNA Evidence: Essential Elements of a Competent Defense Review*: Part 1, 27 Champion 16–18 (2003).
19 Haruo Nishihara: *The Formation and Characteristics of Japanese Criminal Law*, Law Press China, Chengwen Bookstore 1997 edition, p. 432.
20 Mou Lvye: On the Relationship between Defense of Innocence and Sentencing Defense, *Contemporary Law Review*, 2012(1).
21 See Yi Yanyou: *Criminal Procedure in China and Chinese Society* (Beijing: Peking University Press, 2010), pp. 168–172.
22 Yi Yanyou: *Witness Appearance and Safeguarding the Right of Criminal Defendants to Confront Witnesses, China Social Sciences*, 2010(2).
23 Yi Yanyou: Guaranteeing the Appearance of Witnesses and the Right of Confrontation for Criminal Defendants, *Chinese Social Sciences*, 2010(2).
24 Long Zongzhi: On the System of Criminal Confrontation and Its Reform and Improvement, *Law Review*, 2008(5).
25 Guo Tianwu: On the Confrontation Rights of Criminal Defendants in China, *Politics and Law*, 2010(7).
26 Du Zhichun and Liao Genwei: On the Improvement of the System of Forensic Expert Appearance in Chinese Courts, *Law Journal*, 2011(7).
27 Chen Ruihua: *Frontier Issues in Criminal Procedure*, Renmin University of China Press, 2000 edition, p. 562.
28 Du Zhichun and Liao Genwei: On the Improvement of the System of Forensic Expert Appearance in Chinese Courts, *Law Journal*, 2011(7).

9 Judicial Conscience

The Path to Substantive Decriminalization beyond Legal Norms

[Basic Facts of the "Zhao Chunhua Case"] Between August and October 12, 2016, Zhao Chunhua conducted a profitable activity by setting up a shooting booth in a park, which was handed over to him by an old man. There were nine gun-shaped objects in Zhao Chunhua's booth, and she used plastic bullets to shoot balloons. The judgment showed that the public security organs captured Zhao Chunhua during patrol and seized nine gun-shaped objects, related gun parts and plastic bullets on the spot. According to appraisal, six of the nine gun-shaped objects could fire normally and were powered by compressed gas. On December 27, Zhao Chunhua was sentenced to three years and six months in prison for illegally possessing firearms in the first instance. With the announcement of the case, the defendant Zhao Chunhua received widespread sympathy from all walks of life, and many questions were raised about China's criminal justice system. However, so far, the voices have shown that scholars usually use the doctrine of law to analyze and criticize this judgment or continuously explain that "toy guns are not guns" using technical indicators. Little do they know that for someone lacking common sense, all the sophisticated theories seem unnecessary. Constantly entangling with the technical standards of how to identify firearms and exploring in-depth explanations of why toy guns are not firearms only seem like monk-like prattle and repetition. This approach will only exacerbate the bias that "lawyers are technicians", making legal professionals and the legal profession stray further away from the values of fairness, justice, goodness and morality inherent in the law. It is imperative to deliberate on the legal, judicial system and judicial ethics issues raised by this case in order to prevent similar judgments from happening again in the future.

9.1 Judicial conscience beyond the norms of criminal law is needed for justice within the norms

The "Zhao Chunhua Case" is one of the increasing number of cases in China in recent years in which people have been sentenced for using toy guns. Compared with similar cases, the defendant in this case had a pure motive (making a living rather than indulging in play), restrained behavior (only for business purposes and not for personal use), a short period of time (only two months of operation) and belonged to the disadvantaged group (a 51-year-old woman). Therefore, once the judgment

DOI: 10.4324/9781003456773-10

was announced, the public immediately voiced a unanimous opinion that the "Zhao Chunhua Case" should be not guilty and that the court's judgment was wrong. The opposition between judicial and public positions reflected a fundamental question: Did the judgment in this case effectively achieve judicial justice? Why do the people overwhelmingly advocate a not-guilty verdict?

Judicial conscience is the bridge to realizing judicial justice, and justice should be guarded by judicial conscience. The limitations and verbal ambiguity of criminal norms are contradictory with the realization of individual case fairness by the judge. Judicial conscience can precisely reconcile these contradictions and maximally achieve the fairness of individual case and judicial justice. Therefore, "judicial conscience is a necessary professional quality for judges and an inexhaustible source of the rule of law and justice". There is currently a widespread skepticism about judicial fairness, which stems from the unfair judgments in some judicial cases. Although factors such as legal interpretation and application, evidence collection and analysis may influence these judgments, the lack of judicial conscience is also an extremely important factor. Conscience is an essential personal quality unique to humans and an inherent basic attribute of being human. Conscience mainly concerns obligations and responsibilities, and moreover, basic obligations and responsibilities.[1] With regard to judicial conscience, it refers to the legal professional conscience possessed by judges as the subject of the judiciary, which is established on the basis of a deep understanding of secular human nature and a profound insight into human nature. It is a rational judgment of right and wrong, reflecting the judge's judicial philosophy, pursuit of justice, professional ethics, sense of responsibility and humanistic sentiments, which are formed based on a recognition and understanding of the legitimacy and legality of legal rules, as well as self-reflection on their legal life.

Wang Yangming was one of the earlier Chinese scholars to explicitly define the qualities of a person with conscience. He pointed out, "Conscience is the essence of the heart, the so-called constant illumination. The essence of the heart has no starting or ending".[2] Conscience is the most fundamental quality of the human heart. Everyone has conscience, but sometimes people are not aware of it. This means that the formation of a judicial judgment requires questioning the judge's conscience; when the judge's conscience is obscured, a judgment without conscience results. How is judicial conscience formed? Conscience is also known as the "dedication to conscience", in other words, knowing well, and knowing what is good. Judicial conscience comes from grasping the spirit of the law and understanding and applying the law from the perspective of life experience. Judicial conscience stems from grasping the spirit of the law. Under the stable rules of law, making judgments that conform to the basic spirit of social life experience is the embodiment of judicial conscience. If judicial conscience is extinguished and technical skills are prioritized, judicial justice will also cease to exist.

The judge's conscience directly affects the realization of judicial conscience, "judicial judgments are filtered through the judge's conscience". In this regard, whether the judge's conscience exists or not, its level directly determines the effectiveness of judicial conscience. However, the judge's conscience should not be the goal of judicial conscience, which can only be the means of achieving judicial conscience. The ultimate goal of judicial conscience is to achieve judicial justice. In the current era dominated by instrumental rationality, where "most of society has given up thinking about justice and turned to focus on the debate strategy in court, the professional and daily lives of legal professionals", emphasizing that "judicial conscience is more important than judicial skills" is undoubtedly more urgent, and it is also necessary to consider the role of judicial conscience in achieving judicial justice from the perspective of value rationality. If the judiciary does not uphold conscience and repeatedly makes unjust judgments, it means the gradual loss of the judiciary's reputation and the gradual decline of judicial justice. The public's questioning of individual case judgments will escalate to the questioning of the professional and moral conscience of judicial personnel, and ultimately, the entire society will doubt the fairness of the judiciary. The justice required by the rule of law can only be aligned with the justice sought by judges through judicial conscience. The result of this balance means the realization of true judicial justice.

The bottom line of criminal law is also the bottom line of judicial justice. Upholding the bottom line of criminal law is necessary to achieve judicial justice. The bottom line of criminal law is the principle of *nulla poena sine lege*, which solves the problem of how to limit punishment through the characteristic of criminal law. Therefore, the determination of criminal offenses is not verbal match of the simple and technical elements of the offense, but a process of implementing the idea of "how to limit punishment" to effectively and accurately combat crime. This is also the purpose of criminal law. Criminal law is a restrictive law that limits the state's power to infringe on individual rights, rather than encouraging the expansion of state power to combat crime. In fact, the absence of criminal law is most conducive to combating crime. Therefore, to uphold the bottom line of criminal law, we must adhere to the principle of *nulla poena sine lege*; to adhere to the principle of *nulla poena sine lege*, we must adhere to the standard of "punishment is deserved for all kinds of crimes". This is also the reason why the concept of "criminal punishment" has evolved into "criminal punishability" in criminal law theory.

Only by adhering to judicial conscience and upholding the bottom line of criminal law can judicial justice be achieved. Judicial conscience represents the path of achieving justice beyond legal norms, while the bottom line of criminal law represents the path of achieving justice within legal norms. These two paths work together from outside and inside legal norms to achieve judicial justice. Therefore, judicial conscience and the bottom line of criminal law intersect on the path to achieving judicial justice.

9.2 Direct impact of judicial conscience on the realization of judicial justice in individual cases

How does judicial conscience affect the realization of judicial justice in individual cases? How does it permeate the judicial process and influence the justice or injustice of judicial rulings? The "Zhao Chunhua case" provides a good sample for analysis. As a woman who made a living by selling inflated balloons, Zhao used a toy gun and plastic bullets, which were identified by the Tianjin Public Security Bureau's physical evidence appraisal center as six guns that could shoot normally and were powered by compressed gas. However, can Zhao Chunhua be convicted of illegal possession of firearms based solely on this? The answer is no. The guilty verdict in the "Zhao Chunhua case" indicates that the judge not only lacks an understanding of Chinese social experience but also lacks insight into Chinese secular sentiments and human nature. Moreover, the judge lacks the virtue of compassion for the poor and the weak, which leads to such a judgment lacking judicial conscience.

The "balloon-stall shooting case" violates people's understanding of the "common sense, human nature, and common logic" and their judgment of things. Judicial conscience is based on the judge's understanding of "common sense, human nature, and common logic" in social life, including his or her comprehension of social experience and general moral concepts.[3] Professor Chen Zhonglin, who proposed the "common sense, human nature, and common logic" concept, has long held that modern rule of law ultimately relies on the governance of human nature and conscience, and that "common sense, human nature, and common logic" are the soul of modern rule of law.[4] The academic community has mixed views of the "common sense, human nature, and common logic" rule, but it cannot be denied that, like any truth that always has an impure side, any viewpoint that is questioned must have its truthful side. This is also why the "common sense, human nature, and common logic" rule of law concept can become an important content of "judicial conscience" summarized by Professor He Qinhua. At the same time, various astonishing events continue to occur in our society, including various cases and verdicts that violate common sense, are unreasonable and illogical and become important factors that people do not trust in the judiciary. For example, Inner Mongolian farmer Wang Lijun made a living by selling corn but was convicted of illegal business operations by the court.[5] The judge seems to be unaware of the basic provisions of Article 225 of the Criminal Law and treats it same as selling rice and corn and clothes on Taobao (lack of common sense); ignores the norms of the law and lacks a basic understanding of the general buying and selling of goods in the market economy (lack of common logic); interpreted corn as a commodity that is not allowed or regulated by the state and classified the normal purchase, processing, and sale of corn by farmers to make a living as illegal business operations (lack of human nature), ultimately charging an innocent person with a crime in the name of the law. In this way, all buying and selling behaviors can be classified as illegal business operations in society.

The same is true for the "selling balloons and shooting balloons" case. Although the toy guns sold by the vendor met the national standard and the requirement for firearms in the "Firearms Identification Regulations" of more than 1.8 J/cm^2, this regulation obviously violates the fundamental common sense that people have about firearms as weapons with lethal power. Moreover, whether it is a toy gun or a replica gun, as long as the actor is not aiming to commit a crime or illegal act, their own collection, use or shooting balloons has nothing to do with the crimes described in the Criminal Law. Elevating such behavior to a criminal offense is not to maintain but to destroy normal social order. Judgments that violate the "common sense, human nature, and common logic" of the rule of law are common. The headlines and voices from various sectors, such as "Absurd! Elderly woman selling balloon shooting game convicted of illegal possession of firearms", "Weird incidents in a weird society: a person with 6 balloon guns sentenced to 3.5 years, a murder with 1 handgun sentenced to 1.5 years" and the case of 18-year-old Liu Dawei, who was sentenced to life imprisonment for purchasing a replica gun online, indicate how much the judges' ruling in this case goes against society's "common sense, human nature, and common logic". The judgments in such cases reveal that judges lack an understanding of the basic norms of right and wrong and behavioral standards that are commonly recognized in Chinese society, as well as a lack of concern and isolation from the lives of the people. Through these judgments, the serious flaws in China's judicial system, which uses the number of cases as a benchmark, are fully exposed. This means that judicial personnel have lost their understanding of "common sense, human nature, and common logic" recognized by society. A judiciary without common sense is doomed to lack a conscience.

Judicial conscience means the recognition and application of the concept that "the law is the summation of social life experience". The life of the law is not logic but experience. The "Zhao Chunhua case" violated the grasp of legal professionals on social life experience, lacked a deep understanding of secular emotions and a profound insight into human nature, but rigidly applied legal provisions, which lacked the fundamental judgment of right and wrong, and ultimately buried the judicial conscience that should not have been lost. Various street vendors can be found everywhere, which is an existence that cannot disappear on the vast land of China. The lower strata of society rely on them for their livelihoods, and the Chinese people who are fond of enjoying the lively street life seek pleasure through them to relieve the bitterness of life. They are not only a symbol of China's vibrant economy but also an indicator of the problems in the development of the Chinese economy. Judges should not be gods detached from reality, nor should they become "amorphous dummies that are not contaminated by any human emotion". As individuals, judges should respond to the "human situation. They do not reside in a vacuum". Judges, like other people, must have experienced various temptations of consumption and entertainment and have seen (maybe even consumed at) stalls like Zhao Chunhua's balloon stand. Although they may not necessarily empathize, they must know the reasons for the existence of these street vendors. However, when the judge encountered the law, and when the legal text encountered the facts of the case, the mechanical comparison between them quickly led the judge to enter into the guilty verdict of Zhao Chunhua. In this case, the judge did not respond to the human situation of Zhao Chunhua as a fellow human being, nor did he carefully analyze whether the verdict that convicted Zhao Chunhua would be a just judgment or whether it would achieve legal justice. The judges seemed completely isolated from the lives of the people, as if they completely lacked sympathy and compassion for the difficult lives of the lower strata of society. In this case, the judge became a machine that was not emotionally infected, rather than an individual with a soul, brain, emotion and physical body. For judges, Article 353 of the French Code of Criminal Procedure stipulates that "the law only requires them to be calm, focused, conscientious and honest to form impressions based on the evidence of guilt and defense reasons, and make judgments". Where were the honesty and conscience of the judges who sentenced Zhao Chunhua to guilty in the "balloon stand and toy gun" case? A conscientious judge should have insight into the helplessness and hardships of the general public, including Zhao Chunhua, who are struggling to make a living. From this, what should be appreciated is the fact that guns in the "balloon selling" case were just toys, just like the balloons being shot. If the judge regards Zhao Chunhua's toy gun as a firearm, can Zhao Chunhua's balloon also be regarded as an explosive? Because without bullets being shot, no one can guarantee that the balloon will not suddenly explode or self-destruct. Here, as long as the judge takes a closer look at the reality in China, pays attention to Zhao Chunhua's survival needs in shooting balloons with a toy gun, considers the value and significance of the toy gun in the case and analyzes and interprets the legislative value, enforcement orientation and scope of application of Article 125 of the Criminal Law, they can establish their inner conviction that this case should not constitute the crime of illegal possession of firearms. If the judiciary lacks empathy for the people and uses the name of the law to arbitrarily deprive citizens of their rights and living space, the judgment it produces will inevitably be unjust. "If the court's judgment is consistent with the civilized sense of right and wrong, we will say that this is a just judgment; otherwise, we will criticize the injustice of the judgment". Without justice, where is conscience? Judicial conscience is the "perfect combination of law and morality". In the "Zhao Chunhua case", the judge, without the real-life experience of social life, detached from a profound grasp of secular emotions and a deep understanding of human nature, rigidly applied legal provisions, lacked basic judgments of right and wrong and ultimately buried the judicial conscience that should not have been lost. If the judge identifies Zhao Chunhua's toy gun as a firearm, can they also identify Zhao Chunhua's balloon as an explosive? Because without bullets being fired, no one can guarantee that the balloon will not suddenly explode or self-destruct. Here, as long as the judge takes a closer look at the reality in China, pays attention to Zhao Chunhua's survival needs in shooting balloons with a toy gun, considers the value and significance of the toy gun in the case and analyzes and interprets the legislative value, enforcement orientation and scope of application of Article 125 of the Criminal Law, they can establish their inner conviction that this case should not constitute the crime of illegal possession of firearms.

The "Zhao Chunhua case" violated people's basic rational judgment of good and evil, right and wrong, and went against people's value demands for justice and discernment. It hindered the realization of the ultimate goal of pursuing peace through justice. Once exposed, the case triggered heated discussions in various circles. An important and common voice from all sectors of society was that the law "bullied honest people", infringed on the rights and freedoms of the underprivileged and eroded the living space of the lower strata of society. The defendant's voice was, "Please use the gun I bought to shoot me. If you can kill me, I will admit my guilt! If you can't kill me, then let me go home! Playing with toy guns that I bought and using toy guns to shoot at balloons at a booth have no social harm. It's just for my own entertainment. I didn't aim and shoot the gun at others, nor did I use it to commit crimes. What harm did I cause?" However, the verdict judged them guilty, and the public saw the injustice of the judiciary, believing that the judiciary did not distinguish between right and wrong, and that the law did not punish real corrupt officials but instead targeted vulnerable groups. This not only aroused the defendant's dissatisfaction with the verdict but also triggered society's questioning and criticism of the verdict.

From the above, it can be seen that in the "Zhao Chunhua case", the judge lacked conscience as the "essence of the heart", lacked the voice of fairness and justice deep in their soul, lacked a basic understanding of society and social life and lacked the "common sense, common feelings, and common sense" perspective. This directly led to the judiciary's lack of conscience, deviating from the value concept of justice and peace that it should have. If judicial justice does not have the support of judicial conscience, justice will only be reduced to short-term expediency and destined to become "poetry and distance".

9.3 Interpretation of the criminal constituent elements under the indirect influence of judicial conscience

Compared with the somewhat "moralistic" mode of judicial conscience regulation, criminal law regulations are clear and complete. In the face of criminal law regulations, whether the "Zhao Chunhua case" should be convicted has become a practical issue of whether criminal justice has adhered to the bottom line of criminal law.

The court ruled that Zhao Chunhua had committed the crime of illegal possession of firearms, which obviously misunderstood the application of Article 125 of the Criminal Law. Faced with criminal law regulations, judges should not mechanically apply and simply match the legal provisions but should find clear principles and their limitations in the law. In terms of objective illegality and subjective responsibility analysis, the fact that the "balloon-stall case" was convicted means a mechanical understanding of the objective behavior object, which abandoned the substantive consideration of "worth punishing all kinds of crimes" at the level of illegality and responsibility. That is to say, it abandoned the clear understanding and limitations of concepts, such as what constitutes firearms and whether they have the possibility of attribution in the law, and thus exceeded the requirement of the legitimacy of the principle of legality of criminal penalties and criminal law regulations, punished behaviors that should not be punished and crossed the bottom line of criminal law.

Analyzing from the objective illegality aspect, the "Zhao Chunhua case" being criminalized means that toy guns and replica guns are given the same normative evaluation as real guns in criminal law, treating behaviors that do not have punishable illegality as crimes and breaking the provisions of the objective constitutive elements of criminal law.

According to relevant regulations, when the muzzle energy of the fired projectile is greater than or equal to 1.8 J/cm^2, it is universally recognized as a firearm. In the "Zhao Chunhua case", after being appraised by the appraisal center, six gun-shaped objects had a muzzle energy greater than 1.8 J/cm^2, exceeding the national standard. However, relying solely on this, Zhao Chunhua could not be convicted.

Firstly, the toy guns in the "Zhao Chunhua case" only meet China's formal (technical) standards for firearm identification, not the substantive (performance) standards for firearm identification, and cannot be regarded as "firearms" in criminal law. Article 46 of the Firearms Management Law stipulates that "firearms" referred to in this law mean various firearms that use gunpowder or compressed gas as power, use tubular devices to launch metal projectiles or other substances and can cause injury or loss of consciousness to people. Therefore, the performance characteristics of firearms must be such that they can cause injury or loss of consciousness to people. Performance characteristics are the key features that define firearms as strictly controlled items and are defined from the perspective of the effect of the projectile on the person it is aimed at (i.e., lethality). The toy guns in this case only have a muzzle energy of 2.17–3.14 J/cm^2, which is far from being able to penetrate human skin, let alone cause "injury or loss of consciousness". In the "first case of fake guns and real crimes", the first person, Wang Guoqi, conducted an experiment in which he used a replica gun he bought and sold to shoot himself and "at most it was just a little red and painful, without even bleeding". Therefore, the toy guns in the "Zhao Chunhua case" do not meet the substantive standards for firearms.

As can be seen from the above, the toy gun in the "Zhao Chunhua case" is not a firearm in the legal sense and cannot be evaluated as a criminal offense under criminal law. The criteria for identifying firearms must strictly comply with the formal and substantive conditions of laws and regulations, which not only require meeting the technical requirements of a kinetic energy of at least 1.8 J/cm^2 but also require performance that is "capable of causing injury or loss of consciousness". Moreover, the regulation that specifies the requirements for firearms performance is the "Firearms Management Law", which has a higher legal status than the administrative regulations of the "Firearms Identification Regulations". This means that when determining whether toy guns and imitation guns are firearms, strict adherence to the provisions of laws and regulations, from form to substance, must be implemented with dual standards, rather than a single formal standard. Treating all toy guns and imitation guns that exceed the kinetic energy of 1.8 J/cm^2 as firearms in the criminal sense is an expansion of the interpretation of firearms, which improperly expands the scope of punishment for criminal offenses involving firearms.

From a subjective perspective, the "Zhao Chunhua case" being classified as a criminal offense means that the perpetrator's subjective intention is ignored, disregarding the principle of accountability that is linked to the understanding of the illegality and punishability of criminal acts. This punishes behavior that does not have a subjective intent to violate the law or an understanding of its punishability, thus violating the provisions of subjective liability requirements in criminal law. In this case, Zhao Chunhua clearly has the capacity for criminal responsibility, and her behavior is not negligent. Therefore, the issue of whether the perpetrator is capable of being held accountable is actually whether Zhao Chunhua's behavior possesses the element of intent as a responsibility requirement, and precisely in this regard, Zhao Chunhua does not have intent. Firearm crimes are administrative offenses, and their criminal object is firearms. Therefore, Zhao Chunhua's subjective intent requires him to recognize that what she possessed was a firearm in the legal sense rather than a toy gun. The problem is that Zhao Chunhua "thought the gun on his stand was a toy gun", "he didn't even know it was a firearm in the legal sense. If he knew it was a firearm, he wouldn't have touched it". Moreover, "these toy guns did not have testing standards when they left the factory, and there was no indication on the gun box. The people who eventually committed these crimes only found out they had done something wrong after they were caught". This means that Zhao Chunhua could not discern the nature of the toy gun on his stand.

There is no inherent illegal intent, and there is little understanding of the nature of toy guns. Moreover, these toy guns or imitation guns are usually purchased through legitimate channels such as online stores. If that's the case, how can one know whether these toy guns or imitation guns fall under the criminal definition of firearms? China prohibits the circulation of firearms in the market, which means that firearms that circulate in the market should not be prohibited by national law. As a result, there is a paradox in practice: the court convicts without considering the presence or absence of subjective intent, but only the quantity of firearms, which results in the sentencing standard being based more on the quantity of firearms rather than the quality of the case. These cases are "irresponsible violations" and can even be comparable to cases with strict liability. If we want to strictly crack down on firearm-related crimes and increase control over firearms, we should start from the source, the manufacturers of toy guns and imitation guns, rather than blaming innocent users at the bottom of the chain.

As can be seen above, treating actions that do not have illegal intent or criminal intent as actions with possible accountability breaks through the subjective accountability requirements of criminal law. On the level of subjective accountability, ignoring whether the perpetrator has illegal intent means abandoning the standard of "liability and the defendant's malice" or intentional responsibility in the litigation process. The criminal judgment in the "Zhao Chunhua case" broke through the requirements of the subjective responsibility of criminal law, exceeded the provisions of the principle of legality in punishment and crossed the bottom line of criminal law.

9.4 Conclusion

Currently, "gun control" actions similar to those in Tianjin are spreading across the country, and there have even been cases where individuals were prosecuted for buying toy guns online and giving them to children as toys, only to have the toy guns identified as firearms. How to effectively prevent the continued spread of wrongful convictions in such cases and how to effectively protect the human rights and freedoms of citizens are issues that need to be further pondered after the "Zhao Chunhua case".

"The law's extreme is evil's extreme", an ancient legal proverb cited by Cicero in "On Duties", is often mentioned in this noisy era. When used in criminal justice, the connotation expressed precisely reflects the tension between general justice and individual justice, formal interpretation and substantive interpretation. The omnipresence of the law means the loss of freedom, and the rule of law that is beneficial to humanity becomes a harm to human rights. At the same time, it also makes our society extremely prone to "obvious excessive punishment" at least in the field of "gun control". Therefore, in the future, when facing similar cases like the "Zhao Chunhua case" in the field of judicial practice, the judicial sector in our country should adhere to judicial conscience and adhere to the bottom line of criminal law, not abuse the state's criminal punishment power to punish innocent citizens, and not apply excessive punishment to the innocent.

Justice is the primary value of the social system, and judicial conscience is the pursuit of this legitimate and virtuous value of justice, which is the inherent support for realizing judicial justice. The guilty verdict in the "Zhao Chunhua Case" exposed the extreme lack of grasp of social life experience by judicial personnel, their alienation from secular sentiments and human nature and their lack of basic judgments of right and wrong and good and evil. It was a judgment that lost judicial conscience. At the same time, it means that judicial personnel have a mechanical understanding of criminal law provisions and have abandoned the clear understanding and limitations of concepts such as what constitutes a firearm and whether it has the potential for punishable illegality and liability, punishing behavior that should not be punished and crossing the bottom line of criminal law. Only by adhering to judicial conscience and upholding the bottom line of criminal law can judicial justice be achieved. Judicial conscience represents the path to achieving justice outside the legal norms, while the bottom line of criminal law represents the path to achieving justice within the legal norms. The two work together from both the outside and inside of legal norms to achieve judicial justice.

Judicial conscience is a powerful and special force, and if it is destroyed, it is a collective loss for us all. Judicial conscience should be nurtured and can play a role in nurturing judicial conscience in the legislative process, case judgments and other processes. "For all of us, understanding and grasping the power of conscience is necessary, but it is particularly necessary for legislators, law enforcement officers, and law professors". In order to achieve judicial conscience, judges in particular must understand and grasp the power of conscience, respect the feelings of the people, respect common sense and logic, respect social customs and Chinese social moral habits and find the reasons for their own behavior and the true legal basis for the case in the seemingly vague but actually clear guidelines of conscience, accurately applying the law. Judges cannot mistakenly believe that justice can only stand firm by punishing all illegal behavior; this is a misreading of justice and an important element of judicial conscience.

The bottom line of criminal law is the high-voltage line of legal application and a special protection line for citizens. If the bottom line of criminal law is destroyed, it is a tragedy for the rule of law. The bottom line of criminal law must be upheld, and the application of criminal law provisions must not exceed the objective illegality and subjective attribution requirements of criminal law, and also the consideration of criminal punishability must not be abandoned. Toy guns, simulation guns or bamboo guns that meet national firearm technical standards but do not have the essential standard of firearm performance and lethality will not cause harm or threat to public safety and legal interests. The behavior of Zhao Chunhua and his ilk does not have any social harm, and punishing them goes against the criminal standard of punishing behavior that causes harm to legal interests required by criminal law, as well as the substance of the principle of legality and the appropriateness of criminal punishment rules. Judges should strive to find a balance between general (formal) interpretation and balancing (substantive) interpretation, especially when there is a conflict between the spirit of the law and the legal provisions. Judges must reach a reasonable conclusion through a full understanding of legal provisions and a comprehensive consideration of the facts of the case, while balancing the requirements of the wording of the law and the underlying ideas behind the law.

If we want to step into a truly rule of law society and civilized society, we cannot ignore the important role of conscience. If we want to avoid the capriciousness of criminal law sanctions, we cannot ignore the bottom line of the principle of legality. The legal system is to correct people's evil behavior, not to deliberately breed evil behavior; judges should not actively seek cases but actively seek a way out of indefinite sentencing. Only by using the law properly can the law further encourage people to engage in legal behavior. The bottom line of criminal law is the last line of defense for judicial justice. Judges must not exceed the requirements for establishing criminal liability when applying criminal law, and must not exceed the principle of legality, and after the formal consideration of illegality and responsibility requirements, they must then take a position on criminal punishability and make an overall judgment on the criminality of the behavior in cases such as the "Zhao Chunhua case" to avoid making citizens easily culpable. Only in this way can we avoid the "criminal justice machine damaging the emotional needs of victims, offenders, and the public", uphold judicial conscience, uphold the bottom line of criminal law and achieve individual justice and judicial justice.

Notes

1 See He Huaihong: *On Conscience*, Peking University Press, 2009, p. 36.
2 Wang Yangming: *Complete Translation of the Transmission of Knowledge*, Guizhou People's Publishing House, 1998, p. 168.
3 He Qinhua and Qi Kaiyue: *Judicial Conscience: The Perfect Combination of Law and Morality*, *People's Court Daily*, January 15, 2016, 2nd edition.
4 See Chen Zhonglin: Common Sense, Human Nature, and Common Logic: A View of Rule of Law and Legal Education, *Pacific Journal*, 2007(6).
5 See Inner Mongolia Bayannaoer Linhe District People's Court (2016) No. 0802 Criminal Judgment in First Instance No. 54.

References

Cai Daotong: Priority Application of Special Articles over Ordinary Articles, *The Jurist*, 2015(5).

Chen Lixin: *Drunk Driving*, Legal Daily, 8th edition, January 13, 2013.

Chen Ruihua: *Frontier Issues in Criminal Procedure*, China Renmin University Press, 2000 edition, p. 562.

Chen Ruihua: *Criminal Evidence Law*, Peking University Press, 2012 edition, p. 88, 115.

Chen Ruihua: On the Rules of Mutual Confirmation of Evidence, *Law and Business Research*, 2012(1).

Chen Zhonglin: Common Sense, Human Nature, and Common Logic: A View of Rule of Law and Legal Education, *Pacific Journal*, 2007(6).

Chu Huaizhi, Yonghong, Zhang. The Value Connotation of the Proviso to Article 13 of the Criminal Law, *Journal of Jiangsu Police Academy*, 2003(2).

Chu Huaizhi: *Criminal Integration*, Law Press, 2004, pp. 485–486.

Claus Roxin: Die Lehre von der objektiven Zurechnung, translated by Xu Yuxiu, Chengchi Law Review, 1994(50).

Claus Roxin: *General Part of the German Criminal Law*, (1), p. 23.

Du Zhichun, Genwei, Liao: On the Improvement of the System of Forensic Expert Appearance in Chinese Courts, *Law Journal*, 2011(7).

Feng Yadong: Study on the Relationship between Crime Constitution and Its Various Forms, *Chinese Journal of Law*, 2009(5).

Guo Tianwu: On the Confrontation Rights of Criminal Defendants in China, *Politics and Law*, 2010(7).

He Huaihong: *On Conscience*, Peking University Press, 2009, p. 36.

He Qinhua, Kaiyue, Qi: *Judicial Conscience: The Perfect Combination of Law and Morality*, *People's Court Daily*, 2nd edition, January 15, 2016.

He Yuejun: *Study on the Legislative Mechanism of Risk Society*, China Social Science Press, 2013, p. 125.

Haruo Nishihara: *The Formation and Characteristics of Japanese Criminal Law*, Law Press China, Chengwen Bookstore, 1997, p. 432.

Human Rights Watch, interviews with attorneys for both the defendants, Tbilisi, April 2002.

Inner Mongolia Bayannaoer Linhe District People's Court (2016) No. 0802 Criminal Judgment in First Instance, 2016, No. 54.

J. H. Von Kirchmann: The Worthlessness of Jurisprudence as a Body of Knowledge, translated by Zhao Yang, *Journal of Comparative Law*, 2014(1).

Jiao Baoqian: Concept of Legal Dogmatics and Its Evolution, *Studies in Law and Business*, 2006(4).

Kinderhauser: German Criminal Law Dogmatics Between Adaptation and Autonomy, translated by Cai Guisheng, *Journal of National Prosecutors College*, 2010(5).
Leonard Stamm: The Top 20 Myths of Breath, Blood, and Urine Tests, *Champion*, 2005(29), p. 44, 45–46.
Liang Zhiping: Law' Defense, *Social Sciences in China*, 1986(4).
Lin Dan: *Ulrich Beck's Risk Society Theory and Its Influence on China*, People's Publishing House, 2013, p. 169.
Lin Yuxiong: *General Principles of the New Criminal Law*, 2006, p. 483.
Lin Yuxiong: *Strict Proof and Criminal Evidence*, Law Press, 2008, p. 167.
Liu Yanhong: Self-Consistency of the Two-Hierarchy System of Purpose and the "Proviso" Decriminalization Function, *Law Review*, 2002(6).
Liu Yanhong: Study on the Theory of Social Harmfulness, *China Legal Science*, 2002(2).
Liu Yanhong: Misconceptions and Obstacles to Application: General Comments on Judicial Interpretations Since the Promulgation of the New Criminal Law, *Peaking University Law Journal*, 2002(5).
Liu Yanhong: *Views on Substantive Criminal Law*, China Renmin University Press, 2009, p. 91, 92.
Liu Yanhong: Risk Criminal Law Cannot Shake the Modest-and-Restrained Principle, *Studies in Law and Business*, 2011(4).
Liu Yanhong: We Should Stop the Criminal Legislation of Criminalization, *Law Science*, 2011(11).
Liu Yanhong: Evaluation and Reflection on the Current Criminal Status, *Legal Research*, 2013(1).
Liu Yanhong: Research on Criminal Evidence Rules for Drunk Driving Dangerous Driving Crimes, *Legal Science*, 2014(2).
Liu Yanhong: Source, Function and Significance of Formal and Substantive Interpretation of Criminal Law, *Science of Law*, 2015(5).
Liu Yanhong: Strategic Transformation of China's Anti-Corruption Legislation and Its Systematic Construction, *China Legal Science*, 2016(4).
Liu Yanhong: Damage of Symbolic Legislation to the Function of Criminal Law, *Political Science and Law*, 2017(3).
Liu Yanhong: Evaluation and Reflection on the Value of Criminal Legislation for Terrorist Crimes in the Past 20 Years, *Peking University Law Journal*, 2018(1).
Liu Yanhong: The Development Direction of Criminal Law under the Formation of Schools of Chinese Jurisprudence: Doctrinalization, *Politics and Law*, 2018(7).
Long Zongzhi: On the System of Criminal Confrontation and Its Reform and Improvement, *Law Review*, 2008(5).
Long Zongzhi: Research on Several Issues of the Norms and Implementation of Two Evidence Regulations, *Chinese Law*, 2010(6).
Ma Kechang, editor-in-chief, *General Introduction to Foreign Criminal Law (Civil Law System)*, China Renmin University Press, 2009 edition, p. 117.
Mou Lvye: On the Relationship between Defense of Innocence and Sentencing Defense, *Contemporary Law Review*, 2012(1).
Ni Chunle: *Special Litigation Procedures for Terrorist Crimes*, Mass Publishing House, 2013, p. 8.
Qian Mu: *General Introduction to Cultural Studies*, Zhengzhong Book Company, 1981, p. 3.
Shan Sijing, Pengfei, Wang: "Eating Egg Yolk Pie Will You Drive Drunk? Blood Test shall Prevail!", *East Asia Economic and Trade News*, 3rd edition, July 15, 2012.

Song Mengxi: *Walking on the Path to Philosophy*, Dushu, SDX Joint Publishing Company, 2001(6), p. 103.

The Fourth Plenary Session of the Eighteenth Central Committee of the Communist Party of China: Decisions of the Central Committee of the Communist Party of China on Several Major Issues Concerning Comprehensively Promoting the Rule of Law, *People's Daily*, October 24, 2014, p. 1.

Vgl. Vogel: *Einflüsse des Nationalsozialismus auf das Strafrecht Von Professor*, ZStW, 2003, S. 645ff.

Vgl. Sieber: *Grenzen des Strafrechts – Grundlagen und Herausforderungen des neuen strafrechtlichen Forschungsprogramms am Max-Planck-Institut für ausländisches und internationales Strafrecht*, ZStW, 2007, S.27.

Wang Fengxiang: On the Standard of Proof for 'Excluding Reasonable Doubt', *Prosecution Daily*, 3rd edition, May 3, 2013.

Wang Lida: A Preliminary Study on the Research Orientation of Legal Hermeneutics: A Methodological Reflection, *The Law Monthly*, 2000(9).

Wang Liangshun: On the Criminal Liability of Unit Members Participating in the Pure Natural Person Crimes, *Study in Law and Business*, 2013(2).

Wang Yangming: *Complete Translation of The Transmission of Knowledge*, Guizhou People's Publishing House, 1998, p. 168.

Wang Zhigang: On the Characteristics of Blood Sample Evidence and the Improvement of Judicial Procedures for Collection, *Politics and Law*, 2012(3).

William C. Thompson et al, Evaluating Forensic DNA Evidence: Essential Elements of a Competent Defense Review: Part 1, *Champion*, 2003(27), p. 16–18.

Wu Zongxian: On Community Correction Legislation and Criminal Law Amendment, *Justice of China*, 2009(3).

Xi Jinping: Improve the Rule of Law Construction Plan to Increase the Quality and Efficiency of Legislative Work and Foster a Good Legal Environment for Promoting Reform, Development and Stability, *People's Daily*, February 25, 2018, p. 1.

Xi Jinping: Improve the Rule of Law Construction Plan to Increase the Quality and Efficiency of Legislative Work and Foster a Good Legal Environment for Promoting Reform, Development and Stability, *People's Daily*, February 26, 2019, p. 1.

Xi Jinping. Secure a Decisive Victory in Building a Moderately Prosperous Society in All Respects and Win a Great Victory of Socialism with Chinese Characteristics in the New Era. *People's Daily*, October 28, 2017, p. 1.

Xi Jinping: Strengthen the Party's Centralized and Unified Leadership for the Law-based Governance on All Fronts, and Better Harness the Role of the Rule of Law in Solidifying the Foundation, Keeping the Expectation Stable and Seeking Long-term Benefits. *People's Daily*, August 25, 2018, p. 1.

Yi Yanyou: *Criminal Procedure in China and Chinese Society*, Peking University Press, 2010, pp. 168–172.

Yi Yanyou: Guaranteeing the Appearance of Witnesses and the Right of Confrontation for Criminal Defendants, *Chinese Social Sciences*, 2010(2).

Yi Yanyou: Witness Appearance and Safeguarding the Right of Criminal Defendants to Confront Witnesses, *China Social Sciences*, 2010(2).

Zhang Biao: Is It Difficult for 'Bao Qingtian', *Southern Weekend*, May 16, 2013, Edition A1.

Zhang Mingkai: *A Preliminary Discussion on Legal Interests*, China University of Political Science and Law Press, 2000, p. 364.

Zhang Mingkai: *Outline of Foreign Criminal Law* (Second Edition), Tsinghua University Press, 2007 edition, p. 123.

Zhang Mingkai: *Research on Fraud Crime and Financial Fraud Crime*, Tsinghua University Press, 2007, pp. 373–374.
Zhang Xiang: Formal Rule of Law and Legal Dogmatics, *Chinese Journal of Law*, 2012(6).
Zhao Bingzhi: Whether the Elderly Should Be Exempted from Death for Committing Crimes, *Legal Daily*, October 27, 2010, p. 12.
Zhao Bingzhi, Miao, Du: Criminal Law Amendment (9): Prepositioning of Legal Interests Protection to Weave the Counter-Terrorism Legal Net, *Procuratorial Daily*, September 28, 2015, p. 3.
Zhang Zhiming: *Operational Analysis of Legal Interpretation*, China University of Political Science and Law Press, 1999, p. 238.
Zhou Youyong. Five Development Concepts and Rule of Law China Construction, *Law and Social Development*, 2018(3).
Zhou Youyong: *Principles of Administrative Law* (Third Edition), Peking University Press, 2018, p. 83, 258, 358.
Zhou Youyong: New Tasks for Chinese Legal Research and Disciplinary Development in the New Era, *Journal of Wuhan University (Philosophy and Social Science Edition)*, 2019(2).

Index